Gandhi and Gutiérrez

Two Paradigms of Liberative Transformation

Gandhi and Gutiérrez

Two Paradigms of Liberative Transformation

by
John Chathanatt, S. J.

Decent Books
New Delhi -110059

Cataloging in Publication Data — DK

Chathanatt, John, 1947-
    Gandhi and Gutiérrez.
    Includes bibliographical references (p.   )
    Includes index.

    1. Gandhi, Mahatma, 1869-1948 — Philosophy.
    2. Gutiérrez, Gustavo — Philosophy.   3. Liberty.
    4. Liberation theology.   I. Title.

123.5   21

Keywords: Gandhi; Gutiérrez; Liberation theology;
Satya; Ahiṁsā; Ahiṁsātmak Satyāgraha; Rāmarājya;
Spirituality; Transformation; Kingdom; Option for the
poor.

ISBN 81-86921-28-1
First Published in India in 2004
© Author

Published and printed by:
Decent Books
D-36/A-1, Mohan Garden
Najafgarh Road
New Delhi - 110 059
Ph. (011) 2535-3435

Distributed by:
D.K. Printworld (P) Ltd.
Regd. office : 'Sri Kunj,' F-52, Bali Nagar
New Delhi - 110 015
Phones : (011) 2545-3975, 2546-6019; Fax : (011) 2546-5926
E-mail : dkprintworld@vsnl.net
Web : www.dkprintworld.com

Dedicated

to my dear parents, Mary and Augustine,

and

to all my teachers and friends

who helped and guided me
through the life journey to be what I am today

"A Small Body of Determined Spirits
Fired By An Unquenchable Faith In Their Mission
Can Alter The Course of History."
— *Mahatma Gandhi*

Contents

FOREWORD   xi

PREFACE   xiii

KEY TO TRANSLITERATION   xvii

1. THE AGENDA : THE THEME AND THE THESIS   1

2. MEANING OF LIBERATION   14
   Introduction   14
   Gandhian View of Liberation   15
      Liberation as *Swarāj*   15
         Swarāj as Freedom – *Swarāj* as Self-rule – *Swarāj* as
         Mokṣa – *Swarāj* as Transformation
      Conclusion   30
   Liberation According to Gutiérrez   31
      Meaning of Liberation   31
         Liberation as an Aspiration – Liberation as a process
         of Humanization – A New Human Quest – Liberation
         as a Graced "Kairos" – Liberation as Transformation
         – Liberation as Salvation
      Conclusion   43

3. FOUNDATIONAL BASES OF LIBERATIVE   44
   TRANSFORMATION

Introduction   44

Foundational Basis of Gandhian Liberation   45

Gandhi's God   46

    Ultimate End and Final Telos   50

    The One Creator, Master, and Father of us all   52

    God is Present, Active, and interested in Human

        History and Human Affairs   54

    God as Existential Force, Non-embodied

        Consciousness, Unalterable Law, Ultimate

        Value, and Cosmic Pervading Power   56

    God as Protector/Saviour   61

    God as Prime Source and Summit of all

        Moral Norms   61

    A God beyond Morality   62

    A God beyond Reason   63

    God, a Preferential Lover   64

God as Truth   67

Nature of Truth   70

    The Great Reversal   73

    Impact of Truth   79

Gandhian Homo   85

    Human the Brute   86

    The Soul Within   88

    Human Inter-relatedness   93

Theological Origin of Gandhian Socio-political

    Action   96

Conclusion   102

Foundational Bases of Liberation According to

Gutiérrez   102

    A Paradigm Shift   102

    The God of Gutiérrez   106

        God of Life – God in and of History – A God Hidden,

Present, Active and Acting – God of Communion
and Commitment – God of Love – God of Preferential
Love – Jesus Christ the Liberator

Gutiérrez's Homo   118

Created in the Image and Likeness of God – The Fact
of Sin – Saving Action of God – Human Responsibility
– Nature of Human-God Encounter

4. **A SPIRITUALITY OF LIBERATIVE**   **130**
   TRANSFORMATION

Introduction   130

Gandhian Novelty and Contribution   132

Satya and *Ahiṁsā*   134

Ahiṁsātmaka Satyāgraha   141

Origin and Meaning – *Satyāgraha vs* Passive Resistance
vs Pacifism – Positive Meaning – Virtue of the Strong
– Implications of Non-violence – Theory and Praxis
of *Ahiṁsātmaka Satyāgraha* – *Satyāgraha* as a
Technique – Ideal *Satyāgrahī*

A Method of Individual and Social Transformation and Conflict Resolution   160

The Healing Power of *Ahiṁsā*   163

The Law of Suffering and the Way of the Cross   164

Resolution of Conflicts   165

Reasons Against the Use of Violence   167

Means-end Nexus   173

The Non-violent Creed   176

Conclusion   177

Toward a Spirituality of "Drinking from Our   180
Own Wells" In Search of a New Spirituality

The Nature of Liberation Spirituality   183

What it is Not – A Life-affirming Spirituality – A
Dynamic Spirituality – A Christo-Centric Spirituality
– A Way of "Walking According to the Spirit" – A
Grass-root-intimacy Spirituality – An Historically-

involved Community Enterprise – A Preferentially-
opted Spirituality – A Spirituality of Empowerment
– Methodology is Spirituality – A Contemplative in
Action – A Spirituality of Conversion – Magnificat:
An Admirable Expression – Conclusion

Conclusion   205

5. THE GOAL OF LIBERATIVE TRANSFORMATION 207
   Introduction   207
   Gandhian *Rāmarājya*   208
   The Kingdom of God According to Gutiérrez   213
   Conclusion   219

6. EVALUATION AND CONCLUSION   220
   Option for the Poor vs Option for Truth   220
   Swarāj vs Liberation   228
   Kingdom and *Rāmarājya*   229
   Ahiṁsātmaka Satyāgraha and "Drinking from Our
       Own Wells"   230
   Reconciling Communion   235
   Towards a New Agenda of Liberative Transfor-
       mation   237

   GLOSSARY   242

   SELECTED BIBLIOGRAPHY   246

   INDEX   272

Foreword

THE Foreword of a book is not an explicit assessment of its worth. Yet in introducing the present work I cannot help using some words which are partly evaluative. This has to be so because of the quality of what is there in it and how it is put.

As a comparative study of Gandhi, who is basically a man of *religion*, and Gustavo Gutiérrez who may be called (in some of author's own words) the 'Father of Liberation Theology in South America,' this book is unprecedented. What is more, it is thoughtful, comprehensive within the limits of relevance, and neatly written; and so I feel happy in prefacing it.

I say, it is thoughtful, because it proceeds all along by making distinctions which are judicious and no hair-splitting at any point. Thus, whereas we often tend to use the word *swarāj* as a blanket term, the author takes care to show how Gandhi uses it in four distinct senses, — that is, *swarāj* as: freedom (— from, say, alien rule), self-rule, *mokṣa*, and transformation. The inclusion of *transformation* as a possible meaning of *swarāj* perhaps looks a little odd; but it is not really so. Even in the political sense or as riddance from a bad habit, *swarāj* is no mere snapping of chains, but a gain in quality, may be as a heightened, yet deserved sense of self-regard, and so a kind of transformation. Likewise, turning to Gutiérrez, the author clarifies how the eminent theologian speaks of liberation in more than five senses, that is, as aspiration, process of humanization (which is surely not the same thing as just being born as a human), Graced 'Kairos,' transformation, and salvation.

Luckily, the same analytic working of attention is to be seen in Chapter III ('Foundational Bases of Liberative Transformation'), IV ('A Spirituality of Liberative Transformation'), V ('The Goal of Liberative Transformation') where a fascinating comparison is made between *Rāmarājya* (Gandhi) and the Kingdom of God (Gutiérrez), and VI which has fascinated me because of the way it opposes *ahiṁsātmaka satyāgraha* (Gandhi) to "Drinking from Our Own Wells" (Gutiérrez).

As for the work's requisite range, I can vouch for it so far as Gandhi is concerned; for adequate attention has here been paid to the key concepts of his ethico-religious thought as they bear on his philosophy of action, namely, *Satya, Ahiṁsā, God, Satyāgraha*, and the means-end nexus.

Above all, the author's writing is all along pointed and clear, and nowhere ambiguous or rhetorical.

I expect this book to be read widely. I have enjoyed and profited from it, and I am not exceptional as a reader.

16-12-2003   **S. K. Saxena**

Preface

THE yearning for a better living according to the dignity of persons is ever present and persistently operative in the struggles of human history. Though the world is not yet a fitting home for full humanity, history has witnessed the rise of various ideologies, strategies, and utopias for social and material progress and human welfare and liberation. The irruption of prophetic personalities in various places and time has produced new paradigms that reshape society and set things right when the blindness of the human mind failed to find and even blocked the process of liberation. Gandhiji's struggle for freedom and his search for *Rāmarājya* in the midst of British colonialism, and the South American attempt at creation of a liberation theology, especially by Gustavo Gutiérrez, in the context of a Christian, specifically Catholic, doctrinal history in a world of human suffering are two such attempts at liberative transformation. A comparative study of these two paradigm figures may help inform and clarify approaches to social action and towards liberation in India. This is an attempt to work toward a paradigm of liberative transformation in the Indian context which attempts to identify various elements for an economic-political ethics. In a world torn by violence, strife and enmity, a comparative study of these two paradigm figures becomes a fruitful endeavour, especially now when we are groping for effective, non-violent, truthful, and peaceful means of social transformative action and conflict resolution. Irrespective of their cultural, educational and time differences, both can be profitably compared, and be engaged in a mutual conversation to help our search for an adequate and consistent paradigm for socio-economic transformation.

Many persons and events have shaped the making of this book. It is because of the assistance of devoted friends that this work has seen the light of the day. Without their support, inspiration, and encouragement this work would not have been what it is today.

Gandhi has been a fascination for me since my early school days. My quest to come to grips with the thinking and accomplishment of a person who relentlessly worked for the freedom of one sixth of humanity, guided my philosophical studies at Shembaganur, Tamil Nadu. This curiosity and fascination later blossomed in the rich soil and serene climate of the University of Chicago, under the guidance of various professors. I would like to express my sincere gratitude to the three persons who helped me during my research there. Professors James M. Gustafson and David Tracy as Co-directors and Lloyd Rudolph as Reader of my study gave very pertinent and invaluable suggestions as they minutely went through the pages of this study and guided me through out the work. Their constant encouragement and constructive criticism culminated in the completion of the work. I am immensely grateful to them. As teachers, during my years at the Divinity School of the University of Chicago, they have been very liberal with time, pedagogical skills, and intellectual insights. Their guidance is evident in the present work.

Besides, I thank my own family members, my Jesuit Superiors and companions in Patna, Delhi and Chicago Jesuit Provinces, the Woodlawn Jesuit community at Chicago, the Barry Community of the Society of Helpers and the Divinity

School of the University of Chicago for their unwavering
support during this time of transition and growth. To my own
teachers and colleagues at Vidyajyoti College of Theology,
Delhi, I owe a great debt of gratitude for their inspirational
guidance and collaborative support. They allowed me to take
time off during my teaching career at the Faculty and
generously shouldered added responsibility while I was away
to revise the research work done a few years back. I could
also utilize some part of my leave at the Woodstock
Theological Centre, Georgetown University, Washington D.C.
The Director and the Staff of the Woodstock Theological
Centre, Georgetown University, Washington D.C., and the
Woodstock Jesuit community to which I was attached deserve
my heartfelt thanks and sincere appreciation for all the help
they rendered to me when I was a fellow at the Centre. I am
also grateful to Rev. Fr. Hubert Haenggi, S.J. of the Swiss
Province for the encouragement and support for the
publication of the work.

I sincerely acknowledge that this work could not have
been written, much less see it published, without the
considerable help from many other quarters. I owe my
gratitude to Prof. George Gispert-Sauch and Late Mr. T.K.
Thomas for going through the manuscript minutely and giving
me valuable suggestions for its improvement. The
bibliographical and other archival help given by the Gandhi
Peace Foundation, and the Gandhi Smriti/Museum in Delhi
greatly helped in the revision process. My heartfelt thanks to
each of them.

I am also thankful to Ms Preeti, Mr Masroor Ahmad and
Mr. Joshy Jose for their secretarial assistance rendered during
the preparation of the manuscript for publication. I am most
grateful to Prof. S.K. Saxena for writing the foreword for the
book. Mr. Susheel K. Mittal and my publishers M/s Decent
Books, deserve my deep appreciation and heartfelt thanks
for the speedy and flawless publication of the work.

I regret that there is no other way to make my sincere gratitude ardent than a general expression of my whole-hearted appreciation to all my friends and associates who encouraged me to bring this work to its successful completion. Thank you, one and all.

Delhi   **John Chathanatt, S. J.**

Key to Transliteration

अ *a* (b<u>u</u>t)

आ *ā* (p<u>a</u>lm)

इ *i* (<u>i</u>t)

ई *ī* (b<u>ee</u>t)

उ *u* (p<u>u</u>t)

ऊ *ū* (p<u>oo</u>l)

ऋ *ṛ* (<u>rhy</u>thm)

ए *e* (pla<u>y</u>)

ऐ *ai* (hi<u>gh</u>)

ओ *o* (t<u>oe</u>)

औ *au* (l<u>ou</u>d)

क *ka* (s<u>k</u>ate)[1]

ख* *kha* (blo<u>kh</u>ead)[1]

ग *ga* (<u>g</u>ate)[1]

घ *gha* (lo<u>gh</u>ut)[1]

ङ· *ṅa* (si<u>ng</u>)[1]

च *ca* (<u>ch</u>unk)[2]

छ* *cha* (cat<u>ch h</u>im)[2]

ज *ja* (<u>j</u>ohn)[2]

झ *jha* (he<u>dgeh</u>og)[2]

ञ *ña* (bu<u>n</u>ch)[2]

ट *ṭa* (s<u>t</u>art)[3]

ठ* *ṭha* (an<u>thill</u>)[3]

ड *ḍa* (<u>d</u>art)[3]

ढ* *ḍha* (go<u>dh</u>ead)[3]

ण* *ṇa* (u<u>nd</u>er)[3]

त *ta* (pa<u>th</u>)[4]

थ *tha* (<u>th</u>under)[4]

द *da* (<u>th</u>at)[4]

ध* *dha* (brea<u>the</u>)[4]

न *na* (<u>n</u>umb)[4]

प *pa* (s<u>p</u>in)[5]

फ* *pha* (loo<u>ph</u>ole)[5]

ब *ba* (<u>b</u>in)[5]

भ *bha* (a<u>bh</u>or)[5]

म *ma* (<u>m</u>uch)[5]

य *ya* (<u>y</u>oung)

र *ra* (d<u>r</u>ama)

ल *la* (<u>l</u>uck)

व *va* (<u>v</u>ile)

श *śa* (<u>sh</u>ove)

ष *ṣa* (bu<u>sh</u>el)

स *sa* (<u>s</u>o)

ह *ha* (<u>h</u>um)

°   *ṁ* anusvāra (nasalisation of preceding vowel)

:   *ḥ* visarga (aspiration of preceding vowel)

* No exact English equivalents for these letters.

[1] guttural   [2] palatal   [3] lingual   [4] dental

[5] labial

1

The Agenda
The Theme and The Thesis

LIBERATION has been a persistent human quest at every phase
of history. Irrespective of colour, creed, socio-economic status,
place or time of birth, this human quest has been continuously
existent and operative in various struggles in history.[1] A
century ago the interpretation of the "anguished world" was
different from our contemporary assessment. We shifted the
earlier phase of attributing the cause of suffering to nature to
an emphasis on history.[2] Today we increasingly recognize that

---

1. Words like "Development," "Growth," "Welfare," "Progress,"
"Revolution," "Modernization," "Liberation," are repeatedly used in the
contemporary economic language and daily parlance to capture human
yearning for better living in keeping with the dignity accorded to the
human. Though history has witnessed the fashioning of different
ideologies, strategies and utopias to expedite a better world order bringing
about full humanity, yet even today the world of the human is not a home
for full humanity. The trickling-down economic theory, the Marxist's idea
of social and material progress, Gandhi's search for "Rāmarājya," South
American Liberation Theology and the emergence of Basic Christian
Communities, the Nyererean "Ujamaa," down to the present
conscientization attempt through non-formal education in India, all lie
behind the present search for the transformation of the human and of the
universe.

2. The passionate concern evoked by the histories of human suffering
resulting from the natural and environmental calamities is articulated by

the actions of persons, individually and collectively, have contributed to social and historical processes which oppress and dehumanize. This pathological tendency of human existence to convert life into death and good into evil is referred by Paul Ricoeur as *la faute* and by Bernard Lonergan as "bias."[3]

Mathew Lamb. The Lisbon earthquate of 1755 inspired Voltaire in 1756 to eloquently denounce needless suffering. "Compte's eulogy of positive science implemented in technology and industry promised a control of nature which would put an end to disease, plague, famine, and floods by subordinating all the positive sciences and their implementaions in industry to the advancement and progress of human life." Mathew L. Lamb, *Solidarity with Victims: Toward a Theology of Social Transformation* (New York: The Crossroad Publishing Company, 1982), p. 2. Social Darwinism interpreted human development and progress as a struggle for survival against unfriendly environment. A second phase ushered in the explanation of human maladies with the advent of Karl Marx and Sigmund Freud. They "shifted the burdens of human suffering from nature to history." The locus of responsibility has been shifted from the "shoulders of mother nature to the proud shoulders of a male-dominated history." *Ibid.*, p. 3. See also Floyd W. Matson, *The Broken Image* (New York: Doubleday, 1966), and Ernest Becker, *The Structure of Evil,* (New York: George Braziller, 1968).

3. See Paul Ricoeur, *Freedom and Nature* (Northwestern University Press, 1966) and Bernard Lonergan, *Insight: A Study of Human Understanding* (New York: Philosophical Library, 1958). A correlation of Ricoeur's notion of the fault and Lonergan's notion of bias with social sin is insighfully explicated by Patrick Kerans in *Sinful Social Structures* (New York: Paulist Press, 1974). Carl Friedrich von Weizacker, one of the most competent peace researchers, sternly warns humankind, whose aggressivity, violence and sickness of peacelessness got out of control: "In view of his aggressiveness man appears as the sick animal, insane in his innermost being." C.F. von Weizacker, "Friedlosigkeit als seelische Krankheit," in *Der ungesicherte Frieden* (Gottingen: 1979), pp. 32-56, quote 33, as quoted by Bernard Haring, *The Healing Power of Peace and Nonviolence* (New York: 1986). In the same vein Rollo May, a famous psychotherapist, says: "We are the cruellest species on the planet. We kill not out of necessity but out of allegiance to such symbols as the flag and fatherland. We kill on principle." See *Power and Innocence. A Search for the Sources of Violence* (New York: 1972). How would one otherwise explain the Gujarat pogrom of 2002? (For a detailed analytical description of the Gujarat incident and

In the context of such practical human suffering, history has witnessed eruptions in various cultures and times of prophetic paradigm personalities for "thrusting the evil back and setting virtue on her seat again" (*Bhagavad-Gītā*). What follows is an attempt to look closely at two such paradigm figures in their insightful struggle for liberation: Mohandas Karamchand Gandhi who successfully led India's freedom struggle against the British and was called the "Mahātmā" (Great Soul), and Gustavo Gutiérrez whose "attempt at reflection, based on the Gospel and the experiences of men and women committed to the process of liberation in the oppressed and exploited land of Latin America."[4] Their insightful proposals are already bearing fruit of various kinds the world over.[5]

---

other reports see *Gujarat 2002: Untold and Re-told Stories of the Hindutva Lab*, ed. John Dayal, (Delhi: Media House, 2002). Also see David Hollenbach, *Nuclear Ethics* (Ramsey, New Jersey: 1983); Gerard A. Vanderheaar, *Christians and Nonviolence in the Nuclear Age* (Mystic, Conn. 1982). J. Glenn Gray has harsher language: "Human beings can be devilish in a way animals can never be." *The Warriors: Reflections on men in Battle* (New York: 1967), p. 51.

4. Gustavo Gutiérrez, *A Theology of Liberation: History, Politics and Salvation*, trans. & eds. Caridad Inda and John Eagleson (Markyknoll, New York: 1973; original *Theologia de la liberacion: Perspectivas*, CEP, Lima, 1971; 15th anniv. edn. 1988), p. ix. All my references are taken from 1973 edition unless mentioned otherwise.

5. I am grateful to George Gispert-Sauch, a professor of theology, Vidyajyoti College of Theology, Delhi, for calling my attention to the fact that "at first sight it might look 'unfair' to compare Gandhi to Gutiérrez given the fact that there is half a century of difference between them. Gutiérrez is educated in the world of sociology and Marxist analysis and debate. Gandhi's world is that of the law at the end of last century, and his mentors like Tolstoy and a brand of socialism that was more ethical than political. Naturally the outlook is different." All the same, since both are attempts at liberative transformation of the human as well as human institutions, irrespective of their cultural, educational and time differences, both can be profitably compared in our search for an adequate paradigm for socio-economic transformation. There are other instances where comparison has been attempted. Martin Green relates Gandhi to European

India had undergone a process of political transformation since the turn of this century. A democratization process through political conscientization is growing in intensity especially after India's Independence.[6] On the other hand, the social and economic structures are relatively unchanged in many regions of India. A Christian by birth and brought up in the rich and diverse cultural and religious heritage of India, I am interested in helping to clarify the approaches to social action and in working toward a paradigm of liberative transformation in the Indian context, with a view to identify some of the needed features of economic-political ethics.

In order to move toward this paradigm it is important to draw on sources within Indian history, culture and social change, and from Christian faith and theology that influence the transformation process. Thus I have chosen to work on Mohandas K. Gandhi, the "Father of our nation," and Gustavo Gutiérrez, who might be called the Father of Liberation Theology in South America. I have chosen Gandhi because he may be described as the most prominent light of liberation in modern India.[7] Gutiérrez is chosen because his theology of

"counter cultural" currents. See his *The Challenge of the Mahatmas* (New York: Basic Books, 1978), *Tolstoy and Gandhi: Men of Peace* (New York: Basic Books, 1983), *The Origins of Nonviolence: Tolstoy and Gandhi in Their Historical Setting* (University Park: Pennsylvania State University Press, 1986), and *The Mountain of Truth: The Counterculture Begins* (Hanover: University Press of New England, 1986).

6. It is true that political stalwarts like Jawaharlal Nehru, Patel and Kamaraj are not found in today's India. There are no political figures comparable to these powerful personalities in India today. All the same, there is a growing political awareness in the general masses in favour of shaping their own destiny much stronger than what was present.

7. In the contemporary world scene Gandhi is influential abroad as well. The events in the Philippines that brought an end to the regime of Ferdinand Marcos, and in Eastern Europe, particularly in the thought and action of Lech Walesa and Václav Havel bear witness to this. See Rainer Hildebrandt, *Von Gandhi Bis Walesa: Gewaltfreier kampf für Menschenrechte* (Berlin: Verlag Haus am Checkpoint Charlie, 1987). Martin Luther King

liberation[8] exerts a great influence in shaping the process of transformation in many parts of the world today, including India. A comparative study of these two paradigms of liberative transformation could be a positive and useful endeavour, especially now when we are groping for effective, non-violent and truthful means for social transformative action and conflict resolution in a world torn by violence, strife and enmity.

Gandhi is a fascination! As the unnamed hero of many novels written during 1930 to 1950, he was more "present" by his absence.[9] His very life was a miracle to many. My interest in Gandhi goes way back to when I first encountered him through his unfinished autobiographical work. This strange person challenged for fifty years the British masters in South Africa, in India, and even the basic tenets of orthodox economics and politics. A contemporary of political figures such as Tsar Nicholas, Lenin, Stalin, Adolph Hitler, Kaiser Wilhelm, Sun Yat Sen, Chiang Kai Shek, Mao Tse Tung,

---

studied and actively used Gandhian techniques of non-violent resistance in his attempt at the liberation of his Afro-American brethren in U.S.A.

8. Words like "Capitalism," "Socialism," and "Communism" have been worked to death in the last century applying them to any conceivable practice and economic system. In the last three decades or so the word "Liberation" has undergone a similar fate in the theological and ethical circles. I do not intend to add more death blows to this word and the idea inherent in it. Nevertheless, the word and the spirit behind it pose a challenge to this hour of history especially from the standpoint of many nations and peoples that are in the throes of economic development, progress, and cultural revival.

9. Some of the novels where Gandhi remained as the unnamed hero are *Kandan the Patriot*, and *Murugan the Tiller* by K.S. Venkataramani; *Kantapura* by Raja Rao; and *Waiting for the Mahatma* by R.K. Narayan. The biography of Gandhi by Romain Rolland introduced him to Europe and the U.S.A. Gandhi was selected the "Man of the Year" by *Time* magazine (1930). See Lloyd Rudolph "Gandhi in America." Also see Shahid Amin, "Gandhi as Mahatma," in *Selected Subaltern Studies*, ed. Ranajit Guha and Gayatri Chakravorty Spivak (New York: Oxford University Press, 1988), 288-348.

Woodrow Wilson, and Franklin Roosewelt, he bridged the
time span between two world wars, when armies fought first
with rifles and then with atomic bombs.

Gandhi's quest for liberation began with the struggle for
political freedom from the imperial rule. His experience of
living with millions under colonial oppression, starvation, self-
degradation, untouchability, and racism did not smother his
conviction that things need not be as they are, that they should
not and ought not be as they are. In a dialectical process of
meditative reflection and action, he gradually developed a
"conceptual framework" and outlined a comprehensive
programme to re-affirm the dignity and the sacredness of
human beings and to reconstruct society in its socio-economic,
political, and moral aspects.

He attempted the task within a religious and theological
framework. There is a theocentrism in the Gandhian form of
social action giving support to and letting energy flow to the
anthropocentric endeavours. The form and content of
Gandhian ethics of action follow systematically and logically
from his concept of the human person qua moral agent who
always stands in relation to the Absolute Truth (God), to other
human beings and to the universe. One of Gandhi's primary
concerns is to explain how religious life, faith and belief-
systems help to form a responsible self. This implies that the
action of the self as agent in various realms (politics, economics)
has an ethical and religious significance. He translated the
metaphysical doctrine of the sacredness of life into a category
that was ethical and moral in character.

This further implies that responsible action in these areas
of human life has a moral content. Gandhi's views on political
economy and the activities associated with and springing from
such views are rooted in his assumptions and concepts
regarding human nature, human perfectibility, human
fulfillment, and person-to-person and person-to-God
relationships. With his very definite faith-conviction regarding

what the human is in his/her essential nature, what s/he should be and can become, and what his/her place is in the universe, Gandhi realized what a false understanding of the self and a fundamentally flawed organization of the society can do to the human.

To be involved in the public realm was then to be involved in the sacred *dharma* (duty). An involvement in the uplift of all, especially the *Harijan* (the untouchable outcastes = people of God) and in the attainment of freedom, was basically a surrender to God and God's will.[10]

So Gandhi's ardent endeavour for *swarāj* (self-rule or mastery, liberation, freedom, independence, self-determination, self-government, autonomy — in short, freedom from every kind of oppression) is motivated by his anthropological and theological convictions. The political origin and the centrality of his theology of *swarāj* is due to the sacredness he attributes to the person. The same faith-convictions lead him to embrace the means of *ahiṁsātmaka satyāgraha* (non-violent but active search and work for truth and justice) in his liberative transformation programme. Self-suffering (*tapasyā*) and the contritional-conversion model for conflict resolution are the outcome of his meditative wrestling with the mystery of God and human persons who are but "Sparks" of the Absolute One. His preference for the word *swarāj* to *mokṣa* (heaven, salvation) manifests his anthropological emphasis and the importance he gives to "this hour of history."

Individual transformation and institutional reform are two sides of the same coin in Gandhi's theology of social action.

---

10. The Jain concept of liberated life (*jīvanmukti*) has been given a re-interpretation by Gandhi to include socio-political involvement. Concern for salvation (*mukti, mokṣa*) is a paramount search in all systems of Indian philosophical and theological thought — an exception to this is the atheistic trend of Nyāya-Vaiśeṣika system. While Swami Vivekananda democratized the concept of *jīvanmukti*, making the liberated life accessible to every devout Hindu, Gandhi showed its relevance for socio-political action.

Transforming the human meant the creative building of mutual
relationships, which worked for a substantial change in society.
In fact, the whole of Gandhian revolution was ultimately aimed
at resetting humans into that right position from where the
antagonistic forces of an egoistic society had thrown them
away, in that process depersonalizing them.

Gandhi's meaning of *swarāj* therefore needs to be explored.
This is necessary to understand the Gandhi's vision and
proposal for a transformed society of human relationship. In
my attempt to identify the salient features of a paradigm of
liberative transformation for India, such an exploration is all
the more indispensable. The Gandhian notion of *swarāj* is
analysed in the first part of the second Chapter.

South American Liberation Theology has developed in the
context of a specific religious history and practical human
suffering. Gustavo Gutiérrez sets out his liberation agenda in
the Latin American context with the intention of discerning
the meaning of "the signs of the times" in the light of God's
action in history through a Biblical hermeneutics. His starting
point is a critical reflection on the historical praxis, involving
a political hermeneutics of the Gospel. His religious vision is
not focused on a Hidden God, but on one who emphatically
stands revealed in the struggle of the oppressed. History, not
anthropology is the primary reference point in his theological
task. The basic question is to understand God's action in
history and humanity's adequate response to it. Gutiérrez'
historical consciousness seems to be a consciousness of social
conflict; and in a conflictual situation the divine presence is
discerned to be with the poor.

An economic and political transformation of the existing
social structures through an immanent insertion into the world
of the poor is Gutiérrez's liberation agenda. Transformation
of the structure and organization of society seem to have
priority over individual conversion. It is his historical
discernment that the continuation of the present order will

perpetuate hunger and violence. Hence the commitment to liberation through working for the transformation of the existing social order is both urgent and primary. But though history becomes the primary reference point, there is an anthropological agenda lurking, as it were, underneath the call for structural transformation in the paradigm of liberation proposed by Gutiérrez. Here too the notion of Liberation according to Gutiérrez needs analytical study. This will be done in the second part of the second chapter.

In order to assess the adequacy, coherence, consistency, and comprehensiveness of serious theological ethical systems, one needs to explore their foundational bases. Certain "base points" on which an ethics is developed should be looked into.[11] Hence we need to explore the foundational basis of the agenda of liberative transformation as proposed by both Gutiérrez and Gandhi. This is my task in the third chapter.

Both Gandhi and Gutiérrez see the modern world as dehumanizing, in its present form of existence and operation. This calls a right discernment of the signs of the times. This, in turn, calls for a prophetic denunciation in an active effort to effect socio-economic and political structural changes in order

---

11. According to James M. Gustafson "The organizing perspective, metaphor, analogy, or principle of any comprehensive theological ethics must be developed so that four distinguishable base points, or points of reference, are coherently related to each other." The following are the four base points that must cohere with the liberation agenda: (i) The understanding and interpretation of God — the ultimate value and power, God's relations to the world and to humans, and His "moral" and "non-moral" purposes; (ii) the interpretation of the meaning or significance of human experience and human life in world and in history — historical life of the human community, the events and circumstances in which humans act; (iii) the interpretation of persons as moral agents and their acts; and, (iv) the interpretation of how persons ought to make moral choices — moral judgement on their own and on others actions. See *Protestant and Roman Catholic Ethics* (Chicago: University of Chicago Press, 1978), pp. 139-44; idem, "Context vs. Principles: A Misplaced Debate in Christian Ethics," *Harvard Theological Review* 58 (1965): 171-202.

to usher in freedom and to expedite the liberative transformation of the human. Ordinarily the Gandhian *ahiṁsātmaka satyāgraha* (non-violent search for truth) is considered a technique of non-violent action. But it is more than this. I would argue that it is the outcome of a long process of discernment. Gandhi did not separate the final goal from the process of discerning and attaining that goal. There is an intrinsic relationship between means and end. Means modify and constitute the end and have a capacity to create their own ends. The liberation praxis of Gutiérrez, on the other hand, is arrived at by a process of social analysis in the light of a political hermeneutics of the Gospel. Here, too, a process of discernment is involved. The means of attaining goals is crucial in any ethical considerations. Hence an analysis of the proposed means of liberative transformation in the socio-theological agenda of Gandhi and Gutiérrez needs clarification. This is my task in the fourth chapter.

Of course, their liberation agenda is oriented to their respective goals. Both are concerned with what they see as socio-economic and political oppression brought about by an industrialized society and colonial powers. Both long for egalitarian societies (*rāmarājya* for Gandhi; the Kingdom for Gutiérrez), communities structured in freedom, love and brother/sisterhood. Basic virtues such as trust and generosity, especially for Gandhi, could, however, emerge only with the demise of the dreary and despotic institutions of the day. The nature of a liberated society, and the elements of the ultimate goal of action need further analysis. The fifth chapter deals with this.

There are points at which Gandhi and Gutiérrez might be meeting. Yet there are significant differences in their approaches to the liberation process. Concern for freedom is a meeting point. Their differences in social analysis (its sources, what it yields, etc.) and how these differences affect what they take to be prescriptions for action are significant. The ways in which each conceives of human fulfilment have areas of agreement and differences. What difference does the biblical theology of Gutiérrez make in comparison with Gandhi's God (Truth) in each of their concepts of human fulfilment and prescriptions for action?

Oppressive social structures ought to be transformed first and foremost, according to Gutiérrez. On the other hand, Gandhi's perception was that any real and lasting transformation of this world order for the better had to begin with an inner conversion of the heart. Gandhi's vision would not allow actions of violence in the great drama of social transformation. When the adversary is the whole social order, one's strategy for effective change should include every single soul in that social order. Transforming the social order implies changing everyone's way of thinking (of both the powerful and the victims of power): a change — a conversion process — that comes about through understanding and harmonizing opposing points of view. Again and again, without any compromise, Gandhi laid emphasis on his notion of *ahiṁsātmaka satyāgraha*.

Gutiérrez would disagree with Gandhi concerning the means. He can tolerate moments of violence depending on the cultural and contextual situation. Although Gandhi was not against some use of external encouragement (coercion) to spur that change along, it had to be a conversion of the heart first and foremost. Since according to Gutiérrez there is systemic social oppression in the world of human affairs, his approach is (in the last analysis) economic and political, structural and institutional. The major differences between the two are to be found in their primary methods about what is required to transform this imperfect world into a better one. These differences are significant enough to deserve close attention and articulation.

The following two figures illustrate the movements with respect to their respective paradigms of liberative transformation. Gandhi's movement seems to be from person to personal acts (conversion process) and then to the system (structure). On the other hand, for Gutiérrez it seems to be from person to system (structure) first, and only then to personal acts (transformation process) — a movement in the opposite direction.

Here a conversation between the two will be in order. Gutiérrez could ask Gandhi about the role of institutions and structures in the liberation praxis. Gandhi, on the other hand, could ask Gutiérrez about the role of the individual as a responsible agent in the liberative transformation process and social action.

In the light of the analysis and insights drawn from a comparison of the two paradigm figures from two diverse cultural milieus, one could draw various elements for the

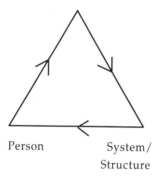

Personal Acts/
Transformation Process

fig. **1.1: Clockwise movement
in the Gandhian Paradigam**

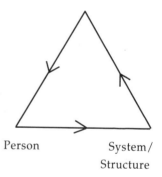

Personal Acts /
Transformation Process

fig. **1.2: Counterclockwise move
in Gutérrez's Paradigm**

contemporary search of more adequate paradigm of liberative transformation and socio-political action.

I propose to combine

(a) the key emphasis given by Gutiérrez to the analysis of "the moment of truth" (the *kairos*) and of the particular contextual, cultural situation, through a right reading of the "signs of the times" in the light of God's action in history, through a critical reflection on historical praxis

and through a political hermeneutics of the Gospel; and
(b) the inviolable *sacredness* attributed to individual persons
by Gandhi, which forms the core of his theological
anthropology, the *antaryāmin* of his socio-economic and
political transformation process and the basis of his
ahiṁsātmaka satyāgraha, together with the redemptive and
reconciling power of self-suffering (*tapasyā*) love with
the contrition-conversion model for conflict resolution.

That way I would be able to analyse the foundations of
the above figures. Therein both persons and systems stand
not in opposition to one another, but in mutual enrichment
giving rise to a better and more adequate paradigm of
liberative transformation. Such a move enable us to be mutually
responsible to the socio-economic and political structures of
our creation, so that structural transformation is then
comparatively easier. Through his social analysis and the
importance given to history, Gutiérrez scrutinizes the value-
laden presuppositions embodied in social structures and
political practices. This is needed to understand and adequately
address the socio-economic and political problems that
confront India today. On the other hand, the enlightened
notion of human agency and responsible freedom, together
with mutual rights and duties in the conflictual world of human
affairs, as emphasized by Gandhi, is a *sine qua non* for the
establishment of a meaningful and sustainable community of
human relationships.

My thesis is that a process of systemic and structural
change simultaneous with a process of individual conversion
(conversion to Truth), can result in a more adequate
understanding of responsible social action which would, in
turn, lead to a better social order and a richer paradigm than
the ones envisaged and proposed separately by either of the
figures under scrutiny. A mutual conversation and the
presentation of such a hypothesis is the task I have set for
myself in the sixth and final chapter, Evaluation and Conclusion.

2

Meaning of Liberation

Introduction

"THEOLOGY of Liberation" had its origin in Latin America. Though the spirit behind it was active and operative in other continents especially in Africa and Asia, a theologizing process making use of the phrase and the spirit it involves has been of rather recent origin; and it "occurs in a defined situation of alienation or dependence such as in regions regarded as 'peripheral' in countries that depend economically, politically, and culturally on the Western world."[1] Though the impulse for such theologies is universal, their historical irruption, as François Houtart points out, occurs in social situations that are very much marked by enslavement, alienation, oppression, dependency, under-development, and acute economic disparity.

Born of this historical consciousness and a lifelong devotion to transformation, Gandhi's theology of liberation is universal and all-encompassing reaching out to all his fellow humans, irrespective of colour, creed, socio-economic or political status. The whole universe, *a fortiori*, the humans, stand in need of liberative transformation.

---

1. Ignatius Jesudasan, S.J., *A Gandhian Theology of Liberation* (Maryknoll, New York: Orbis Books, 1984), p. 2.

Gandhian View of Liberation

LIBERATION AS SWARĀJ

The one word that captures the quintessence of the Gandhian vision of liberative transformation is *swarāj*.[2] As a constant

2. The Sanskrit word *swarāj* is associated to the term *swarājya* which means belonging to one's own country and refers to a particular mode of attaining self-determination in a polity. A systemic presentation of Gandhi's notion of *swarāj* is found in his *Hind Swarāj*, first published in his mother-tongue, Gujarati. Using the Socratic method of dialogue between "Reader" and "Editor," Gandhi wrote this work on board the steamer, *Kildonan Castle* in November 1909 on a return voyage from England to South Africa. It is historically inaccurate to say that the original work in Gujarati was written in 1908 — as Jesudasan (with many others) mentions in Endnote No. 9, p. 145 of *A Gandhian Theology of Liberation*, probably following what Gandhi himself said. Haridas T. Mazumdar is correct in pointing out this chronological discrepancy. Gandhi went on a deputation to London in July 1909 and his return trip to South Africa was in November 1909 [Cf. *Sermon on the Sea* (Chicago: Universal Publishing Co., 1924), footnote No. 1, p. xvi].

Published in December (1909) in two parts in the 11th and 18th issues of *Indian Opinion*, a weekly that Gandhi was editing and publishing in South Africa, it was first published as a book in January 1910. Undeterred by the proscription of the book by the government of Bombay in March 1910, Gandhi hastened to publish an English translation of it the same month (published by the International Printing Press, Phoenix, with a foreword by Gandhi dated March 20, 1910). There were many subsequent editions of this seminal work. Ganesh and Co., Madras, brought out the first Indian edition in English in 1919. By 1924 six editions of the book had been issued. A U.S. edition of the work, ed. Haridar T. Mazumdar, the author of "Gandhi the Apostle," under the title, "Sermon on the Sea," was published in 1924 with an introduction by John Haynes Holmes, minister, Community Church, New York City. The revised new edition brought out in 1939 is what the *Collected Works* series has adopted (see M. K. Gandhi, *Collected Works of Mahatma Gandhi*, 100 vols., New Delhi: Publications Division of the Ministry of Information and Broadcasting, Government of India, 1958), 10: 6-68.

Hind Swarāj forms the basis of all his subsequent conceptualized articulations of *swarāj*. With regard to the ideas expressed in the book Gandhi writes in the preface, "These views are mine, and yet not mine. They are mine because I hope to act according to them. They are almost a part of my being. But they are not mine, because I lay no claim to originality.

seeker and a persistent experimenter, Gandhi sought to find
a term from the indigenous tradition that would adequately
capture the notion of freedom and liberative transformation
swelling in his heart and mind and which, at the same time,
would be part of the common language and intelligible to the
ordinary masses. Already popularized by Annie Besant, the
foundress of the Theosophical Society, *swarāj* was the word
that he chose.[3] Aware that an erosion of the true meaning of

... The views I venture to place before the reader are, needless to say, held
by many Indians not touched by what is known as civilization, but I ask
the reader to believe me when I tell him that they are also held by thousands
of Europeans."

Concerning the origin of the work Gandhi says in *Young India* (January
26, 1921) that this work was written "in answer to the Indian school of
violence and its prototype in South Africa. I came into contact with every
known anarchist in London. Their bravery impressed me, but I felt that
their zeal was misguided. I felt that violence was no remedy for India's ills,
and that her civilization required the use of a different and higher weapon
for self-protection." With respect to its content he opines that "it is a book
which can be put into the hands of a child. It teaches the gospel of love in
place of that of hate. It replaces violence with self-sacrifice. It pits soul force
against brute-force. It has gone through several editions and I commend
it to those who would care to read it. I withdraw nothing except one word
of it, and that in deference to a lady friend." The lady friend Gandhi
referred to is Annie Besant who took objection to Gandhi's use of the
word "prostitute" in speaking of the British Parliament (the Mother of
Parliaments).

What one finds in *Hind Swarāj* is Gandhi's profound reflection. The
soul of the book is the soul of Gandhi's theology. Even after decades the
central foundational message of the "gospel of love in place of that of
hate" is not only not changed but rather emphasized by Gandhi. After
twenty-nine years of its publication Gandhi wrote in his "Message" sent
to the special Hind Swarāj Number of *Aryan Path* that if he were to rewrite
the book he would change the language here and there: "(B)ut (even)
after the stormy thirty years through which I have since passed, I have
seen nothing to make me alter the views expounded in it." (July 14, 1938)

3. Gandhi pays due respect to Annie Besant, the British theosophist,
for taking this term to the millions in India (see *CW* 14:50; Also see
Jesudasan, *A Gandhian Theology of Liberation*, p. 48). To this politico-theological
term Gandhi gave an ethico-religious character in his application of the
term to popular, daily actions. This will be clear in the subsequent analysis.

the word had taken place, Gandhi's first attempt was to restore the original meaning and, in the process, go beyond it if possible.

This Sanskrit term was in use to exclusively identify the goal of national political independence connoting "self-government," "self-rule." Dadabhai Naoroji and Bal Gangadhar Tilak had used it in that sense long before Gandhi's arrival on the Indian political scene.[4] Earlier than the term *swarāj* became prevalent in common parlance, the Bengālī patriots had, toward the end of the nineteenth century, "sought to justify their doctrine of boycott of British goods in the name of *swadeśī* or patriotism."[5] It should be mentioned here that, given the exclusive identification of *swarāj* with independence, the emphasis in both Tilak and Naoroji was shifted from a positive to a negative connotation of the term. Subsequently, the emphasis was entirely changed from its individual to its collective significance and scope.[6]

In the early Greek and Indian thought, the idea of self-rule was applied to the collectivity of various members of a polity and related to the self-rule involved in the moral growth of individuals. In this early philosophical thinking "The maturity and development of a polity were regarded as a reflection as well as an index of the degree of moral maturity and self-cultivation of an elite or a generality of individuals."[7] Gandhi's contribution lies in the restoration of this former meaning of *swarāj*.[8] It is an attempt to take the self-rule concept

4. In his Presidential address at the Calcutta Congress in 1906 Naoroji used the term in this sense. See Yesudasan, *A Gandhian Theology of Liberation*, p. 47; see also Raghavan Iyer, *The Moral and Political Thought of Mahatma Gandhi* (New York: Concord Grove Press, 1983), p. 347.

5. Iyer, *The Moral and Political Thought of Mahatma Gandhi*, p. 347.

6. *Ibid.*, p. 347.

7. Iyer, *The Moral and Political Thought of Mahatma Gandhi*, p. 346.

8. Because of the charismatic leadership of Gandhi, this polysemic word *swarāj* was linked in the minds of ordinary peasants with the name of Gandhi. It was "Gandhiji's Swarāj" or the "Mahātmājī's Swarāj" that

from its association with a few elites to the reach of general masses. His originality consists in giving a theological and an ethico-religious character to the politically popular term *swarāj*.

Whenever Gandhi speaks of *swarāj* he means to apply it both in its individual and social character and significance. The expression of the social and institutional dimensions of *swarāj* are dependent upon and (should) spring from the individual personal dimension. This implies that the seed of *swarāj* should germinate first in the soil of individual consciousness. "The outward freedom . . . that we shall attain will only be in exact proportion to the inward freedom to which we may have grown at a given moment."[9] Thus, Gandhi does not rely on the working of an "invisible hand" to give a principled direction to the collective endeavour of various individuals in their struggle for liberative transformation. The principles should be present beforehand in the character of individuals as inherent virtues to give self-direction to both individuals and the nation-state. The development of polity should be a reflection as well as an index of the degree of maturity of the individual moral agent.

Here we see how the Kierkegaardian insight of the personal-universal inter-relationship is operative in Gandhi's concept of *swarāj*.[10] The primacy as well as the importance of

---

they were looking for; see Shahid Amin, "Gandhi as Mahatma," in *Selected Subaltern Studies* (New York: Oxford University Press, 1988), p. 338. Such a political caricature of *Hind Swarāj* as "Gandhi-Raj" was deeply resented and vehemently rejected by Gandhi."In the first instance," Gandhi quipped, "India is not striving to establish Gandhi-Raj. It is in dead earnest to establish swarāj and would gladly and legitimately sacrifice Gandhi for the sake of winning swarāj." (CW 23: 37-39). It is interesting to note here that his reply to the political caricaturing of the term gave rise to his own authentic hermeneutic of *Hind Swarāj*.

9. *Young India*, November 1, 1928.

10. In a sublime moment Kierkegaard writes: "He who regards life ethically sees the universal, and he who lives ethically expresses the universal in his life; he makes himself the universal man not by divesting

the Aristotelian understanding of the person is also emphasized and articulated by Gandhi.

Swarāj is an evolving concept. There were modifications in Gandhi's concept first expounded in his seminal work, *Hind Swarāj*. *Swarāj* is the condition, relative to "that status of India which her people desire at a given moment." In this respect it is not possible to define *swarāj* in a narrow, univocal way. It evolves with time and with the raised level of consciousness. In 1917, eight years after writing *Hind Swarāj*, Gandhi outlined his programme of *swarāj* at a Political Conference held at Godharā in Gujarat.[11]

In Gandhi's ethico-religious category, then, *swarāj* connotes a variety of notions: autonomy, self-determination, self-government, freedom, independence, liberation, transformation, and ultimately *mokṣa* (salvation) itself.

Swarāj as Freedom

Freedom is not a gratuitous privilege nor a by-product of some social contract. As an inherent characteristic of human nature, the inalienable right and privilege of every individual grounded in moral autonomy of essence of one's existence bestowed by the Almighty in the action of creation.[12] Freedom

---

himself of his concretion, for then he becomes nothing, but by clothing himself with it and permeating it with the universal. For the universal man is not a phantom, but every man as such is the universal man, that is to say, to every man the way is assigned by which he becomes the universal man. . . . He who lives ethically labors to become the universal man." (as quoted by Iyer, *The Moral and Political Thought of Mahatma Gandhi*, p. 345).

11. Enumerated in detail by Jesudasan; see *A Gandhian Theology of Liberation*, p. 54.

12. Gandhi has more affinity for the *exitus et reditus* pattern of the human relationship with God as seen in Aquinas than the Barthian biblically backed interpersonal view of God commanding or speaking and wo/man hearing and obeying. For Gandhi, as it is very clear for Thomas, the objective norms of ethics and morality and the source of knowledge of

as an inherent virtue of human nature is true *swarāj*.[13]

Traditional political theories have grappled with individual freedom and external authority in human society. From the standpoint of the individual moral agent, the major problem of a political community has been to ensure freedom or to justify its restriction. Viewed from the State's or the community's angle, the problem is to get the individual subjects to identify themselves and their long-term interests with the wider community and to comply with the state authority. Depending upon the reciprocal relationship between the moral status of a person as a free agent and one's enlarged role in a polity because of an enhanced status as member of the community and a State, different concepts of liberty and different theories of society and State emerge. Utilitarian ethics and "the confusing impact of the methods of the natural sciences upon social studies" have questioned the very idea of Kantian autonomy of the individual and the Platonic and Stoic ideals of self-rule.[14] Precisely here comes Gandhi's contribution.

In his theological category, freedom has a specific use as a moral and social concept. The "freedom from" and the "freedom for" aspects are clearly conceived. Very definitely Gandhi's notion of freedom goes beyond Graham Wallas' articulation of freedom as the "capacity for continuous initiative," or, for that matter, Bertrand Russell's oft-quoted definition of freedom "as the absence of obstacles to the

---

these norms are not only accessible to human beings but are to be found in large part in the moral ordering of nature, particularly human nature. This would take one to Gandhi's notion of human agency and action. Of course, it goes without saying that the very nuanced human-Divine relationship as articulated by the theologian Aquinas is not exactly the same as the *ātman-Brahman* union envisaged by the political activist Gandhi. All the same it should be mentioned that for both, the human stands in the horizon of the Absolute.

13. See Raghavan Iyer, "Introduction," in *The Moral and Political Writings of Mahatma Gandhi*, 3 vols. (Oxford: Clarendon Press, 1987), 3: 8.

14. See Iyer, *The Moral and Political Thought of Mahatma Gandhi*, p. 346.

realization of desires."[15] Besides the negative connotation, referring to the absence of obstructions, interference, coercion or indirect control, there is the positive aspect of the process of choosing and acting on one's own initiative.

Negative freedom refers primarily to a condition wherein there is absence of coercion or constraint imposed by the will of another person. A person is said to be free to the extent that s/he can choose goals or courses of conduct, or can choose between available alternatives. One is not forced to act as one would not oneself choose to act, or prevented from acting as one would otherwise choose to act, by the will of another person, polity or any other authority. It is the horizon of one's conduct wherein each one chooses the course of conduct and is protected from restraint.

Coercion is not only direct like in commands and prohibitions, but also indirect through manipulation and manoeuvering the conditions that affect the available alternatives. The opportunity to know and to understand the available alternatives is needed to make an informed choice. Since knowledge augments our capacity for acting freely, an important pre-condition of the exercise of freedom is the availablity of education, literacy and learning. So, not only the suppression of facts but also their distortion and misrepresentation and all untrue propaganda, restrict the freedom of individuals. They manipulate the range of alternative choices no less effectively than direct coercion could.

Besides the absence of human coercion, there has to be

(a) the absence of other limitations like lack of knowledge or such things as "fear" that diminish one's capacity to choose, and

---

15. See P.H. Partridge, "Freedom," in *The Encyclopedia of Philosophy*, 8 vols., ed. Paul Edwards (New York: Macmillan Publishing Co., Inc. & The Free Press, 1967; rpt. edn. 1972), 3: 222.

(b) the power or means to make the choice between
    alternatives in order to attain the objective one chooses
    on one's own accord.

This implies that economic destitutes and those who have a
low level of education, implying an absence of a discerning
capacity for truth, cannot really be free in the sense that they
are not free to be, or to act, because they are "not able," they
do not "have the means" or the "power" to act. Thus for
Gandhi "being free to" implies "having the capacity or the
power to." Such a connotation of freedom — to be free from
coercion to achieve chosen ends and to positively possess the
power and social means necessary for their achievement —
would, as de Jouvenel points out, set a new standard as to
how various satisfactions are to be maximized.

What is being forcefully advocated by Gandhi is that we
need such an economic and political arrangement wherein
persons may be redeemed from those circumstances that are
dehumanizing. Gandhi realized very well the realistic fact that
the world of the human is not yet a home for humanity.

Going beyond the narrower negative meaning of
individual or national independence, Gandhi showed the
significance and fuller moral connotations of positive freedom.
Since freedom in the positive aspect is the capacity to choose
for oneself and act on one's own initiative, the existence of
negative freedom is a necessary condition for the attainment
of the positive aspect of freedom.

It goes without saying, thus, that Gandhi preferred
positive freedom to negative liberty. Though an individual is
free to choose to enter or not to enter into an association with
other particular agents, one cannot isolate oneself entirely or
live as an island. The same is true for nations. By equating
freedom with *swarāj* Gandhi built into the concept of freedom
the notion of obligation to oneself and to others, while keeping
the aspect of voluntariness as the very basis of freedom. One
could express the word *swarāj* in two ways then: as *swa-rāj*,

(ruling one's self, have rights with responsibility), and as *swarāj* (freedom in general). Self-rule at the personal level implies the voluntary interiorizing of one's obligation to others. The presence of selfish desires will obscure such an obligation. In other words, a really free person or a truly free nation cannot be selfish and must not be isolationist. To the extent that a nation follows a particular policy of making all its choices only on the basis or the norm of "self-interest," to that extent that nation is not really "free" in the Gandhian understanding.

Gandhi was, at times, adamant about holding on to *swadeśī* and its derivatives of spinning wheel as a symbol of the spirit of self-determination.[16] It represents self-reliance in the area of employment and income generating capacity of the villagers who, in Gandhi's time, constituted over 80 per cent of the people of India. In 1936 Gandhi settled in Sevāgrām village to live with the poor and become part of their daily struggle for survival. By his personal example and service he wanted to "show them how to live" in dignity even in destitution. In the limited resource and meagre income of the village set-up, the "showing" consisted in the limiting of wants to allocate the simple resources of the village meaningfully to a dignified existence. Besides, he worked along with them for continued growth of real income generation through his advocacy of *carkhā*[17] and boycott, even to the extent of irritating those who were hopelessly eager to achieve *swarāj* in the formal sense of

---

16. Gandhi was not a sophisticated economist to undertake a cost-benefit analysis of *"carkha* (spinning wheel) technology" and its impact on economic independence. But there is a case for labour intensive, nature affirming and preserving "development." See F. Schumacher, *Small is Beautiful: Economics as if People Mattered* (New York: Harper & Row, Publishers, 1973).

17. "Limiting" one's wants, in the sense of what one can do without, is the key element. This is something to be pondered seriously in today's world of incessant consumption and creation of unlimited wants resulting in continued borrowing to buy products of alien extraction which, in turn, leaves one in deeper debt and dependency climaxing in non-freedom.

national independence. This shows clearly how much Gandhi valued and cherished self-determination. He showed the close connection between *swarāj* and *swadeśī*, between individual self-rule and individual self-reliance, between national self-government and national self-dependence. Here too it was not just the defensive notion of "negative" liberty but the conception of positive freedom that Gandhi upheld.

Gandhi united these two notions (*swarāj* and *swadeśī*) in a very significant way. The pursuit of *swarāj* necessarily involves the acceptance of *swadeśī*, though the former is morally prior to the latter. Gandhi related the notion of *swadeśī* to his concept of *ahiṁsā* by analogously correlating the link between *swarāj* and *swadeśī* to the relation between *satya* and *ahiṁsā*. By grounding *swarāj* upon *satya*, he linked the notion of positive freedom to truth. The moral priority of *swarāj* is preserved by basing it upon *satya*, i.e., by basing freedom on truth, and by linking *swadeśī* to *ahiṁsā*. Further, Gandhi distinguished between "national *swarāj*" and "individual *swarāj*" in order to prevent the complete fusion of the individual into an organic concept of society.

Though *satya* is the end and *ahiṁsā* the means, the immediate requirement and the *only* legitimate means to pursue *satya* is the practice of *ahiṁsā*. Hence the means "became even more important than the end at the level of conduct and morality."[18] Analogously *swadeśī* has more immediate significance than *swarāj*. If *Swarāj* is the end, *swadeśī* is the only legitimate means. In other words, though freedom has priority over patriotism, the latter is the way to freedom.

Essential to his political ethic, such an interpretation has institutional implications in his notion of a non-violent society and a decentralized polity comprised of numerous village *pancāyat*s. It was becoming more and more evident to him that there could be no complete political independence (*pūrṇa*

---

18. Iyer, *The Moral and Political Writings of Mahatma Gandhi*, 3: 348.

swarāj) without the real participation of the masses. The expression of their self-rule in its socio-institutional dimension was not embodied in the contemporary category of nation-state. It was a bold move on Gandhi's part to go beyond the existing system of nation-state whereof one's autonomous freedom is expressed in a democratic form of government. He envisioned a "democracy" beyond the contemporary democratic form of government.[19]

Swarāj as Self-rule

Swarāj is that "status of India which her people desire at a given moment."[20] The phrase "at a given moment" is important. Depending upon the raised level of consciousness at any particular time of history, people should have the freedom to exercise their *swarāj*. In the early 1920s Gandhi conceived *swarāj* in very practical terms, consisting of three things:

(1) Truthful relation between Hindus and Muslims,

(2) bread for the masses, and

(3) removal of untouchability.[21]

These three items were considered very essential for the political independence from England. When he assumes "the capacity of the people of India to enforce their demands,"[22] in

---

19. With the emergence of large nation states, the quest for direct democracy has disappeared. The resulting radical shift was the emphasis placed on the notion of "representation" rather than "participation." Gandhi's emphasis seems to be on "participatory representation." Hence his concern with various ways of awakening the millions in the villages to the consciousness of their strength so that even civil disobedience, not to speak of violence, could be eliminated in the process of a transformed relationship (CW 64: 195). They ought to be "taught to know what they should want and how to obtain it in the shape of sanitation and hygiene, improvement of material conditions and social relations." (CW, 64: 71).

20. *Young India*, July 17, 1924; CW, 24: 396.

21. *Ibid*.

22. *Young India*, December 15, 1921; CW 22: 18.

his description of *swarāj*, what is implied is the capacity at a
given moment. There is an empowerment of the masses even
at the very initial level of *swarāj* as "bread with dignity" that
enable them to resist authority when it is abused. In other words
"swarāj is to be attained by educating the masses to a sense of
their capacity to regulate and control authority."[23] To claim such
a birth-right of *swarāj* is a sacred duty.[24] This implies that without
basic economic independence and satisfaction of the basic
human need of "bread for the masses," it is illusory to speak of
higher social freedom. Gandhi is very emphatic in his assertion:
"To me it has but one meaning; the eradication of the poverty
of India and freedom for every man and woman. Ask the
starving men and women of India, they say that their swarāj is
their bread."[25] Self-rule is incompatible with every form of
exploitation. Common sense dictates that "when you demand
swarāj, you do not want *swarāj* for yourself alone, but for your
neighbour, too."[26] Reading correctly the mind of Gandhi, Iyer
says that "*Swarāj* which is the hallmark of the free individual is
the basis for communitarian *swarāj*, which in turn lays the
foundation for national *swarāj*, which could, in its turn, in a
world dedicated to *satya* and *ahimsa*, become the basis of global
swarāj, a universal *Rāmrājya* or golden age."[27]

Swarāj as Mokṣa

The earlier analysis of the grounding of *swarāj* on *satya* takes
us to the transcendental dimension of *swarāj*. In contrast to

---

23. *Young India*, January 29, 1925; CW 26: 50.

24. *Young India*, March 3, 1927; CW 33: 138-40. *Young India*, March 17,
1927; CW 33: 133.

25. *Navajivan*, May 4, 1924; CW 23: 538. This conviction of Gandhi
reminds me of a sentence by a village farm-worker in Bihar: "For a starving
person the groaning of an empty stomach is louder and clearer than the
voice of God."

26. *Harijan*, March 1, 1935.

27. Iyer, "Introduction," in *The Moral and Political writings of Mahatma
Gandhi*, 3: 10.

the Jain goal of *kevalajñāna* (pure knowledge) Gandhi does not see the ultimate goal in terms of personal attainment but in terms of the liberation of all. He equated *swarāj* and *mokṣa*. Literally *mokṣa* is the classical Hindu term for the Christian notion of "salvation."[28] The Gandhian usage of the term has a different connotation. For Gandhi *mokṣa* is not a "pie-in-the-sky-when-you-die" — that "something out there" for the attainment of which one struggles. It is realizable, in partial form at least, right here in history. Life is to be lived along the way not just at the end of the road.

His choice to focus specifically on *swarāj* rather than on *mokṣa* shows the importance he has given to the concrete historical, socio-economic, political and incarnate liberation. This further reveals the importance of the enfleshed existence right here in history but in relation to a liberation beyond history, showing a continuum in an unbroken way. The representation of Gandhi's theological ethics in a political category is manifested in his choice of the term *swarāj*.[29] Gandhi rejects a theology that does not encompass politics and the political arena. To the Gandhian way of thinking the break up

---

28. A clarification is needed here. The Christian symbols of salvation, the "Final Bliss," does not have the same signification in Indian philosophical thinking. Indian religious ethical thinking recognizes four *puruṣārthas* (*dharma, artha, kāma,* and *mokṣa*) as the basic ends of the human life. The first three are not ends in themselves but are means to the attainment of the fourth, the ultimate end of the human life. The word *mokṣa* is derived from the root *muc*, meaning to let go, to set free, deliver, release. Hence *mokṣa* is understood as spiritual freedom and redemption, salvation-liberation, spiritual autonomy, absolute freedom, transcendental bliss, the final human good, the ultimate aim of human life, a total absorption into the oneness of all reality. So *mokṣa* for Gandhi signifies the vision of the Absolute Truth to be attained by means of *tapas* or self-suffering. In the preface to his autobiography Gandhi declares that the aim of all his strivings is to attain *mokṣa* or self-realization.

29. One could agree with Jesudasan that it is specifically Gandhi's theology that is actualized in political terms in his choice of the word *swarāj*. To be more specific, it is the doing of that theology (theological

into political life, theological life, and religious life is unnecessary. In fact such a break up is an artificial compartmentalization of life.

A contemplative in action, like Ignatius of Loyola, the locus of his encounter with God is the community of oppressed people to which he is committed. Within this commitment he could see the realization of *swarāj* as the enjoyment of *mokṣa*. His belief in God, active as an existential force, finds expression in his commitment to work for truth and justice in his community. In the struggle of the Indian community against the Transvaal government in south Africa, Gandhi exhorted them, "Truth and justice are on our side. I believe God is always near me. He is never away from me. May you also act in this faith. Believe that God is near you and always follow the truth."[30] His faith is an active faith in the sense that it is inextricably bound up with concrete action and conduct of life. Developed by prayer,[31] faith works as an inner strength and as the force behind non-violence.[32] Several events of his life unfold the working out of his faith and belief system. Hence Gandhi's emphatic assertion, "I cannot find Him [God] apart from humanity."[33] Though God appeared in many and varied forms and ways, the most obvious and evident pattern of God's presence was the poor, the oppressed, the frightened, the untouchable and the social outcasts.[34] Though Gandhi never theologized professionally but the theological considerations were embedded in his theories of political and socio-economic action. In his system of belief the economic and political arena

---

ethics of action) that is manifested in the adoption of a theo-political term like *swarāj*.

30. *Indian Opinion*, January 12, 1907; CW 6: 265.

31. *Harijan*, January 28, 1939; CW 68: 271 in his interview to Chinese delegates.

32. *Collected Works*, 69: 226.

33. *Harijan*, August 29, 1936; CW 63: 240.

34. *CW*, 65: 134 — Gandhi is not alone in having such an insight.

are the testing ground of a person's overall value system and goals in life.

Swarāj as Transformation

Against the people's "hopeless unwillingness . . . to better their lot" and their tendency to "hug their ignorance and dirt as they do their untouchability," Gandhi sought the cooperation of any willing hand to collectively work for the eradication of destitution and the removal of untouchability. He did this with the hope of setting up a transformatory process in human life that would usher in real and a true freedom fitting, as R. Niebuhr says it, to the children of God.[35]

In the Gandhian concept of *swarāj* there are certain inner attitudes that must express themselves outwardly. The "state of the soul" achieved through self-purification and self-realization is a liberative condition for a transformative process. Freedom from fear, a feeling of capacity and worth, a capacity to direct one's life and actions, are some of these inner attitudes. *Abhaya* (fearlessness), which is "indispensable for the growth of other noble qualities,"[36] "connotes freedom from all external fear."[37] It is the cultivation of self-confidence.[38] Constant intelligent, responsible and conscious choices and the self-awareness involved in them make one fearless and enable one to be an actor rather than a re-actor.

Further, Gandhi demands that we overcome inordinate attachment to the body and the physical aspects involved therein.[39] Quite a number of external fears are precisely because

---

35. Gandhi sought Christian cooperation in such a task in his address at the Leonard Theological College in Jabalpur in 1933.

36. M.K. Gandhi, *Selected Works of Mahatma Gandhi*, ed. Sriman Narayan, 4 vols. (Ahmedabad: Navajivan Publishing House, 1968), 4: 232. Henceforth cited as *Selected Works*.

37. *Selected Works*, 4: 232.

38. *Ibid.*, 4: 233.

39. *Ibid.*, 4: 234.

of the consideration of the physical body as the "centre" (nucleus, the "Ultimate Concern") of one's life. The moment God (Absolute Truth) takes that centre stage of one's life, such external fears disappear: "*Swarāj* is the abandonment of the fear of death."[40] Hence, the capacity for a dispassionate self-assessment, a continuous self-restraint, a ceaseless self-purification, a progressive self-awareness, self-reliance, and self-realization are attitudes and qualities related to true *swarāj*. This inner freedom can "be attained only by him who has realized the Supreme."[41] Thus when "we cease to be masters or self-conscious owners and reduce ourselves to the rank of servants, humbler than the very dust under our feet, all fears will roll away like mists; we shall attain ineffable peace, and see *Satyanarayan* (the God of Truth) face to face."[42]

In the 1920s Gandhi articulated in three "pillars of *swarāj*": hand-spinning, removal of untouchability and Hindu-Muslim unity. He related the attainment of *swarāj* to the progress in these three concrete areas.[43]

CONCLUSION

The above analysis leads to three important conclusions:

(a) The desire to dominate over others is in inverse proportion to the existential experience of real freedom, just as dependence on others shows also the range of one's non-freedom.

(b) Freedom attained through the benevolent effort of others, however generous it may be, will not be retained when such effort is withdrawn. The others' effort may expedite the process of attainment of freedom. Nevertheless, every individual singly and the people of

---

40. *Young India*, October 13, 1927.

41. *Selected Works*, 4: 233.

42. *Ibid.*, 4: 234.

43. *Young India*, December 1921; CW 22: 15. *Young India*, March 9, 1922; CW 23: 53. *The Hindu*, April 19, and May 3, 1929; CW 40: 259, 316.

a nation collectively have to undergo the agonizing experience of carrying the cross of one's life toward the journey of true and complete freedom, renouncing any and every desire to dominate others and refusing to be dominated by others, and thus being attuned to the capacity of self-rule, raising the level of consciousness to the true meaning of freedom.

(c) The internalization of our obligations to others will be obstructed if we are at the mercy of our selfish desires. A truly free person cannot be selfish, and must not be an isolationist. Both remain temptations to freedom.

Liberation According to Gutiérrez

As mentioned above the historical irruption of what is formally known as "Theology of Liberation" occurred in the concrete Latin American social situations that are marked by grave inequality, oppression, enslavement, alienation, underdevelopment, dependency, subtle forms of imperialism, repression of freedom and dehumanizing attitudes and actions. Reflecting on these concrete historical realities in the light of the Christian faith, a new awareness arose in the believing community that things need not be, and ought not to be, as they are. Such reflecting-searching community tried to articulate this belief through theological spokespersons like Gutiérrez. The outcome is the "doing" of the Theology of Liberation.[44]

MEANING OF LIBERATION

The symbol of liberation is indeed a fundamental issue in the liberation theology of Gutiérrez. "In a sense, the very nature of Christianity is being reinterpreted through the lens of the

---

44. The title of José Miguez Bonino's book, *Doing Theology in a Revolutionary Situation* (Philadelphia: Fortress Press, 1971), is indicative of the doing aspect of such a theology. The expression theology of Liberation was first used by J. Cone in the title of his book *A Black* Theology of Liberation. 1968.

symbol of liberation."[45] Precisely because this notion is so central to the whole theologizing of Gutiérrez in the Latin American context, it functions at a number of different levels. It is also experienced as being more adequately illuminative of the basic Christian experience at various spheres of existence and reality.

Gutiérrez does not reduce the rich and profound theological and religious symbol of "liberation" to any one concrete definition. He employs the liberation paradigm to interpret the central Christian mystery of grace and salvation. The success of Gutiérrez lies in his recognition of the profundity of the liberation symbol and in his attempt to isolate and interrelate various spheres of meaning and significance.

Gutiérrez distinguishes three reciprocally overlapping levels in the liberation symbol.[46] They give three interpenetrating spheres of meaning for the term liberation. These three interdependent levels pertain to a single complex process of liberation that finds its full completion in the saving work of Christ. The three distinct, but not separate, dimensions or levels of liberation are: "liberation of a social, political, cultural, and economic kind; specifically human liberation with its various aspects; and liberation from sin."[47] In other words, it is a total "integral" liberation, and "the process is single but not monolithic; various dimensions, aspects, or levels must be distinguished and not confused with one another. Neither separation nor confusion, neither verticalism nor horizontalism."[48] An analysis of these levels of liberation can give us an insight into the full significance of the symbol of

45. Roger Haight, S. J., *An Alternate Vision: An Interpretation of Liberation Theology* (Maryknoll, New York: Orbis Books, 1985), p. 45.

46. Gutiérrez, *A Theology of Liberation*, pp. 21-37; also pp. 149-78.

47. Gutiérrez, *The Truth Shall Make You Free* (Maryknoll, New York: Orbis Books, 1990), p. 14.

48. Gutiérrez, *The Truth Shall Make You Free*, p. 14. See also Gutiérrez, *A Theology of Liberation*, pp. 172-74.

liberation as articulated by Gutiérrez.

Liberation as an Aspiration

First of all, liberation "expresses the aspirations of oppressed peoples and social classes, emphasizing the conflictual aspect of the economic, social, and political process which puts them at odds with wealthy nations and oppressive classes."[49] As a reaction to the problem of dependence, the symbol of liberation points to freedom from concrete social oppressions. In this context words like "development" (*Entwicklung, desarrollo*), "progress," "growth" or the policies characterized as "developmentalist" (*desarrollista*), or "developmentalism" (*desarrollismo*), do not adequately capture the "more universal, profound, and radical perspective of liberation."[50]

---

49. Gutiérrez, *A Theology of Liberation*, p. 36.

50. The developmentalist approach interpreted the different types of political, economic, cultural and social advancement evident in various countries as different stages on a continuum from primitive to modern societies. The "advanced" nations were depicted to have attained the last stages in such developmental process. This very process itself was conceived as primarily internal to nations, though foreign countries could help or hinder this process of progress in various ways. While some theorists emphasized the social, economic and political measures in the developmental process [e.g., W.W. Rostow, *The Stages of Economic Growth: A Non-Communist Manifesto*, Cambridge: Harvard University Press, 1960)], others argued for conversion to modern values as the key to development [e.g., Max Weber, *The Protestant Ethic and the Spirit of Capitalism*, tr. Talcott Parsons with an Introduction by Anthony Giddens (New York: Charles Scribner's Sons, 1976)]. The assumption of these theorists was that development in a capitalist mode of economic arrangement together with democratic political structures had improved life for all who lived in countries having such political and economic arrangement. Such countries were christened as "First World." The so- called "Third World" countries too (who haven't made it) could enjoy the benefits of the trodden path of development if only they would embrace the appropriate policies. Statements abound for and against these views. For influential assertions of these views, vide Daniel Lerner, *The Passing of Traditional Society: Modernizing the Middle East* (New York: Free Press, 1958); David C. McClelland, "The Impulse to Modernization," in *Modernization: The*

Liberation as a Process of Humanization

At the second level, liberation as a generalized symbol, points
to a theory of general human history, wherein the process of
humanization or the assumption of conscious responsibility
for one's own destiny are given paramount importance. In
this process of liberation the unfolding of different human
dimensions would usher in "the creation of a new man and a
qualitatively different society."[51]

Dynamics of Growth, pp. 28-39; Rostow, *The Stages of Economic Growth: A
Non-Communist Manifesto*; Talcott Parsons, "Evolutionary Universals in
Society," *American Sociological Review* 29 (1964): 339-57; Parsons, *Societies:
Evolutionary and Comparative Perspectives*; Alex Inkeles, "The Modernization
of Man," in *Modernization: The Dynamics of Growth*, ed. Myros Weiner
(New York: Basic Books, 1966); Irwing Louis Horowitz, *Three Worlds of
Development* (New York: Oxford University Press, 1966). For critiques of
these views, vide Andre Gunder Frank, "Sociology of Development and
Underdevelopment of Sociology," in *Dependence and Underdevelopment*
by James D. Cockroft, Andre Gunder Frank, and Dale L. Johnson (New
York: Doubleday, Anchor, 1972), pp. 321-98; Susanne J. Bodenheimer,
"The Ideology of Developmentalism: American Political Science's
Paradigm-Surrogate for Latin American Studies," *Berkeley Journal of
Sociology* 17 (1972-73): 517-34; Theotonio Dos Santos, "The Crisis of
Development Theory and the Problem of Dependence in Latin America,
in *Underdevelopment and Development*, ed. H. Bernstein (Harmondsworth,
England: Penguin, 1973), pp. 57-80; Samir Amin, *Accumulation on a World
Scale: A Critique of the Theory of Underdevelopment*, 2 vols., tra. Brian Pearce
(New York: Monthly Review Press, 1974); Immanuel Wallerstein, *The
Modern World System: Capitalist Agriculture and the Origins of the European
World Economy in the Sixteenth Century* (New York: Academic Press, 1974);
Immanuel Wallerstein, "The Present State of the Debate on World
Inequality," in *World Inequality: Origins and Perspectives on the World System*,
ed. Immanuel Wallerstein (Montreal: Black Rose Books, 1975), pp. 12-28;
Alejandro Portes, "On the Sociology of Natural Development: Theories
and Issues," *American Journal of Sociology* 82 (July 1976): 55-85; Muhbub Ul
Haq, *The Poverty Curtain: Choices for the Third World* (New Delhi: Oxford
University Press, 1978); Lee Cormie, "The Sociology of National
Development and Salvation History," in *Sociology and Human Destiny*, ed.
Gregory Baum (New York: Seabury, 1980), pp. 56-85.

51. Gutiérrez, *A Theology of Liberation*, pp. 36-37.

A New Human Quest

A new awareness of the quest of the poor, or the "non-person," for *self-realization* in history is the most important contemporary event of the Latin American theologizing process. This quest is termed as the "irruption of the poor" by Gutiérrez.[52] Such an "irruption" is a struggle not only for economic justice, but also for a new way of becoming human. This human quest to be human is popularly called "Liberation." It calls for better economic, political, cultural, educational, psychological conditions. Such a liberation process attempts "solidarity with the poor, with their struggles and their hopes . . . (and hence) an authentic solidarity with everyone — the condition of a universal love that makes no attempt to gloss over the social oppositions that obtain in the concrete history of peoples, but strides straight through the middle of them to a kingdom of justice and love."[53] Hence the central claim of the new human quest is that the "irruption of the poor" qualitatively changes history, Christianity, and theology. Such a claim, from which Gutiérrez never wavered, implies a real break with the past reading and interpretation of history, and the understanding of Christianity and, further, offers a new way of doing theology. This new way of understanding and doing theology is perceived as contradiction of what has previously been done.

It is, therefore, a conversion. The "new event of the poor," the "new praxis of Christian faith," and the "new way of doing theology," are the paradigm shift demanded by the theology of liberation as proposed by Gutiérrez. Only through the

52. See Gustavo Gutiérrez, "The Irruption of the Poor in Latin America and the Christian Communities of the Common People," in *The Challenge of Basic Christian Communities*, ed. Sergio Torres and John Eagleson (Maryknoll, New York: Orbis Books, 1981), pp. 107-23.

53. Gustavo Gutiérrez, *The Power of the Poor in History*, tr. from the Spanish by Robert R. Barr. Second Printing (Maryknoll, New York: Orbis Books, 1983), p. 129.

"viewing point" of the eyes of the poor can the contemporary of the historical praxis be exposed. As active subjects of their own history, the "other" side (the exploited poor human being who reveals the totally "Other") is forging towards a radically different society.[54]

Liberation as a Graced "Kairos"

The aforementioned "irruption of the poor" as a new experience and expression of Christianity is a moment of *kairos*, a special, graced moment, when God is experienced as appearing in history in new ways. God "pitches his tent" (*shekina*) among the poor and challenges our structures and relationships so that in the midst of many and varied forms of suffering something new is being born in the countries of Latin America. This is what prompts the talk of a *kairos*, a favourable time, a moment when the Lord knocks on the doors of the ecclesial community that lives in Latin America (and elsewhere) in order that they open the doors so that He may come and dine there (Rev. 3,20).[55] Such a graced *kairos* calls for a new way of being a human and a Christian. It calls for a transformation.

Liberation as Transformation

As we have seen in Gandhi, there is also a transformation process in the liberation agenda of Gutiérrez. The liberating praxis counteracts the historical praxis. In other words, the

---

54. Gustavo Gutiérrez, "Liberation Praxis and Christian Faith," in *Frontiers of Theology in Latin America*, ed. Rosino Gibellini. Second Printing (Maryknoll, New York: Orbis Books, 1979), pp. 1, 16. There are three basic claims by Gutiérrez. (1) There is a new subject of history. (2) There is a new experience of Christianity. (3) There is a new form and purpose for theology. An analysis of these three claims can reveal the fundamental structure of liberation theology.

55. Gustavo Gutiérrez, *We Drink From Our Own Wells: The Spiritual Journey of a People*, tr. Matthew J. O'Connell (Maryknoll, New York: Orbis Books, 1984), p. 136.

old Christendom model of being a Christian is contradicted by and even negated in the new way of Christian love. The journey of a people in solidarity with the poor replaces the Christendom movement. Such a new liberating praxis of the experience of God with the poor ruptures the previous patterns and transforms them anew to a new way of being Christian. Rupturing the wall of political and theological distinctions created artificially between the spiritual and temporal planes, the spiritual is being mediated through the temporal in this new understanding.[56] A theological reflection on the intrinsic relationship of the church and the world resulted in a prophetic call to the church to be with the poor. The participatory involvement of many Christians in the struggle of the poor made them reflect on the meaning of this new experience of faith. In this process "the New Christendom movement was ruptured and transformed by Christian action and reflection within the liberating praxis of the poor."[57] The radical historical contradictions — between the poor and the rich, between the non-person and the person, between those who are "absent" from history and the victors of history — irrupt into the new historical consciousness becoming possibilities for a liberative transformation of socio-economic and political systems, new ways of doing theology, new patterns of religious practices, and other various modes of being human. The total liberation in Christ includes a "transformation of concrete historical and political conditions on the one hand but also leads that history above and beyond itself to a fulfilment that is not within the reach of human foresight or any human effort."[58] Bringing us liberation, Christ is the one who truly freed us from "the ultimate root of all disruption of friendship and of all injustice

---

56. Gutiérrez, *A Theology of Liberation*, pp. 63-66.

57. Rebecca S. Chopp, *The Praxis of Suffering: An Interpretation of Liberation and Political Theologies* (Maryknoll, New York: Orbis Books, 1986), p. 51.

58. Gutiérrez, "Liberation Praxis and Christian Faith," pp. 28-29.

and oppression."[59] He is the one who transformed us to be really and truly free; that is, to enjoy a freedom that "presupposes the going out of oneself, the breaking down of our selfishness and of all the structures that support our selfishness."[60] Here openness to others becomes the foundation of a freedom which enables us to partake of the fullness of liberation. The fruit of such a fullness of liberation offered to us by Christ is communion with God and with one another.[61]

At a deeper level, it is the complete and full transformation of the human through an encounter with Jesus Christ. Here the symbol of liberation is used as a hermeneutic device to interpret the meaning of Christian salvation. A profound understanding of human dignity, a realization of the way the dehumanizing social conditions choke human potentialities and a conscious awareness of the need for radical structural change lead a person to hear the call of liberation in Jesus Christ. Liberating every person from sin, "which is the ultimate root of all disruption of friendship and of all injustice and oppression,"[62] Christ the Savior makes people truly free, enabling them to live in harmony and communion.

Liberation as Salvation

As Gandhi has used the symbol of *swarāj* as an explicit hermenutical principle to interpret the meaning of *mokṣa,*

59. Gutiérrez, *A Theology of Liberation*, p. 37.

60. Gutiérrez, *A Theology of Liberation,* p. 36.

61. Here Gutiérrez is in full agreement with Bonhoeffer when the latter asserts: "In the language of the Bible freedom is not something man has for himself but something he has for others. . . . It is not a possession, a presence, an object, . . . but a relationship and nothing else. In truth, freedom is a relationship between two persons. Being free means 'being free for the other,' because the other has bound me to him. Only in relationship with the other I am free." *Creation and Fall, Temptation* (New York: The Macmillan Company, 1966), p. 37, as quoted by Gutiérrez, *A Theology of Liberation*, p. 36.

62. Gutiérrez, *A Theology of Liberation,* p. 37.

Gutiérrez working on a more specific theological level uses the symbol of *liberation* to elucidate the meaning of Christian *salvation*. Salvation includes many domains of liberation. It is not an exclusive but an inclusive concept.

The language of salvation is expressed by means of two symbols — exodus and promise. Exodus relates creation and salvation through liberation. Thus liberation is understood as a process. Liberation becomes the link in the continuum of creation and salvation. Exodus reveals this creation-liberation-salvation continuum. It symbolizes continual transformation of history as re-creation.

Gutiérrez looks into the foundational interpretation of the notion of salvation. He re-examines the explanations, that have been taken for granted, of this theological concept which are based on "untested assumptions and vague generalities."[63] A recovery of the idea of salvation as an intrahistorical reality simultaneous with the development of its meaning as the communion of persons with God and their communion among themselves, transforming, orienting and guiding history to its eschatological fulfilment, leads Gutiérrez to redefine the meaning of salvation. He replaces the historical *quantitative* and *extensive* notion of salvation by a *qualitative* and *intensive* explanation.[64] The former notion "cure for sin in this life to be attained beyond this life" is replaced wherein salvation is not regarded as "something otherworldly, in regard to which the present life is merely a test," but positively is the communion of all with God and with one another that transforms the human reality and leads it to its fullness in Christ.[65] By being the centre of God's salvific design, Jesus Christ, through the paschal mystery, transforms the universe and makes it possible for the humans to

---

63. Gutiérrez, *A Theology of Liberation*, p. 149.

64. The quantitative and extensive explanation implies three things: (1) the number of person saved; (2) the possibility of being saved, and (3) the role which the church plays in this process.

65. Gutiérrez, *A Theology of Liberation*, p. 151.

achieve full humanity in such aspects as "body and spirit, individual and society, person and cosmos, time and eternity."[66]

Since salvation is total, absolute and complete, it can never be reduced to any particular instance of fulfilment. Drawing on the biblical symbols of "Exodus" and "promise," Gutiérrez attempts to articulate "creation-liberation-salvation continuum" showing the new way of being a Christian and revealing the dynamic character of salvation as a process.

In the process of liberation from slavery to freedom, creation is transformed. The Exodus event symbolizes the nature and goal of true human participation in creation: "the liberation from Egypt, linked to and even coinciding with creation, adds an element of capital importance: the need and place of man's active participation in the building of society."[67] The Exodus reveals the character of "redemption" as the fulfilment of creation through re-creation or as the fulfilment of creation through transformation of concrete situations. The Creative action of God is involved to His salvific work. The necessity of human participation is linked to the process of the gradual transformation of history.

Humans participate in God's creative, redemptive and salvific work through their participation in the transformation of history. As God's creative, liberative and redemptive work is *already* fulfilled in historical events and yet as it is awaiting its full eschatological fulfilment because of its *not yet* character, Christian praxis is expressed by the symbol of promise. "The promise is gradually revealed in all its universality and concrete expression: it is *already* fulfilled in historical events, but *not yet* completely; it incessantly projects itself into the future, creating a permanent historical mobility."[68] Hence salvation "which is the goal of history is not merely external to history; it is at the same time internal and active within it.

66. Gutiérrez, *A Theology of Liberation*, p. 151.

67. Gutiérrez, *A Theology of Liberation*, pp. 158-59.

68. Gutiérrez, *A Theology of Liberation*, p. 161.

Salvation is not just an extrinsic term outside human history; it is also its intrinsic motive, its reason for being and its meaningful or meaning-giving power."[69] Such an understanding implies that salvation itself is a historical agenda becoming a process (at least a possible process) within the framework of history itself.

Awareness of the process character of salvation makes us understand it as a continuum. Thus a complete discontinuity between history and its goal (salvation) is not only meaningless but also the denial of the transformatory process that is inherent in the nature of being human. Salvation is a humanization process. Humanization is here understood in the way Roger Haight has succinctly described it as

> a movement toward a greater degree of human freedom, the essence of what means to be human. . . . The process of humanization occurs in history when human freedom is opened up and allowed to expand in possibility and option, rational deliberation and choice, the discovery of truth and value that leads to creative action. Since the essence of human existence is freedom, the process of humanization is liberation; the process of becoming free and responsible. Salvation in this world, in history, is liberation, and its ultimate goal is final liberation and freedom.[70]

This implies that salvation, which God as the ground of the meaning of human historical existence offers, must also be understood in anthropological terms. Understood thus, salvation would imply the eschatological fulfilment and completion of human existence wherein the human spirit is being opened up to an absolute submission and responsible commitment within and beyond history. Thus "salvation in its most general or basic would consist in the fullness of human freedom."[71]

---

69. Roger Haight, *An Alternative Vision: An Interpretation of Liberation Theology* (Maryknoll, New York: Orbis Books, 1985), p. 39.

70. Haight, *An Alternative Vision*, p. 39.

71. Haight, *An Alternative Vision*, p. 38.

All the same, salvation cannot just be equated with
liberation; but liberation is the experience of salvation at
particular instances.[72] As life reaches its fullness in Christ,
"(S)alvation is not something other-worldly, in regard to
which the present life is merely a test. Salvation — the
communion of men with God and the communion of men
among themselves — is something which embraces all human
reality, transforms it, and leads it to its fullness in Christ,"
who, by his death and resurrection, transforms the universe
making it possible for humans to reach fulfilment as human
beings.[73] As an intrahistorical reality, salvation — human
openness to God and to one another and human communion
with God and among themselves — transforms, orients and
guides the course of history to its eschatological fulfilment.[74]
As the history of salvation lies at the very heart of human
history and as the salvific action of God undergirds all human
existential undertakings, the historical destiny of humanity
ought to be placed in the "salvific horizon". In this "salvific
horizon" and within an all-embracing salvific process, any and
every act and work that transforms this world into a human
community, opening it to God and people to one another, is a
salvific act, a saving action which is moving toward its complete
fulfilment into a Kingdom of full communion and love.

Both human liberation and the growth of the Kingdom
are, thus, directed toward total human communion of people
among themselves and with God. The growth of the Kingdom
occurs historically in liberation.[75] One could say that "the
historical, political liberating event *is* the growth of the

---

72. In his *A Theology of Liberation*, Gutiérrez has devoted a whole
chapter (Chapter nine, "Liberation and Salvation") to explain these two
symbols of Liberation and Salvation. See Gutiérrez, *A Theology of Liberation*,
pp. 149-87.

73. Gutiérrez, *A Theology of Liberation*, p. 151.

74. *Ibid.*, p. 152.

75. Gutiérrez, *A Theology of Liberation*, p. 177.

Kingdom and *is* a salvific event; but it is not *the* coming of the Kingdom, not *all* of salvation. It is the historical realization of the Kingdom and, therefore, it also proclaims its fullness."[76] This is where the difference lies. A concrete historical realization is a proclamation, as well, of a further fuller realization.

CONCLUSION

Thus for Gutiérrez, salvation is operative as a process of humanization or the liberative transformation within the confines of history, that challenges the human to a mode of being and acting in the world of human affairs, wherein Christ becomes the central liberating symbol of specifically Christian faith in God. Gutiérrez makes it very clear that this process is not just limited to the historical becoming. Unexhausted in its historical repression, this process continues to its eschatological fulfilment in the day of the Lord.

---

76. Gutiérrez, *A Theology of Liberation*, p. 177.

3

Foundational basis of
Liberative Transformation

Introduction

As mentioned earlier the foundational bases of the liberation agendas of Gandhi and Gutiérrez need to be explored in order to assess their adequacy, coherence, consistency, and comprehensiveness as serious systematic theological ethical undertakings. When I speak of foundational basis, I mean the following broad areas or points of reference:

(i) The interpretation of God and His relation to the world and specifically to humans, i.e., the nature of God's relationship to and the presence in the world of human affairs;

(ii) The understanding and interpretation of God's actions in history and the significance of such actions to the historical life of the human community;

(iii) The significance and interpretation of the world and of human life therein;

(iv) The interpretation of the human person qua moral agent;

(v) The explanation of how religious life, faith, and the belief-system form the essence of a responsible self; and, finally,

(vi) The interpretation of how persons *ought* to make moral choices in their interaction with one another, judge their own and other people's actions and the world of human interaction.

The coherence and interrelationship (or lack of it) of the above six points of reference will reveal the adequacy (or inadequacy) of a theological ethical agenda. The nature of various activities (political, economic, social), the relationship between such activities and the human moral nature and the identification of sets of principles for judging those activities cannot be understood without delving into the depths of what Romain Rolland called the vast religious crypt below the edifice of moral and political thought. In the following pages I will attempt to take such plunge into the bases of the liberative transformation process as understood and practised by both, Gandhi and Gutiérrez.

Foundational Basis of Gandhian Liberation

Speaking of the foundational bases, the first question to be asked is: Who (or What) is the God of Gandhi and what difference does his understanding of God make in the human qua moral agent ? As mentioned earlier, there is a theocentrism that gives support to and let energy flow into the anthropocentric tasks of the Gandhian social action and liberative transformation process. Gandhi's deep faith in an Absolute, the belief-system that emanates from such a faith, and the ensuing religious life guiding him onto socio-political life and liberative transformative actions need to be spelled out in order to assess their formative influence on the responsible self.[1] The form and content of Gandhian liberation

---

1. It should be mentioned right at the outset that no system of religious inquiry could "contain" Gandhi. Rev. Joseph J. Doke, an admirer of Gandhi who wrote his first biography, makes a very perceptive remark about Gandhi: "I question whether any system of religion can absolutely hold him. His views are too closely allied to Christianity to be entirely Hindu; and too deeply saturated with Hinduism to be called Christian, while his sympathies are so wide and catholic that one would imagine he has reached a point where the formulae of sects are meaningless." Joseph J. Doke,

agenda and the corresponding ethics of action follow
systematically and logically from his concept of God as Truth
and his notion of the human person qua moral agent who
(should) always stand in relation to the (Absolute) Truth (God),
to other human beings and to the universe. One of Gandhi's
primary concern is an explanation of how religious life, faith
and belief-systems form a responsible self. It is my contention
that it is Gandhi's idea of Truth and his theological
anthropology, i.e., his notion of the humans based on a theology
and philosophy of religion — that form the underlying force
of his economic-political ethics, and, the consequent *raison d'être*
of his attempted action at liberative transformation.[2] Gandhi's
understanding of the nature of God and the humans, his
exposition of human-divine relationship and what that entails
in terms of prescription for action in his advocacy for a
transformed society of human relationship (*Rāmrājya*) need to
be analysed. To these tasks I now turn.

Gandhi's God

If one looks for neatly presented and tightly argued doctrinal
consistency and systematic exposition in Gandhi, one will be
disappointed. Largely unintelligible outside the framework and
infrastructure of the Indian religious tradition, Gandhi's
conception of God is very rich and deeply nuanced. The
formulation is unsystematic, sporadic, to a certain extent
problematic, at times even contradictory. It is rich because of
the many nuances attached to the qualitative aspects of God —

M.K. Gandhi — An Indian Patriot in South Africa, reprinted by Publications
Division (Delhi: Government of India, Sept. 1967), p. 106.

2. Arthur C. Danto is correct in saying that in Indian thought
"philosophy and religion were never separate enterprises nor independent
concerns." *Mysticism and Morality: Oriental thought and Moral Philosophy*
(New York: Harper & Row, 1972), p. 23. Preoccupation with *mokṣa* prevented
Philosophy from becoming an independent system of mere abstract
conceptual inquiry. Nor was Theology pursued in its own right either.

God considered as *saguṇa Brahman*.[3] It is problematic on two accounts. First of all it is difficult to assign clear and distinct meaning to it. Secondly, it is differently defined in various

3. The Supreme Power (*Brahman* = God) is conceived both in personal and impersonal terms in Indian religious traditions right from its recorded beginning. The Supreme Power or God is conceived both in personal (*saguṇa*, i.e., with qualities) and impersonal (*nirguṇa*, i.e., without qualities) categories. Accordingly, the Vedas conceived God as both *ṛta*, the objective and impersonal law regulating the universe (the Cosmic order) which is the aspect of *nirguṇa Brahman*, and Viśvakarmā, the supreme creator of the universe (the aspect of *saguṇa Brahman*). From the Vedāntic philosophy of *prasthānatrayī* — consisting of Upaniṣads, the *Brahma-sūtra*s and the *Gītā* — different schools of thought, initiated by such men as Śaṅkara, Rāmānuja, Madhva and Vallabha, looked at God both personally and impersonally.

Śaṅkara's conception of the distinction was something akin to Hegel's distinction of the Absolute and God, and Spinoza's substance and God. *Brahman* was primarily *nirguṇa* — without qualities. Hence the Supreme Power could only be described in terms of *neti, neti* — not this, not that; since "It" is beyond description, "That" cannot adequately be explained by the limited human mind. It is beyond good and evil; hence a dispassionate and detached witness. It is embodied in the humans as *ātman*. This *ātman* is *Brahman*; as the Upaniṣadic thinkers put it: *tat tvam asi* (Thou Art That) and *aham brahmāsmi* (I am *Brahman*).

The contingent human mind used to the world of qualities and categories need a quality-bearing personalized *Brahman*, the *Brahman* considered from the worldly, human, practical point of view (*vyāvahārika-dṛṣṭi*) to quench intellectual curiosities and to seek guidance and solace from a transcendental source. This is *saguṇa Brahman*. An emphasis on *saguṇa Brahman* by subsequent thinkers such as Rāmānuja, the most powerful critic of Śaṅkara, resulted in stressing the notions of creation, love, mercy, divine grace (prasad), worship, self-surrender (*śaraṇāgati*), resignation to the will of God (*ārtta-prapatti*) and devotion.

Later Indian thinkers and seekers, including Gandhi, were attracted to both the *nirguṇa* and *saguṇa Brahman*. Though difficult to grasp God as *nirguṇa Brahman*, individual persons, endowed with the capacity of self-transcendence, transcend the consciousness of self-hood and, as if capturing eternity in a moment, can experience "Pure Consciousness Itself." On the other hand, *saguṇa Brahman* makes comprehension easier; indeed even necessary to be a stepping stone to the adequate experience of Pure Consciousness Itself. Perhaps the head and the heart of humans, the seat

Indian traditions and by different thinkers who have clearly influenced Gandhi's understanding and from whom Gandhi borrowed for his articulations. Given Gandhi's *equal-path* approach toward religions and his deep respect to religious traditions and religious thinkers, he made a syncretistic selection of notions and meanings useful to him on various occasions. Gandhi's concept of God was thus profoundly influenced by various religious traditions and thinkers, and consequently the Gandhian God cannot be contained in any specific theological bag! Nor can his notions be fully aligned to a particular system of thought. As a "seeker" trying to articulate insights inspired by metaphysical views and concerns, and as a "doer" more interested in action than in theory, Gandhi cared little for neat and tight theological arguments and abstract speculations concerning God, universe or the humans.

What God is in His essence is not fully and adequately comprehensible to the human mind since, according to Gandhi, "man can only conceive God within the limitations of his own mind."[4] Since "God transcends description,"[5] and is

of intellect and of feeling respectively, have their own distinct requirements in the ways of comprehending "That." While *niruṇa Brahman* provided philosophical coherence satisfying the intellect, human religious aspirations for excellence and virtue were met by *saguṇa Brahman* which satisfies the heart. One can find traces of this thinking in Gandhi.

For a detailed discussion see Bhikhu Parekh *Gandhi's Political Philosophy: A Critical Examination* (Notre Dame, Indiana University of Notre Dame Press, 1989), pp. 68-70. Also see Chandradhar Sharma, *A Critical Survey of Indian Philosophy* (Delhi: Motilal Banarsidass, 1976); Surendranath Dasgupta, *A History of Indian Philosophy*, vols. 1-V (Cambridge University Press, 1922); M. Hiriyanna, *Outlines of Indian Philosophy* (London: Allen & Unwin, 1932); Paul Younger, *Introduction to Indian Religious Thought* (Philadelphia: Westminster Press, 1972; V.S. Naravane, *Modern Indian Thought* (Bombay: Asia Publishing House, 1964); Rama Shanker Srivastava, *Contemporary Indian Philosophy* (Ranchi: Sharda, 1984).

4. M.K. Gandhi, *In Search of the Supreme*, 3 vols. (Ahmedabad: Navajivan Publishing House, 1962), 1: 18.

5. Gandhi, *In Search of the Supreme*, p. 10

"the mystery of mysteries,"[6] Gandhi attaches no special
importance to the term which one uses to address God
(personal or impersonal) Rām, Allāh, Yahweh, Truth or
whatever.[7] Though religious life, in accord with his Jain beliefs,
is a life of self-purification and constant seeking after virtue,
especially *ahimsā* and ruth, it is a life of dedication to God and
the humans. God as *ātmā* is not simply a question of *thought*,
but the very *breath* of life, the quintessence and fragrance of
whose radiation fills the universe.[8] Concern for comprehensiveness makes Gandhi grapple with qualitative attributes
of God resulting in such recurrent expressions: "God, the
Good, the Just, the Compassionate, the Bountiful, the Giver
of the daily bread, the Help of the helpless, the All powerful,
the All-knowing, the Ever-vigilant, the Whole Truth."[9] Nonetheless, he prefers to call God "Truth" and claims "to throw a
new light on many old truth," and endeavours "to follow and
represent truth as I know it."[10] It is clearly evident, then, that
he does have a theology, a science of God, unquestionably
manifested in his innumerable writings and speeches.[11]

6. Gandhi, *In Search of the Supreme*, p. 19.

7. It depends on the individual concerned to hold on to his or her
experiential understanding. As far as Gandhi is concerned his term for
God is "Truth." The Gandhian notion of Truth will be dealt with in detail
later.

8. God as *ātmā*, conscience, is within and among us, which makes
satyāgraha possible, and which helps us to find truth/Truth in this world.

9. Gandhi, *Collected Works*, 52: 301.

10. Iyer, *The Moral and Political Thought of Mahatma Gandhi*, p. 4.

11. Here I am using the word 'Theo-logy' and theo-logical reflection
in the sense Victorio Araya has used: "it pertains to the *logos* (reflection,
intelligence, understanding, reasoned word, discourse) on God (*Theos*)."
See Victorio Araya, *God of the Poor* (Maryknoll, New York: Orbis Books,
1987), p. 1.

Though Gandhi has used the term *Brahman* to designate God, he was
more at ease to use such terms as "Eternal Principle," "All-Powerful"
(Speech at public meeting in Comilla, Jan. 5, 1927; *Amrita Bazar Patrika*, Jan.
7, 1927; *Young India*, Jan.13, 1927; *Collected Works* 32: 511, 571-72),

ULTIMATE END AND FINAL TELOS

> What I want to achieve and what I have been striving and
> pining to achieve these thirty years is self-realization, to see
> God face to face and to attain *Moksha* (salvation). I live and
> move and have my being in pursuit of this goal. All that I do
> by way of speaking and writing and all my ventures in the
> political field are directed to this same end.[12]

"Viswanath" (Lord of the Universe) (*Collected Works*, 56: 246), "Supreme
Consciousness," "Pure consciousness" (*Collected Works*, 11: 92),
"Intelligence," "Mysterious Force," "Cosmic Power," "*Śakti* or spirit"
(*Young India*, October 11, 1928; *Harijan*, August 18, 1946), "*ātman* that has
attained *mokṣa*" (*Collected Works*, 11: 126), and "*caitanya*" (principle of life
and consciousness) (*Collected Works*, 11: 189). On many occasions he has
used other terms to designate that Ultimate Reality, that Ṣupreme Being
whom we call God: "Divine Mind" (*Harijan*, August 19, 1939) or simply
"Divinity", "Invisible Power" (*Harijan*, August 19, 1939), "Guide" (*Young
India*, May 8, 1930; *Collected Works*, 43: 215 — at the time of one of his
arrests Gandhi consoled his satyagrahis saying, "Let not my companions
or the people at large be perturbed over my arrest, for it is not I but God
who is guiding this movement. He ever dwells in the hearts of all and he
will vouchsafe to us the right guidance if only we have faith in Him"), "the
Monitor within each one of us" (*Collected Works* 30: 493), "Witness of all
our actions" (*Collected Works*, 30: 493), "Supreme Potter" (Letter of Feb. 16,
1931; *Collected Works*, 65: 180-81), "True Friend" (*Collected Works*, 69: 248),
"Most exacting Master" (*Harijan*, May 6, 1933; *Collected Works*, 55: 121), "a
'Being' who is formless and all-pervading" (Letter to Kasamali, June 13,
1926; Iyer I: 577), one who is 'perfect' and who is 'responsible' for the
wonderful phenomenon, the world" (Letter to Nirmal Chandra Dey,
December 21, 1927; Iyer, *The Moral and Political Writings of Gandhi*, I: 578),
"First Cause" (Letter to Shankaran, April 8, 1928; Iyer, I: 579), "the King of
kings," (*Young India*, October 11, 1928; Iyer, *The Moral and Political Writings
of Mahatma Gandhi*, I: 584), "Life Force" (*Harijan*, August 18, 1946; Iyer I:
592), and "Ultimate arbiter" (*Gandhi's Correspondence with the Government
1942-4*, 2nd edn. (Ahmedabad: Navajivan Publishing House, September
1945), p. 88. All these descriptive categories of God fade into oblivion in
the presence of God as *satya* (Truth). Positively Gandhi preferred to use
the term *satya* to designate God, since it was the "only correct and
significant" description of God.

12. M.K. Gandhi, *Autobiography: The Story of My Experiments with Truth*,
tr. Mahadev Desai (Ahmedabad: Navajivan Publishing House, 1945.
Reprint. New York: Dover Publications, Inc., 1983), p. viii. The God-talk

This remark of Gandhi in the introduction to his autobiography manifests the ultimate goal of Gandhian journey and the foundation of his belief-system. As we have seen above, Gandhi's notion of *swarāj* is a God-oriented liberation. It is no Kantian autonomy without God that is the centre as well as telos of the liberation motif. Apart from a God-oriented self-realization, there can be no autonomy or adequately genuine realization of full freedom in the liberative transformation agenda of Gandhi.[13] The Augustinian call "become what thou art" could very well be applied to Gandhi's notion of self-realization. A pattern somewhat similar to neo-Platonic Aristotelian and Thomistic thought of everything coming from and returning to God, *exitus et reditus*, is discernible in Gandhi. Such a teleological theme gives ground to a theological conviction that all things, including the world of humans, have their *proper ends* towards which they are naturally oriented. When individual humans are oriented toward the end of merging into *Brahman* for which they have a natural inclination, that is, when they are directed by and toward this truth, they are *rightly ordered* morally and spiritually on the right path. The ultimate end of human is the attainment of God:

> Man's ultimate aim is the realization of God and all his activities, social, political, religious, have to be guided by

that gushed out from the depth of his encounter with God and his continuous experiments with Truth was so connatural to Gandhi that inexperienced minds found his overflow very difficult to digest! So much so that once an irate English correspondent wrote to Gandhi about the "God stunt" in *Young India* referring to the numerous citations on God that so abound in Gandhi's mature writings. Gandhi's publication of the same without any apologetic arguments leaving to history to make any judgements if needed and his continuation of Truth-experiments with added intensity manifested Gandhi's inner experience of the power and depth of God's relation in human affairs. See *Young India*, Oct. 11, 1928; CW 37: 347.

13. In this respect Ignatius Jesudasan is correct in calling Gandhi "a theologian of politics and liberation rather than a prophet of secularization." Jesudasan, *A Gandhian Theology of Liberation*, p. 66.

the ultimate aim of the vision of God. The immediate service
of all human beings become a necessary part of the
endeavour, simply because the only way to find God is to
see Him in His creation and be one with it. This can only be
done by service of all. I am a part and parcel of the whole,
and I cannot find Him apart from the rest of humanity.[14]

THE ONE CREATOR, MASTER, AND FATHER OF US ALL

One of Gandhi's fundamental premises was that God is the
creator of all of us. Though the "invisible" and "indefinable"
God has as many names as there are human beings on earth,
and different people worship God under different names. God,
as creator, is *one* and the *same* for all.[15] From this "one fountain-
source," "one complete whole," different forms of worship
have irrupted in history; to this one "invisible and indefinable,"
many names have been given by various people of the earth.[16]
As Viśwanāth God is Lord of the entire universe.

In his conversation with some Muslim friends Gandhi
articulated his notion of God in very clear terms:

God is certainly One. He has no second. He is unfathomable,
unknowable and unknown to the vast majority of mankind.
He is everywhere. He sees without eyes, and hears without
ears. He is formless and indivisible. He is uncreated, has no
father, mother or child; and yet He allows Himself to be
worshipped as father, mother, wife and child. He allows
himself even to be worshipped as stock and stone, although
He is none of these things. He is the most elusive. He is
nearest to us if we would but know the fact. But He is farthest
from us when we do not want to realize His omnipresence.[17]

14. *Harijan*, August 29, 1936.

15. This should not give us an impression that Gandhi considers God
as a person in the way Christians do and address Him (Her) accordingly
by using terms like Father, Creator, Friend, evoking a personal
relationship.

16. Mahadev Desai, *Epic of Travancore* (Ahmedabad: Navajivan
Publishing House, 1937), pp. 169-71; *CW* 64: 254.

17. *Young India*, Sept. 25, 1924; Iyer, 1: 567-68. While publishing this
conversation in *Young India*, Gandhi quoted a poem from Goethe's *Faust*

Though "we may all have different definitions for 'God'. . . . behind all that variety of definitions there would also be certain sameness which would be unmistakable. For the root is one."[18] In his answer to Tagore's quarrel with him for considering the 1934 Bihar earthquake as a punishment, Gandhi articulated his sense of the Divine in his firm belief that God's finger guides the entire field of life:

> If God is not a personal being for me like my earthly father He is infinitely more. He rules me in the tiniest detail of my life. I believe literally that not a leaf moves but by His will. Every breath I take depends upon His sufferance. . . . He and his law are one. The Law is God. Anything attributed to Him is not a mere attribute. He is the Attribute. He is Truth, Love, Law and a million things that human ingenuity can name.[19]

If God is the only *one* creator, the Father of us all and we are his children, then, there cannot be inequality among the creatures and worshippers of this one and only God.[20] God does not treat some children as untouchables from birth and hence as [the] low[est], and others as the high[est].[21] He made us *all* equal. In the order of creation, there cannot be high or low:

> No matter by what name we describe Him, He is the same without a second and if we are all children of the same Creator, naturally there cannot be any caste amongst us. We are one brotherhood and sisterhood, and there cannot be any distinction of high and low amongst us. There are no *savarnas* and *avarnas*, or all are *savarnas* or all are *avarnas*.[22]

---

that chimes the omnipresence of God in resonance to his own divine reverberations.

18. *Young India*, March 5, 1925; Iyer 1: 571.

19. *Harijan*, February 16, 1934.

20. *Harijan*, December 22, 1933; *CW*, 56: 332-33.

21. *Collected Works*, 56: 485-86.

22. Desai, *Epic of Travancore*, pp. 169-71; *CW*, 64: 254.

So all persons are equal before God just as the children are equal before their parents.[23] The social problem of caste system and untouchability was thus challenged and condemned by Gandhi on a sound theological basis. Gandhi condemned the prohibition of Harijans from entering temples and considered it a sin. If God is Viśwanāth, Lord of the entire universe, then to exclude one segment of society with whom he is specially present,[24] from entrance into the special place of his presence and worship is a contradiction of the very meaning of the name of God itself. It is interesting to note that, because of his association with Harijans, Gandhi himself was barred from entry into many temples, including the temple at Guruvayur, considered to be very sacred, holy and important.[25]

GOD IS PRESENT, ACTIVE, AND INTERESTED IN HUMAN HISTORY AND HUMAN AFFAIRS

Gandhi's God is latent or active in human affairs. His God is *not* someone who is in "heaven," heaven considered here as independent of human history. He has nothing to do with a God who is just "out there" or "in heaven" only and for whose realization countless sages have flocked the Himālayan caves. His God is right here in human history. He can be served and realized only by serving the individual persons around. Tagore's poetic musings would very well be welcomed by Gandhi as sound theological meditation concerning God's presence in human undertakings:

"He is there where the tiller is tilling the hard ground and where the path-maker is breaking stones. He is with them in sun and in shower and his garment is covered with dust."[26]

---

23. *Collected Works*, 56: 409.

24. *Ibid.*, 56: 247-48.

25. See *Harijan*, June 20, 1936; *CW*, 66: 35-36. Gandhi himself was not a regular temple goer.

26. Rabindranath Tagore, *Gitanjali* (Song Offerings). Introduction by W.B. Yeats. Reprint (Delhi: The Macmillan Company of India Limited, 1980), p. 7.

Gandhi would join Tagore in challenging the person standing in the "lonely dark corner of a temple with doors all shut . . . chanting and singing and telling the beads," as the sole sign of worship, and would ask the same poetic question, "What harm is there if thy clothes become tattered and stained?" in the process of meeting him and standing by him "in toil and in sweat of thy brow."[27]

God's immanent presence was articulated by Gandhi in 1936:

> The only way to find God is to see Him in His creation and be one with it. . . . I cannot find Him apart from the rest of humanity. My countrymen are my nearest neighbours. They have become so helpless, so resourceless, so inert that I must concentrate on serving them. . . . If I could persuade myself that I should find Him in a Himalayan cave I would proceed there immediately. But I know that I cannot find Him apart from humanity.[28]

In his dialogue with Dr. Charles Fabri, published in *Harijan*, August 19, 1939, Gandhi says, "The Divine Mind is unchangeable but that Divinity is in everyone and everything — animate and inanimate."[29] Gandhi's experiment lies in finding his God in and through his interaction with others in society. In his service to others, especially the poor, Gandhi finds his God. God's presence is experienced right here in human history. On E.S. Montague's enquiry in 1938 how a social reformer like Gandhi had "strayed" into politics Gandhi replied:

> Politics is an extension of my social activity. I could not be leading a religious life unless I identified myself with the whole of mankind and that I could not do unless I took part in politics. The whole gamut of man's activities today constitute an indivisible whole. . . . I do not know any religion apart from human activity. It provides a moral basis to all

27. Rabindranath Tagore, *Gitanjali* (Song Offerings). Introduction by W.B. Yeats. p. 7.

28. *Harijan*, August 29, 1936.

29. Iyer, *The Moral and Political Writings of Gandhi*, 1: 558.

activities which they would otherwise lack, reducing life to a maze of 'sound and fury signifying nothing'.[30]

GOD AS EXISTENTIAL FORCE, NON-EMBODIED
CONSCIOUSNESS, UNALTERABLE LAW, ULTIMATE VALUE,
AND COSMIC PERVADING POWER

As early as 1907, Gandhi captured the glimpse of the existential force of God's presence in his vision of liberation and justice. "Truth and justice were on our side," said Gandhi in reference to the struggle of the Indians in South Africa against the Transvaal government; "I believe God is always near me. He is never away from me. May you also act in this faith. Believe that God is near you and always follow the truth."[31]

Brahman as cosmic spirit is *nirguna*: "Fundamentally God is indescribable in words. . . . The qualities we attribute to God with the purest of motives are true for us but fundamentally false."[32] "Beyond the personal God there is a Formless Essence which our reason cannot comprehend."[33] The Formless essence, the cosmic spirit, is "pure" or non-embodied consciousness, not the consciousness of some *Being*, but consciousness *simpliciter*.[34] As an existential force it is active and represents infinite energy (*śakti*). This active "energy-spirit" pervades structures and informs the universe operating in it in a law-like manner: "I do *dimly perceive* . . . a living power that is changeless, that holds all together, that creates, dissolves and recreates. That informing Power or Spirit is God. . . . He alone is."[35]

---

30. M.K. Gandhi, *Nonviolence in Peace and War*, 2 vols. (Ahmedabad: Navajivan Publishing House, 1948), 1: 170-71.

31. *Indian Opinion*, January 12, 1907; *CW*, 6: 265.

32. *Collected Works*, 50: 200.

33. *Harijan*, March 23, 1940; Also see *Harijan*, July 28, 1946.

34. If it were consciousness of some being, it would then have to be other than consciousness. But the cosmic spirit is pure consciousness.

35. *Young India*, October 11, 1928; See Gandhi, *In Search of the Supreme*, 1: 5-6. See also *Young India*, November 24, 1927.

God is "mysterious" in the sense that its nature and manner of operation can never be adequately grasped by finite minds, though one can acquire some knowledge of it. His existence cannot just be reasoned out.

> Whilst it is laudable and legitimate to bring everything under the dominion of reason we must be humble enough to recognize that there must be things beyond reason, seeing that man is an imperfect being.[36]

Even if one is not able to reason out God's existence, "I must accept the experience of and the belief of mankind in the First Cause."[37]

There was no doubt in Gandhi's mind that "this universe of sentient beings is governed by a Law. If you think of Law without its giver I would say that the Law is the Lawgiver, that is God. He and His Laws are one. The Law is God."[38]

Though God acts in accord with immutable laws,[39] He and His laws are benevolent:

> That Law . . . which governs all life is God. Law and the law-giver are one. I may not deny the Law or the Law-giver, because I know so little about It or Him. Even as my denial or ignorance of the existence of an earthly power will avail me nothing, so will not my denial of God and His Law liberate me from its operation; whereas humble and mute acceptance of divine authority makes life's journey easier. . . . I do dimly perceive that whilst everything around me is ever changing, ever dying, there is underlying all that change a living Power that is changeless, that hold all together, that creates, dissolves and recreates. That informing Power or Spirit is God. And since nothing else I see merely through

36. Gandhi, Letter to Shankaran, April 21, 1928; Iyer, *The Moral and Political Writings of Mahatma Gandhi,* 1: 580.

37. Gandhi, Letter to Shankaran, April 8, 1928; Iyer, *The Moral and Political Writings of Mahatma Gandhi,* 1: 579.

38. *Harijan,* March 23, 1940; February 16, 1934; Cf. also *Young India,* October 11, 1928; *CW,* 77: 390.

39. *Navajivan,* October 25, 1925.

the senses can or will persist, He alone is. . . . I see It as purely benevolent. For I can see that in the midst of death life persists; in the midst of untruth, truth persists; in the midst of darkness light persists. Hence I gather that God is Life, Truth, Light. He is Love. He is the supreme Good.[40]

This Power of God must be manifested in various ways. For Gandhi

He must rule the heart and transform it. . . . He must express Himself in even the smallest act of His votary. . . . It is proved not by extraneous evidence but in the transformed conduct and character of those who have felt the real presence of God within. Such testimony is to be found in the experience of an unbroken line of prophets and sages in all countries and climes. To reject this evidence is to deny oneself. This realization is preceded by an immovable faith. He who would in his own person test the fact of God's presence can do so by a living faith. And since faith itself cannot be proved by extraneous evidence, the safest course is to believe in the moral government of the world and therefore in the supremacy of the moral law, the law of truth and love. Exercise of faith will be safest where there is a clear determination summarily to reject all that is contrary to Truth and Love. . . . Faith transcends reason (but need not negate it). . . . I am fortified in the belief by my own humble and limited experience. The purer I try to become, the nearer I feel to be to God.[41]

There is one major difference between human actions, which are also governed by laws, and God's actions:

As our laws and our knowledge are imperfect, we can violate these laws in a civil and uncivil manner. Being all-knowing and omnipotent God never violates His own laws. These admit of no improvements or additions. They are immutable.[42]

---

40. *Young India*, October 11, 1928; Iyer 1: 584-85; see also Iyer 1: 589.
41. *Young India*, October 11, 1928; Iyer 1: 583-86.
42. *Navajivan*, October 25, 1925.

Hence, it is self-contradiction to think of changes in God's law because God himself *is* the law.[43]

As the supreme principle of order; as the supreme intelligence guiding and regulating the universe from within, God is not some person outside ourselves or away from the universe. He pervades everything and is immanent in all things.[44] Immanent in the universe, he infuses and evolves order and hence law from within the universe.

The power of God's existential presence transforms human nature itself. The transformed conduct and character of a person blessed with God-realization manifests that God verily is:

> God to be God must rule the heart and transform it. He must express Himself in even the smallest act of His votary. This can only be done through a definite realization, more real than the five senses can produce. . . . Where there is realization outside the senses it is infallible. It is proved not by extraneous evidence, but in the transformed conduct and character of those who have felt the real presence of God within.[45]

Transcending the senses this mysterious Power pervades every reality:

> God is an indefinable mysterious Power that pervades everything. I feel it, though I do not see it. It is this unseen Power which makes itself felt and defies all proof, because it is so unlike all that I perceive through my senses. It

---

43. Gandhi's notion of "immutable laws" of God is akin to the conception of Divine Law in Thomas Aquinas. For his treatment on law see *Summa Theologiae*, 1a, 2ae, Qq. 90-97 (Treatise on Law); See Anton C. Pegis, ed., *Basic Writings of Saint Thomas Aquinas*, 2 vols. (New York: Random House, 1945), 2: 742-805.

44. According to Bhikhu Parekh, a Gandhian analyst, Gandhi's God "was not a creator." But there are positive references in Gandhi where he calls God creator. See Parekh, *Gandhi's Political Philosophy*, p. 73.

45. *Young India*, October 11, 1928; Iyer 1: 585; *In Search of the Supreme*, 1: 6.

transcends the senses.[46]

As power immanent, "God abides in our hearts."[47] Because God is beyond the reach of our senses, we cannot truly describe him adequately:

> As a matter of fact we are all thinking of the Unthinkable, describing the Indescribable, seeking to know the Unknown, and that is why our speech falters even inadequate and often contradictory.[48]

Consideration of God as Ultimate Value has ethical implications for Gandhi. God makes a claim on us to direct our values in accordance with this Ultimate Value. Even Nietzsche spoke of the trans-valuation of old values (*Umwertung alter Werte*) in the sense that there are times of alteration in our valuation. Directing one's action in accord with absolute values can be subversive. Every authentic appeal to ultimate values can have a corrosive action on the established order.[49] Gandhi himself was convinced that

---

46. Gandhi, *In Search of the Supreme*, 1: 5.

47. *Collected Works*, 50: 203.

48. *In Search of the Supreme*, 1: 23. Gandhi would agree with Gabriel Marcel when he says, "God can only be given to me as Absolute Presence in worship; any idea that I form of Him is only an abstract expression or intellectualisation of the Presence." See *Being and Having*, Fontana Library, 1963, p. 184, as quoted by Suman Khanna, *Gandhi and the Good Life* (New Delhi: Gandhi Peace Foundation, 1985), footnote 8, p. 98.

49. Albert Camus has strongly stressed this in his *L'Homme revolte*: In every act of rebellion, the man concerned experiences not only a feeling of revulsion at the infringement of his rights but also a complete and spontaneous loyalty to certain aspects of himself. Thus he implicitly brings into play a standard of values so far from being false that he is willing to preserve them at all costs. . . . An awakening of conscience, no matter how confused it may be, develops from any act of rebellion and is represented by the sudden realization that something exists with which the rebel can identify himself — even if only for a moment. Cf. *The Rebel* (English tr.), Hamish Hamilton, 1953, pp. 19-20; as quoted by Iyer, *The Moral and Political Thought of Mahatma Gandhi*, p. 118.

religious beliefs or the ways we look upon God matter greatly
and affect our lives:

> There is no doubt that mankind is affected largely by the
> way it looks upon God. So far as India is concerned the vast
> majority think of God as the Monitor within each one of us.
> Even the illiterate masses know that God is only one, that
> He is all-pervading, and therefore, is the witness of all our
> actions.[50]

GOD AS PROTECTOR/SAVIOUR

Another powerful symbol of God is God as Protector (Help
of the helpless/Saviour). Though the use of this symbol is not
as common as his references to God as Truth, there are quite
a number of references to God as the help of the helpless.
They occur especially when Gandhi speaks on the *Harijan* issue.
Basing themselves on the *karma* theory, many orthodox Hindus
argued that the Harijans were in the current existential
condition because of their past sins. Gandhi argued that, if
this is the case then the Harijans should all the more be allowed
to enter the temple to offer worship in order to atone for
their past sins as "God has been described by all scriptures of
the world as a Protector and Saviour of the sinner."[51] There
are other references to God as Saviour and to the saving
presence and activity of God. God is also described as the
only true healer or doctor.[52]

GOD AS THE PRIME SOURCE AND SUMMIT OF ALL MORAL NORMS

One of Gandhi's important understandings is of God as both
moral agent and the prime source of all norms of morality.
Gandhi emphasized that "God is ethics and morality."[53] This
connotes the linkage of God with the moral law of the human
universe. "And what is God but the law?" he asks and goes

50. *Collected Works*, 30: 493.
51. Speech at Mandla, December 6, 1933, *CW*, 56: 304.
52. *Collected Works*, 62: 119.
53. *Collected Works*, 26: 224.

on to say that "to obey God is to perform the law."[54] In a short reply to Mr. Nadkarni's "Letter to the Editor of *Young India*" inquiring about the reasons of Mr. Bradlaugh's atheistic denial of God, Gandhi wrote:

> I present Mr. Nadkarni with these definitions of God: The sum total of *karma* is God. That which impels man to do the right is God. The sum total of all that lives is God. That which makes man the plaything of fate is God. That which sustained Bradlaugh throughout all his trials was God. He is the Denial of the atheist.[55]

A GOD BEYOND MORALITY

And yet Gandhi's God is a God beyond morality. A type of Aristotelian notion and argument is present in Gandhi. While Aristotle attributes contemplation (*theoria*) to the gods, he denies to them production and moral action. In His *Nicomachean Ethics*, Aristotle says that the gods have no need of action (*praxis*), since they already possess that happiness (*Eudaimonism*) which is the end of all action. Happiness displays "activities in conformity with virtue." Thus happiness is for Aristotle synonymous with "living well" (*eu zen, kalos zen*) or "acting well" (*eu prattein, eupraxia*) and "acting well" is equivalent to "faring well." The aim of human life, according to Gandhi, is to merge into *Brahman*, to become what we are (*tat tvam asi*) or that the self becomes the Self. Moral actions are necessary means to the end of merging into God. Since God is in Himself, we are not yet "That," we need moral/ethical actions that necessarily help us in union. On the other hand, God who is/exists in Himself need not necessarily act (since God does not have to act to exist because he is pure Act) and since ethics and morality have to do with the realm of action, God is beyond morality and ethics. Nevertheless, He is the Norm for human actions. He is the Law guiding human actions.

---

54. *Harijan*, April 24, 1937; *CW*, 65: 111.
55. *Young India*, April 30, 1925; Iyer 1: 575.

A GOD BEYOND REASON

Being beyond and above reason, God cannot be proved by reason; the existence of the cosmic spirit is incapable of rational demonstration.[56] Though "reason may be a useful instrument of knowledge at one stage,"[57] faith and experience to which faith leads are the two stages of knowledge of God:

> Just as hearing is not the function of the eyes, so also knowing God is not the function of the senses or of reason. (At the same time) to say that reason cannot know God betrays ignorance. . . . To know Him a different faculty (of unshakeable faith) is required.[58]

The truth is that "belief in God is a function not of the intellect but of faith."[59] By and of itself reason just cannot prove the existence of God (nor deny His existence) and for that matter, of anything.

At the same time Gandhi could not see why only what satisfied reason should be deemed to exist. In fact Gandhi rejected the view that reason was a person's highest faculty.[60] In his reply to Ibrahimji Rajkotwala's query about the rational proof of the existence of God, Gandhi retorts:

> If you say that nothing is beyond rational explanation, you will certainly run into difficulties. If we give the highest place to reason, we shall be faced with serious difficulties. Our own *ātman* is beyond reason. People have indeed tried

---

56. *Young India,*, January 21, 1926.

57. Gandhi, Letter to Ibrahimji Rajkotwala, May 5, 1932; Iyer 1:588.

58. *Ibid.; Ibid.*

59. *Young India,* January 21, 1926; Iyer 1: 589.

60. Here Gandhi is in direct contradiction with Aquinas. For Thomas the essential human nature is distinguished by rationality and freedom. Rationality is associated to corporeality too. But they agree in their fundamental source for ethics: their reflective (more experiential for Gandhi) understanding of what "the human" or "human nature" comprises, not in an actual so much as in an ideal sense. Cf. Lisa Sowle Cahill, *Between the Sexes: Foundations for a Christian Ethics of Sexuality* (New York: Paulist Press, 1985), pp. 105-19.

to prove its existence with logical arguments, as they have tried to prove the existence of God. But he who knows God and the *ātman* only by his intellect does not know them at all. Reason may be a useful instrument of knowledge at one stage. But anybody who stops there will never enjoy the benefits of true spiritual knowledge in the same way that intellectual knowledge of the benefits of eating food does not by itself help one to enjoy those benefits.[61] God or the *ātman* is not an object of knowledge. He Himself is the Knower. That is why we say that He is above reason.[62]

Knowing God is not the function of the senses or of reason. To know Him a different kind of faculty is required, and this is unshakeable faith.[63]

And hence

belief in God is a function not of the intellect but of faith. Reasoning is of little help to us in this matter and once we accept God the ways of the world cease to bother us. Then we have to accept that no creation of God can be purposeless.[64]

GOD, A PREFERENTIAL LOVER

. Gandhi often speaks of God as *daridranārāyana* (Lord of the poor). God is "a servant of his servant."[65] Such a concept is

---

61. Gandhi's food analogy is very appropriate indeed. One can never be intoxicated by an intellectual knowledge of the taste of wine! One can surely and to a certain extent adequately, explain its taste as well as describe the drunken state of a person subsequent to drinking. But one can never get drunk by the knowledge of the taste of wine or by the intellectual understanding of the after-effect of drinking. One has to *drink* the wine in order to get drunk. Similarly one has to *taste* God, in Gandhian terms, to know who God really is and what he can do to we humans. Simply put, true knowledge is a relational reality. One could very well say that in speaking thus Gandhi is in a mystical realm.

62. *Mahadevbhaini Diary*, 1: 136-37; Iyer 1: 588.

63. *Ibid.; ibid.*

64. Letter to Bhuskute, *Mahadevbhaini Diary*, 1: 364; Iyer 1: 589.

65. *Collected Works*, 49: 92.

essential to the one dedicated to the path of love and service. His discussion of God as *daridranārāyaṇa* is mainly to derive the ethical motivation to serve the poor and the oppressed: "He (God) can be served in one way alone. To serve the poor is to serve God. . . . In serving those who suffer, one serves God."[66] Even worship is offered through service:

> The best and most understandable place where He can be worshipped is a living creature. The service of the distressed, the crippled and the helpless among living things constitutes worship of God.[67]

Thus the human being, not the lord of creation but the servant of God's creation, stands as God's steward and co-worker "to serve all the lives and thus to express God's dignity and love."[68] Gandhi's own personal conviction that we serve God through service, especially of the victimized, gushed from the depth of his heart in his press meeting of 1939 while breaking one of his numerous fasts:

> I claim to know my millions. All the 24 hours of the day I am with them. They are my first care and last, because I recognize no God except the God that is to be found in the hearts of the dumb millions. They do not recognize His presence; I do. And I worship the God that is Truth or a Truth which is God through the service of these millions.[69]

Echoing the supplication of Tagore in his *Gītāñjali*, "Give me the strength never to disown the poor or bend my knees before insolent might" and the wisdom of the Tamil Śaivite poet Appār, Gandhi could point out that "the servant of God

---

66. *Navajivan*, October 25, 1925; Iyer 1: 577.

67. *Navajivan*, May 6, 1928; Iyer 1: 582.

68. *Young India*, March 24, 1927; *CW*, 33: 186.

69. At the same time one should work and earn one's living: "It is sin to provide food for an idle person who makes no effort and depends on others for food. It is a meritorious act to provide him with an occupation and, if he refuses to work, to let him starve is to render service to him. However, ceremonial worship by itself does not constitute the service of God." *Navajivan*, October 25, 1925.

will never consent to be the slave of any man."[70] The service rendered to God should be out of undivided loyalty. This is clear in one of his statements:

> I have realized that those who wish to serve God cannot afford to pamper themselves or to run after luxury. Prayers do not come easily in an atmosphere of luxuries. Even if we do not ourselves share the luxuries, we cannot escape their natural influence. The energy that we spend in resisting that influence is at the cost of our devotional efforts.[71]

Gandhi's best articulated description of God is given in his answer to a "conscientious objector" to the introduction of God's name into the Congress pledge of non-cooperation. It is so captivating that I feel obliged to quote him at length:

> We all may have different definitions of 'God.' If we all could give our own definitions of God there would be as many definitions as there are men and women. But behind all the variety of definitions there would be also a certain sameness which would be unmistakable. For the root is one.
>
> God is something undefinable which we all feel but which we do not know. . . . To me God is truth and love; God is ethics and morality; God is fearlessness. God is the source of light and life and yet He is above and beyond all these. God is conscience. He is even the atheism of the atheist. For, in His boundless love He permits the atheist to live. He is the searcher of hearts. He transcends speech and reason. He knows us and our hearts better than we do ourselves. He does not take us at our word for He knows that we often do not mean it, some knowingly and others unknowingly. He is a personal God to those who need His personal presence. He is embodied to those who need His touch. He is the purest essence. He simply is to those who have faith. He is all things to all men. He is in us and yet above and beyond us.

---

70. Jesudasan, *A Gandhian Theology of Liberation*, p. 67.

71. *Indian Opinion*, August 7, 1909; CW, 9: 277.

One may banish the word "God" from the Congress but one has no power to banish the Thing Itself. What is a solemn affirmation if it is not the same thing as in the name of God? And surely conscience is but a poor and laborious paraphrase of the simple combination of three letters called God. He cannot cease to be because hideous immoralities or inhuman brutalities are committed in His name. He is long suffering. He is patient but He is also terrible. He is the most exacting personage in the world and the world to come. He metes out the same measure to us that we mete out to our neighbors — men and brutes. With Him ignorance is no excuse. And withal He is ever forgiving for He always gives us the chance to repent. He is the greatest democrat the world knows, for He leaves us 'unfettered' to make our own choice between evil and good. He is the greatest tyrant ever known, for He often dashes the cup from our lips and, under cover of free will, leaves us a margin so wholly inadequate as to provide only mirth for Himself at our expense. It is thus that Hinduism calls it all His sport — *lila*, or call it an illusion — *maya*. We are *not*, He alone *Is*. And if we will be, we must eternally sing His praise and do His will. Let us dance to the tune of His *bansi* — lute, and all would be well.[72]

GOD AS TRUTH

All other articulations of God are eclipsed, when Gandhi starts speaking of God as Truth. As early as 1908 Gandhi very clearly expressed his firm conviction of the relation of God with truth:

> Where there is God there is truth, and where there is truth there is God. I live in fear of God. I love truth only, and so God is with me. Even if the path of truth does not please the community it pleases God. Therefore, I will do what pleases God even if the community should turn against me.[73]

It should be mentioned here that it was Gandhi's search for a firm foundation for his political programme of action that resulted in the centrality of his notion of truth.[74]

---

72. *Young India*, March 5, 1925; Iyer 1: 571-72; *CW*, 26: 224-25.

73. *Indian Opinion*, December 9, 1908; *CW*, 9: 107-08.

74. In this respect Gandhi agrees and echoes Hans Barth when the

Whereas Max Weber analysed the relationship between the Protestant ethic and the spirit of capitalism without making any judgement upon it, Karl Marx introduced an insoluble contradiction between religious faith and the process of social transformation and took a committed stand in favour of the dispossessed proletariat, Gandhi attempted successfully to resolve the apparent contradiction between religion and social sphere by a recourse to religious faith itself, and put it at the service of the liberative transformation of human beings in the social, political and economic spheres. In this process of transformative undertakings, perhaps, intuitively, he received an "insight" into the meaning and the power of truth.

As the supreme value in politics, religion and ethics, and as the ultimate source of appeal and authority, *satya*[75] is the foundation of all reality. Throughout his life Gandhi struggled for the realization of Truth through *ahiṁsā*. His life-experience convinced him, as he confessed at the end of his autobiography,

---

latter affirms, "Every political theory absolutely depends on a theory of truth whether it makes it explicit or not. As a basis for a program of action, it always conceals a theory of truth. . . . Whatever the doctrine of truth may be, it has certain inevitable and determinable consequences for political theory . . . the difference between an absolute and relative theory of truth is . . . of decisive, constitutive importance in establishing institutions which form the public will. Man has always justified unlimited coercion by rightly or wrongly assuming monopolizing the possession of some political truth." As quoted by Raghavan N. Iyer without giving reference. See Iyer, *The Moral and Political Thought of Mahatma Gandhi*, p. 149.

75. The Sanskrit word *satya* is derived from *sat*, which means being. *Sat* also means abiding, actual, right, wise, self-existent essence, as anything really is, as anything ought to be. (Cf. Monier-Williams, *Sanskrit-English Dictionary*). Generally translated as truth, the primary meaning of *sat* is "existing" (from the root *as* = to be; the noun form *satya* means "Being"). Gandhi describes God as truth in the sense of being that which is, whose essence it is to be (*sat*). In the Indian definition changelessness is an inherent quality of being, and therefore truth and God also have the qualities of changelessness. The implication of the derivation of *satya* from *sat* is that "nothing exists in reality except Truth, everything else is illusion." (Shukla,

that "there is no other God than Truth."[76] On deeper analysis one would find that *"Satya* is the only correct and fully significant name for God."[77] His relentless life of contemplative-action is a saga of the pursuit of Truth. From his deep conviction that "morality is the basis of things and truth is the substance of morality,"[78] search for Truth became the sole objective of his life. As he grew in wisdom and knowledge, "truth began to grow in magnitude and everyday my definition of it has been widening,"[79] until he reversed the expression "God is Truth" to "Truth is God" in order to make, as it were, the absolute and ultimate foundation of all life and actions.[80] He claims that "This truth is not only truthfulness in word, but truthfulness in thought also and not only the relative truth of our conception but also the absolute Truth, the Eternal

---

Conversations with Gandhiji, Vora, 1949, p. 35). As *parama satya, satya* is the highest of human ends transcending all other ends and hence endows value to *dharma* (moral law and cosmic order), *artha* (material welfare), *kāma* (human affections and happiness), and to *mokṣa* (salvation and eventual emancipation). Besides the normal meaning of veracity, *satya* has a variety of connotations, viz., real, sincere, pure, good, existent, effectual, and valid. *Sat* in its highest sense stands for the absolute, archetypal Reality and for the absolute, archetypal Truth. Going beyond and standing behind the "illusory flux of fleeting phenomena," there exists an eternal substratum of noumenal reality, the one and only bedrock of supernatural Truth. This *Satya* is the source of eternal and universal values like truth, righteousness and justice. See Nirmal Minz, *Mahatma Gandhi and Hindu Christian Dialogue* (Madras: The Christian Literature Society, 1970), p. 2. See also Iyer, *Moral and Political Thought of Gandhi,* pp. 150-51.

76. Gandhi, *Autobiography,* p. 453.

77. Letter to Narandas Gandhi, July 22, 1930; Iyer 2: 162.

78. Gandhi, *Autobiography,* p. 30.

79. *Ibid.*

80. Gandhi's manifest claims of the reversal could be seen in many of his letters and speeches. The following could be a selective sample: Speech after morning prayers, July 22, 1930; Letter to Narandas Gandhi MMU/I; Iyer 2: 162-64; Speech at Meeting in Lausanne, Mahadev Desai's Diary, December 8, 1931; Iyer 2: 164-70; Letter to Boys and Girls, March 21, 1932, Mahadevbhaini Diary; Iyer 2: 172.

Principle, that is God."[81] His depiction of truth as a goal to be approximated rather than an archetype or a full revelation given at a particular moment of history speaks of his understanding of Truth as a final telos that sparks out in the partial truths found in human hearts and manifested in various faiths. At the same time Gandhi found difficulty in articulating truth/God adequately. Construing reality with Hegelian completeness is foreign to Gandhi. The Gandhian conception of truth goes beyond a Lockean love of stability and entails a constant, spiritual Augustinean restlessness to finally "rest in Thee, my Lord."[82] At the same time Gandhi existentially experiences that Truth can be found in every heart. The truth-content is manifested and is present in all religious traditions. Beyond their particular cultural and historical religious expressions, Gandhi finds a common element in the religion of humanity which is reflected as faith in the moral order governing the universe. According to Gandhi this religious belief is common to all religions. This moral order is *satya*, and the process by which life is continued is *Ahiṁsā*.

Nature of Truth

> But for me, truth is the sovereign principle which includes numerous other principles. Thus truth is not only truthfulness in word but truthfulness in thought also and not only the relative truth of our conception but the Absolute Truth, the Eternal Principle, that is God.
>
> In fact it is more correct to say that Truth is God than to say that God is Truth. . . . My uniform experience has convinced me that there is no other God than Truth.
>
> I endeavor to follow and represent truth as I know it. I do claim to throw a new light on many an old truth. . . . The little fleeting glimpses, therefore, that I have been able to have of Truth can hardly convey an idea of the indescribable luster of Truth, a million times more intense than that of the

---

81. Gandhi, *Autobiography*, p. ix.
82. See Augustine, *Confessions*, especially Ch. XIII.

sun we daily see with our eyes. In fact what I have caught is only the faintest glimmer of that mighty effulgence. But this much I can say with assurance, as a result of all my experiments, that a perfect vision of Truth can only follow a complete realization of Ahiṁsā.

These three passages succinctly articulate Gandhi's notion of the nature of Truth, and the relation of that Truth to moral/ethical considerations. As we often experience a moral uncertainty regarding good and evil, we experience a cognitive confusion in regard to the true and the false. These moral and cognitive ambiguities are explained by Gandhi in terms of the partiality and fragmentariness of our knowledge of truth. His change from "God is Truth" to "Truth is God" made him consider the major religions of the world as cultural and historical phenomena, offering their allegiance to the God of Truth in diverse ways. Gandhi endeavoured for the integration of truth into his thought and actions, indeed, his very life-process.

Gandhi described God as truth in the sense of being that which is, whose essence is *sat* (to be). This primary ontological meaning of *satya* (derived from *sat*), meaning "to be," "to exist," connotes the idea of changelessness. Therefore truth (hence God) has the qualities of changelessness. This intrinsic characteristic, "to be," of God is exclusively his: "Only God is, nothing else is."[83] Everything else is momentary and fleeting.

Moreover, Gandhi speaks of truth as *sat*, being the ontological absolute. What characterizes Gandhi's approach, in keeping with the Hindu tradition, is to consider the continuous quest of *sat* as the goal of every human endeavour. Gandhi was so rooted in his own traditional heritage that to consider persons as founded in the ontological was connatural to him. But Truth is not a substitute for God. It is meant to elucidate the meaning of God.

---

83. Letter to Amrit Kaur, *CW*, 64: 432.

This ontological meaning is never divorced from that of the moral realm. When Gandhi very emphatically says that "the essence of religion is morality,"[84] he affirms the quality of God through the religious expression of His immanence. This immanent presence of God in all of us; his presence and activity in us all binds us all to Him. God's presence, thus, becomes a unitive presence. "God is present in all of us. For my part, every moment I experience the truth that though many we are all one."[85] And further, "He is not outside of us. He is in the hearts of us all."[86] He affirms this singular guiding presence of God's finger in the *Satyāgraha* movement when he consoles his followers perturbed over one of his arrests: "It is not I but God who is guiding this movement. He ever dwells in the hearts of all and he will vouchsafe to us the right guidance if only we have faith in Him."[87] There are occasions when Gandhi experienced God face to face in his meeting with ordinary people. To cite one such instance, Gandhi himself describes his meeting with some peasants in Campāran as follows: "It is no exaggeration but the literal truth to say that in this meeting with the peasants I was face to face with God, Ahiṁsā and Truth."[88]

The *esse* of ontological reality implies an *ought* to the fact of its being what it is, i.e., to its very esse. The ethical/moral is intertwined with the ontological. There is a dialectical relation between the two. Gandhi would agree with James M. Gustafson that "the religious dimensions have priority over the moral."[89] For Gandhi, Truth as sovereign principle "includes numerous other principles."[90] And also, "This Truth

---

84. Gandhi, *Autobiography*, p. viii.

85. *Navajivan*, March 16, 1930; *CW*, 44: 82.

86. *Collected Works*, 45: 22.

87. *Young India*, May 8, 1930; *CW*, 43: 215.

88. Gandhi, *Autobiography*, p. 370.

89. James M. Gustafson, *Can Ethics Be Christian?* (Chicago: The University of Chicago Press), p. 173.

90. Gandhi, *Autobiography*, p. ix.

is not only truthfulness in word but truthfulness in thought also and not only the relative truth of our conception, but also the Absolute Truth, the Eternal Principle, that is God."[91] So Truth as ontological reality is the overriding principle of conduct. It is the reason for being moral. It becomes a scale to evaluate conduct.[92] This explanation of ontological reality as a "principle" (and *not* as a person), makes it rather easy for Gandhi to make the interconnection between the ontological and the ethical. So ". . . without Truth it is impossible to observe any principles or rules of life."[93]

As far as Gandhi is concerned, the most perfect term which describes God fully and adequately is Truth. Each and every devotee of this "Ultimate reality," this "ultimate concern," gives it a symbolic form by his or her worshipping imagination and so long as the symbolic images meet the spiritual needs of worshipper, they are true.

THE GREAT REVERSAL

At one stage of his "experiments" with truth Gandhi came to realize that the formulation "Truth is God" is preferable to "God is Truth." As mentioned earlier, Truth is not a "substitute word" for God, but it serves to elucidate what "God" means for Gandhi. His firm faith in God underlies not only his theological statements but also all his thoughts and acts, his commitment to working for truth and justice in his community. Though traces of the two formulations mentioned above can be found in earlier reflections,[94] the origin of this reverse

---

91. Gandhi, *Autobiography*, p. ix.

92. For Gustafson too religion qualified morality by providing (1) the reasons for being moral, (2) the character of the moral agent, and (3) the points of reference used to determine conduct. Cf. *Can Ethics be Christian* ? p. 173.

93. M. K. Gandhi, *The Selected Works of Mahatma Gandhi*, ed. Sriman Narayan, 5 vols. (Ahmedabad: Navajivan Publishing House, 1968), 4: 214.

94. Speaking at a reception given to him at Johannesburg in 1908, Gandhi explained the true meaning of religious faith in God. Consoling

formulation could be traced back only to 1930.[95] This reversal could be explained as a process of understanding of his believing faith in God.[96] Confronted by conscientious atheist objectors in Lausanne, Switzerland, on December 8, 1931, Gandhi told the story of his finding the name for God:

> In my early youth I was taught to repeat what in Hindu scriptures are known as the one thousand names of God. But these . . . were by no means exhaustive. We believe — and I think it is the truth — that God has as many names as there are creatures and therefore, we also say that God is nameless and since God has many forms we also consider Him formless, and since He speaks to us through many tongues we consider Him to be speechless and so on. . . . I would say, to them those who say God is Love, God is Love. But deep down in me, I say God may be love but God is Truth. If it is possible for the human tongue to give the fullest description of God, for myself I have come to the conclusion that God is Truth. But two years ago I went a step further

those who suffer oppression and injustice and are denied their legitimate rights, he emphasized: "Where there is God there is truth, and where there is truth there is God. I live in fear of God. I love truth only, and so God is with me. Even if the path of truth does not please the community it pleases God. Therefore I will do what pleases God, even if the community should turn against me." *Indian Opinion*, December 9, 1908; *CW*, 9: 107-08.

95. I am referring to the letter to Narandas Gandhi that Gandhi wrote after his morning prayer on July 22, 1930. Here he very emphatically says: "Nothing is or exists in reality except Truth. That is why *sat* or *satya* is the right name for God. *In fact it is more correct to say that Truth is God than to say that God is Truth.*" Letter to Narandas Gandhi, MMU/I, Iyer II: 162. (emphasis mine). In his famous speech at a meeting in Lausanne, Switzerland, on December 8, 1931, Gandhi told the confronting conscientious atheistic objectors his discovery of the name of God after a continuous, relentless search after Truth. Cf. Iyer 2: 165.

96. Gandhi seems to have undergone a similar experience to that of Anselm. The irresistibility of the force of what "daunted" Anselm made him determine to take the positive step of proving to the "imaginary fool" the existence of God that he already knew and believed in his faith. Similarly, confronted by real, convinced, and conscientious atheists, Gandhi affirmed that Truth is God.

and said Truth is God . . . and I came to that conclusion after a continuous, relentless search after Truth which began so many years ago. . . . I never found a double meaning in connection with Truth and not even atheists have denied the necessity or power of Truth. In their passion for discovering Truth, they have not hesitated even to deny the very existence of God — from their own point of view rightly. And it was because of their reasoning that I saw that I was not going to say 'God is Truth', but 'Truth is God'.[97]

Thus, in the morning of his life he had learned the thousand names of God (*sahasranāma*) from the scriptures of his religion. Later on he discovered many more names of God in Islam. The significant implication of all this for him is that God has as many names as there are creatures: each creature being a name of God. On the other hand, he himself had, at first, concluded that God is truth.[98]

As a law student in London Gandhi had come across a lot of free-thinkers. For an adolescent from the small town of Porbandar, who had been protectively brought up under the watchful eye of his religious-minded mother and nurtured in the traditional Vaiṣṇava cult of Hinduism, pre-atheistic tendencies of an otherwise Christian West were, indeed, puzzling. Yet, when he saw the moral earnestness of committed

97. Speech at Meeting in Lausanne, Mahadev Desai's Diary (MSS), December 8, 1931; Iyer 2: 164-65. See also Bose, *Selections from Gandhi*, pp. 3-4.

98. The Indian Sacred Scriptures, especially the Upaniṣads, make clear mention of God as Truth. For instance the *Muṇḍaka Upaniṣad* (III.1.6.) announces: "Truth alone prevails and no untruth. Truth is the pathway which learned men tread. It is by this path that the sages, satiated in their desires, have obtained salvation in Him who is the infinite ocean of Truth." The very first injunction given to a disciple after he has taken the sacred thread in the initiation ceremony is: "Speak the Truth, observe duty, do not swerve from Truth." (*Taittīrīya Upaniṣad*, I.II.I). Again the *Taittīrīya Upaniṣad* (II.I) proclaims, "*Brahma* is Truth eternal, intelligence immeasurable." Truth is the very foundation of everything: "Everything rests on Truth. Therefore they call Truth the highest." (*Mahānārāyaṇa Upaniṣad*, XXVII.I).

atheists like Charles Bradlaugh, whose funeral he happened
to attend, he could not help but admire him and look for
another name for the Absolute whom he called God. Gandhi's
hermeneutic intuition in the spirit of continuous search has
debated as to whether other sincere seekers including those
who professed no religious belief at all "were on the track of
truth, and that this was a term which best expressed the central
thrust of man's striving for better things, whether this be a
new social order or a new personal style of life."[99] Truth seekers
include scientists, artists, poets, mystics, lawyers and even
the village farmers who go about their ordinary routine of
life. What gives unity to all these seekers? What is the
sovereign principle of all that is? What is that which in fact be
said to determine the behaviour of one and all? Margaret
Chatterjee is right in pointing out that Gandhi's central insight
from all such inquiries is that a person is one, a creature, who
has *aspirations*, who has a *goal*. Gandhi could include even his
atheist friends in this category of persons having aspirations.
The determinant of these form of faith cannot be said to be
God in the ordinary sense or the God of particular religious
affiliations because there are persons who deny the very
existence of any such "religious" God. On the other hand,
even in their most vehement denials they, as convinced
atheists, are convinced that the view they uphold is the *truth*
of the matter.[100] Hence truth is that toward which every human

---

99. Margaret Chatterjee, *Gandhi's Religious Thought* (Notre Dame:
Indiana University of Notre Dame Press, 1983), p. 59.

100. Gandhi asserts, very emphatically, "I never found a double
meaning in connection with Truth and not even atheists have denied the
necessity or power of Truth. Not only so. In their passion for discovering
Truth, they have not hesitated even to deny the very existence of God —
from their own point of view rightly. And it was because of their reasoning
that I saw that I was not going to say 'God is Truth,' but 'Truth is God.'
(Speech at Meeting in Lausanne, December 8, 1931. *Mahadev Desai's Diary*
(MSS); Iyer, 2: 165). Yet in another place Gandhi says about Charles
Bradlaugh's denial of God as "a denial of Him as He was known to
Bradlaugh to have been described. His was an eloquent and indignant

being aspires. In fact, it is that which is said to determine everybody's behaviour. As far as Gandhi is concerned, this common goal, this determining principle of all, is God. Gandhi thus comes to the conclusion: Truth is God. Gandhi's reversal of 'God is Truth' to 'Truth is God' is simply a consistent philosophical argument embedded in a sustained theological journey.

He was, thus, led to the conclusion that Truth is God:

> I saw that Truth is the only perfect description of God. All other descriptions are imperfect. Even the word *Ishvar* is a descriptive term, applied to an omnipotent something which cannot be described by human speech. . . . Thinking of God as a ruler does not satisfy our mind. . . . The statement that Truth itself is God is a perfect statement as far as human speech can express anything perfectly. We shall come to the same conclusion if we consider the etymological meaning of the word *satya*. It is derived from the root *sat*, which means to exist eternally.

> That which exists eternally is *satya*, Truth, it can be nothing else. . . . We may find difficulty in understanding what 'seeing God' means; there can be no difficulty in understanding the meaning of 'seeing Truth'. Seeing Truth may itself be difficult, it is so. But as we go nearer and nearer towards It, we can have an increasingly clearer vision of Truth that is God, and that strengthens our hope and faith that one day we shall have a full vision of It.[101]

As far as Gandhi is concerned, the most perfect human expression of "That," is Truth.

If God is the universal principle, in the sense of actually determining our many and varied endeavours, then Truth is the appropriate name of such a God. Thus he makes the "Great

---

protest against the then current theology and the terrible contrast between precept and practice." See *Young India*, March 5, 1925.

101. Letter to Purushottam Gandhi, *Mahadevbhaini Diary*, 1: 105-07; Iyer 2: 174-75.

Reversal" from "God is Truth" to "Truth is God."[102]

In conclusion, the principle of Anselm, "God is something than which nothing greater can be conceived," could be paraphrased in Gandhian terms as, *God is the Truth than which no other greater truth can be conceived.*

Thus Gandhi seems to enclose three connotations in the various facets of his experiments with truth:

1. truth as what facts are (in a relational dimension with events) — truth as veracity;
2. truth as that to which one holds fast (a person's "ultimate concern," value commitment), and
3. truth as *sat*, or Being, in the ontological sense, the God of common parlance, the Unchanging Ultimate Reality.[103]

When Gandhi speaks of the truth of atheists, the meaning of this truth is in the second category. When the merging of the second and third takes place, i.e., when that to which one holds fast is *sat* (Truth, God) one necessarily finds meaning in Gandhi's passionate proclamation that Truth is God. Then it affects the first interpretation too in the sense of seeking a "kingdom of transformed relationships." Gandhi, like Anselm, is attempting to understand that by his reason which he already believed by his faith, i.e., a philosophical argument is embedded in a theological/spiritual/religious — even mystical — journey.

---

102. Speech at Meeting in Lausanne, Mahadev Desai's Diary, December 8, 1931; Iyer 2: 165.

103. Here I am at variance with Dr. Michael W. Sonnleitner of the Department of Political Science, University of Northern Iowa. In a paper entitled "Gandhian Satyagraha & Swarāj: A Hierarchical Perspective," presented at the 15th Annual Conference on South Asia, University of Wisconsin at Madison, on November 8, 1986, he categorises the *sat* (truth) (of *satyāgraha*) into three hierarchical levels, viz., "secular", "religious" and the "mystical". He does the same with *ahiṁsā*. I don't think such a "sacred-secular" dichotomy is in keeping with the spirit of Gandhian understanding.

In this light, the Gandhian theories of trusteeship and non-cooperation reveal a deeper meaning. Gandhi's vows at various stages of his life are endeavours in his life-journey to attain the Ultimate Bliss. Self-sacrificial, active and compassionate love becomes a possibility. His undaunted faith in the redemptive power of Truth is revealed. His distinction between sinner and sin, his non-cooperation with sin and love of the sinner, his condemnation not of the individuals but of their maliciously-motivated and evil-intended actions become clear.

The Gandhian search for Truth shows that there has to be a gradual evolutionary process in every person endowed with the inborn capacity for moral progress and a life-call to transcendent life. This self-transcendence is manifested in a passion for *satya*, through *ahiṁsā* which is self-purificatory active love and ready to suffer, in working for a kingdom of transformed relationships (*Rāmarājya*), experiencing and expressing that Augustinian "thirsting restlessness" or "restless thirsting" of the soul, until the person, at home in the community, finds perfect rest in the Ultimate Truth (*parama satya*). The one who catches a glimpse of this *parama satya* in a flash, can speak of this God of Truth (or Truth-God) only as *neti, neti* — not this, not that.

IMPACT OF TRUTH

Gandhi's shift from "God is Truth" to "Truth is God" helped him synthesize his ontological vision of Reality with his religious insight based on his own experience, tradition and the sacred scriptures. This, in turn, helped him to introduce into "human politics the strongest of religious impetus of the last two thousand years,"[104] laying thus a strong religious ethical foundation to political actions. A strong case could be made that in the *vyāvahārika* level of human life, it is Gandhi's moral understanding of God that prevails. God as Sovereign Principle, Ultimate Law and Norm, determines the morality

---

104. Romain Rolland, *Mahatma Gandhi* (London: Allen & Unwin, 1924), p. 4.

of our actions and endeavours. We test the appropriateness of all our activities against this Principle. Truth, then is the right name for such a God; and since Truth is the appropriate name for God, God is experienced and explained in moral terms, becoming the Norm, as it were, for human practical life. God is, thus, the *telos* and determines the ultimate *ought* of every human undertaking.

This is why Gandhi fought against "godlessness" (absence of a sense of divine or sacredness; absence of a principle and/ or ideology in life) not atheism *per se*: "You may call yourself an atheist, but so long as you feel akin with mankind you accept God in practice." His religious awareness was revolutionary in the sense that, though he called himself an "orthodox Hindu," he included under Hinduism the teachings of Jesus and Mohammed without experiencing or seeing any thing illogical or any inner contradiction.[105] He could treat Buddha as the great reformer of Hinduism because "You believe in some principle, clothe it with life. . . . I should think it is enough."[106] He had the firm conviction that the moral and ethical values he strove to translate into his personal and political acts could be appropriated by all. This translation (application) was necessary for the transformation of human relationships and socio-economic and political activities. The ethical necessity of this application made him portray himself as a humble searcher after truth, and disclaim the popular titles of *mahātmā*, "saint," "ascetic" or *saṁnyāsī*.[107]

Gandhi was convinced that the realization of Truth would make a person a redemptive lover having the capacity of loving an opponent (an enemy or a misguided person) to the extent of transforming him/her into a friend. His principle was to

---

105. He did not need any "anonymous Hindu" theory to give coherence to his religious system and belief.

106. *Harijan*, July 17, 1939.

107. *Young India*, March 2, 1922. Clothed in a mystique of sainthood and divinity, Gandhi has been denied the practicality and effectiveness of

get rid of an "enemy" by getting rid of "enmity" (and not by getting rid of the enemy person, as so often happens in the contemporary world especially in the political arena) and thus to transform the "enemy" into a "friend." He manifested in his life the redemptive power of love. Love builds bridges of human relationship. The last respect paid to Abraham Lincoln by Stanton standing near the dead body of the man he (Stanton) once hated, was that "he now belongs to the Ages," a living historical example of an "enemy" becoming a "friend."[108]

Gandhi's undaunted devotion to truth convinced him of the healing power of *ahiṁsā*. The attention of the world was drawn to Gandhi in his *ahiṁsātmaka Satyāgraha* (non-violent endeavour for truth) and to the healing power of the non-violent approach to personal as well as institutional relationships and conflict resolution. Though Bernard Häring argues that this approach is very Christocentric in character, Gandhi has clearly translated this power into his concrete

---

his experiments. Gradually people came to emphasize the high caliber of his moral attainments and religiosity to the detriment of the mundane practical efficacy of his experiments. Gandhian excellence seemed to induce amazement and a holy reverence rather than comradeship and sympathetic cooperation, and, *a fortiori*, critical analysis. Many in contemporary India and the world at large would echo the sentiments of the first Prime Minister of independent India, Jawaharlal Nehru: I am not a Gandhi — implying that I am not a person of such a lofty character and deep-seated virtues. Gandhi needs to be demystified to become a dialogue partner, so that he could better influence the modern world from a human platform and not from the top of a saintly pedestal. (Cf. Amin, "Gandhi as Mahatma," pp. 288-348).

108. Stanton was Abraham Lincoln's presidential opponent. For some reason Stanton hated Lincoln. He missed no opportunity to degrade Lincoln about his physical appearance and used every ounce of his energy to embarrass Lincoln. But when Lincoln, after winning the election named Stanton his Secretary of War, in spite of the uproar of his inner circle of friends, Lincoln transformed an enemy into a friend even if one were to admit that Lincoln's appointment was meant to be a strategic move. See Martin Luther King, Jr., *Strength to Love*, Third Printing (Philadelphia:

historical situation.[109] He himself acknowledges that he is in his own way trying to "apply the eternal truths to our daily life and problems. . . . I have nothing new to teach the world. Truth and Non-violence are as old as the hills."[110]

Gandhi was absolutely convinced that suffering is a necessary condition for the realization of Truth. It is because of the suffering-truth relationship, he could not admit any form of violence even to one's opponents, and he insisted that, the "pursuit of Truth did not admit of violence being inflicted on one's opponent but that he must be awakened from error by patience and sympathy. . . . And patience means self-suffering."[111] Hence the closest paraphrase of *ahiṁsā* in the Gandhian spirit would be "redemptive self-suffering love."

The non-violent approach to the healing power of Truth does not mean a withdrawal into inactive pacifism. Gandhi shared, with the psychotherapist Rollo May, the concern not to belittle or deny the need for and the efficacious character of that power.[112]

Fortress Press, 1983), p. 52.

109. Häring writes, "When we come to a deep trust in him (Christ), to a deeper knowledge of his healing and redeeming love, we reach a deeper knowledge of self, through him, and understand our need to be more completely healed from our violence. . . . Discipleship of Christ, 'life in Christ Jesus,' has the quality of a new creation, of new healing powers prospering in healthy and healing relationships." Häring, *The Healing Power of Peace and Non-violence*, p. 67.

110. *Harijan,* March 1936, p. 49. Also See *Young India,* December 2, 1926, p. 419.

111. Bose, *Selelctions from Gandhi,* p. 17.

112. Rollo May in his *Power and Innocence: A Search for the Source of Violence,* p. 14, speaks about "power analogous to the healing power by which one overcomes tuberculosis, not analogous to military power." Speaking of the aggressiveness of humankind that is already out of control, May warns, "We are the cruellest species on the planet. We kill not out of necessity but out of collegiance to such symbols as the flag and fatherland. We kill on principle." as quoted by Häring *The Power of Peace and*

Gandhi's pursuit of Truth was a total commitment. The commitment involves every moment of his being and existence. Like Ramakrishna, the mystic, he was *drunk* with the religious experience of the reality of Truth. This is the sentiment he expressed when he says:

> What I want to achieve, what I have been striving and pining to achieve these thirty years is self-realization, to see God face to face, to attain *Moksha*. I live and move and have my being in pursuit of this goal. All that I do by way of speaking and writing and all my ventures in the political field are directed to this same end. I am but a weak aspirant, ever-failing, ever trying. My failures make me more vigilant than before and intensify my faith. I can see with the eye of faith that the observance of the twin doctrines of Truth and Non-violence has possibilities of which we have but very inadequate conception.[113]

He associated knowledge of God with the heart rather than with reason: "Faith in God cannot be reasoned out. It does not come from the head but from the heart, and, things of the heart are spontaneous and instinctive."[114] God would not be God if he allowed himself to be an object of proof by

---

Nonviolence, pp. 5-6. In the same vein Weizacker warns humankind, "in view of his aggressiveness man appears as the sick animal, insane in his innermost being." as quoted by Häring, *op.cit.*, p. 4.

113. Gandhi, *Autobiography*, p. viii. Gandhi's expression of the "eye of faith" reminds me of the lines of George Santayana:

> Columbus found a world, and had no chart,
> Save one that faith deciphered in the skies;

To trust the soul's invincible surmise
> Was all his science and his only art.

As quoted by N.A. Palkhivala, "Relevance of Gandhi Today," *Gandhi Marg* (April 1984), pp. 4-5. Goethe, the German thinker, said that epochs of faith are epochs of fruitfulness; while epochs of disbelief, however glittering, are devoid of any permanent good. If today the world has a number of problems which seem insoluble, it is because ours is an age of disbelief. Gandhi's undaunted faith in the power of suffering love to get to the rock-bottom Truth did bear abundant fruit.

114. Letter to Janakadhari Prasad, May 28, 1928; *CW*, 36: 338.

his creatures. Since emotion and feelings are also things of the heart, purity of the emotions was important for faith.[115]

His continuous experiments with and the inner experience of the immediate presence of truth schooled him in a process of discernment. Gandhi knew how "to trust the soul's invincible surmise," (to borrow a line from George Santayana). Gandhi had in a pre-eminent degree what we call in Sanskrit *buddhi* (Intuitive understanding),[116] which is the result of meditative contemplation, concentration, dedication and devotion over the years. Gandhi's high level of moral refinement and subtlety of spiritual insight enabled him to easily discern *good* from *evil* and thus radiate what Aquinas called the "impression of divine light in us." The smoother the surface of the radiating mirror of the heart, the sharper will the reflecting images be.

When Tagore said "Every child who is born in this world brings a message from God that He is not discouraged with man," he articulated his intuitive understanding of the inherent dignity of the human person recognized by the God in whom Tagore believes. In this no one would perhaps agree more with Tagore than Gandhi.

One of the reasons why one fails to be a votary of Truth is that one does not apprehend Truth in the right perspective. Gandhi gives the benefit of the doubt to the person in error who does not apprehend the Truth in the right perspective, or, perhaps, is incapable of right apprehension because of variables like pride, arrogance, self-righteous attitude, apathy, thirst for power, lack of conducive or even sinful social structures and environments. Persons may erroneously, but

---

115. Letter to Esther Menon, May 29, 1932; *CW*, 49: 490.

116. The conceived meaning of this word cannot be captured in an equivalent word in any European language. An approximate equivalent may be "intuitive understanding." Dr. Raynor Johnson, an eminent scientist from Australia, needed six lines in his book *The Imprisoned Splendor*, even to paraphrase this word.

earnestly and sincerely, accept that as Truth which is not really the Real (Truth). For example, the opposition to God by the atheists is merely because of an inability to recognize the really True or the truly Real. In their journey through life, atheists become satisfied with a contingent reality they "pick up" somewhere on the way, and are satisfied with it and embrace it as their "Ultimate." Their journey is incomplete, as far as Gandhi is concerned. Atheism is thus seen as an epistemological problem. It falls short of the final Telos, because of its inability to "see" the really Real Truth. The really Real and True has a compelling force, as was experienced, say by Augustine of Hippo or Ignatius of Loyola, and the person who rightly *sees* such Truth is naturally attracted towards It. And once a person experiences the compelling force of this Other (the Holy), one will feel the irresistible need to act according to the dictate and spell of that One. The commands of such a One would, as Barth shows, make a claim on the human.[117]

Thus the Gandhian notion of God is very much linked to his interpretation of human nature, human qua moral agent. The Gandhian interpretation of human nature needs further clarification.

GANDHIAN HOMO

In his idea of the human Gandhi takes into account one's true and real self, the spiritual element inherent in the person. He is not just concerned with the static human nature, but tells us how one can mould oneself so as to become what one is capable of becoming. Hence the human is not just a being, but a *becoming being,* a perfectible being, whose nature is more naturally inclined to do good than to be evil. The divinity inherent in a person does distinguish the human from brute creation. But, for Gandhi, human nature does not consist in

117. Though Barth's Christian doctrine of God ["the knowledge of the electing grace of God in Jesus Christ"; see *Church Dogmatics*, 2 vols. (Edinburgh: T.T. Clark, 1957), 2: 543] and the God (Truth) of Gandhi are different, there seems to be some affinity between them with regard to

the dualistic Manichean experience of "perpetual pull-and-haul" between the two forces of Light and Darkness, Good and Evil, God and the Devil, that make of human life a vast, perpetual battleground. The Hobbesian "homo hominis lupus" state of nature that places human life in an inevitable condition described as "solitary, poor, nasty, brutish and short," is absolutely foreign to Gandhi. His faith in the inherent goodness of human nature is evident in his assertion, "(T)hat in mankind moral qualities and social virtues, love, co-operation and the like, preponderate over violence, selfishness etc., is proved by the fact that life exists amidst destruction."[118] Gandhi's frank optimism rests on his belief in the infinite possibilities of the individual to develop non-violence. We are born in order to realize God who dwells in us. Human is divine in the sense that s/he is "capable of realizing His kingship with the whole of creation especially the rest of humanity."[119]

Human the Brute

At the same time, there is a beastly and brutal element in human nature: "We were perhaps, all originally brutes. I am prepared to believe that we have become man by a slow process of evolution from the brute."[120] The best of all possible actions and the worst of bestial undertakings are inherent in human capacity. It depends on the individual in which direction one's action should move. Reflecting on the ordinary experience of humankind and drawing lessons from the historical process Gandhi comes to his conclusions. Bernard Häring also speaks in the same spirit when he says,

---

the compelling force of their God.

118. G.N. Dhawan, *The Political Philosophy of Mahatma Gandhi* (Bombay: The Popular Book Depot, 1946), p. 100. Of course, humanity has not committed suicide *en masse* though historically humans have shown and are showing even now the brutal fact of human capability for mass torture, murder and pogrom!

119. Iyer, "Gandhi's View of Human Nature," *Gandhi Marg* (January 1962), p. 143.

The sane human being is gifted with speech, with power to communicate within the stream of tradition, able to share with others in the search for saving truth. Those who lack the faculty for truthful communication in the search for peace belong to the most demented species of animal.[121]

In his autobiography Gandhi writes that the brute by nature knows no self-restraint. It is our capacity to exercise self-restraint that makes us human.

Every one of us is a mixture of good and evil. Is there not plenty of evil in us? There is enough in me . . . and I always pray to God to purge me of it. The difference that there is between human beings is the difference of degrees.[122]

Ordinarily one is prone to choose the easy path:

Man must choose either of the two courses, the upward or the downward, but as he has the brute in him, he will more easily choose the downward course than the upward, especially when the downward course is presented to him in a beautiful garb.[123]

In all humility Gandhi admits, "I wear the same corruptible flesh that the weakest of my fellow beings wear, and am therefore as liable to err as any."[124] Though we are in a human form, we still share the qualities of "our remote reputed ancestor, the ourang outang."[125]

THE SOUL WITHIN

A person is not merely a bundle of flesh; nor is s/he the embodiment of the brute either. Behind all this visible but ephemeral and unconscious matter there is a spirit, a soul — invisible, eternal, all-pervading and self-conscious. It is part and parcel of the Supreme. He believes that

120. *Harijan*, April, 1938. See also *Harijan*, October, 1938.

121. Häring, *The Healing Power of Peace and Nonviolence*, p. 4.

122. *Harijan*, June, 1939.

123. *Harijan*, February, 1935.

124. *Young India*, p. 946.

125. *Harijan*, October, 1938.

The soul is Godhead within man; it is self-acting; it persists
even after death; its existence does not depend upon the
physical body; it is matter rarefied to the utmost limit. Hence
whatever happens to one body must affect the whole of
matter and the whole of spirit.[126]

Following the Hindu concept that the divine soul is present
in the human soul (*ātman* as the participating spark of
Brahman), Gandhi believes that the *ātman* is the same in all
giving unity to all humans. Hence, humankind constitutes an
organic whole of inter-dependent entities.

This theological notion of the unity of being has moral

---

126. *Harijan*, November, 1938. I do not wish to go into the whole of
Indian philosophical/theological notion of the "self," that definitely exerted
its influence on Gandhian understanding. All the same, I would like to
make the following observation to make Gandhi's notion clear. Gandhi
made a distinction between "self" and "*ātman*" following the orthodox
Hindu tradition. *Ātman* is *Brahman*, present in the human. *Ātman* is identical
in all persons. The presence of the same *ātman* in all persons is what gives
unity to all human beings — "Thou art That," implying every thou is That.
At the same time there is a principle of individuation that provides the
basis of individuality to all humans. This cannot be *ātman* — because it is
same in all persons. Hence, what makes persons distinct selves; what
gives unique psychological and spiritual constitution, giving distinctive
dispositions, tendencies, propensities and temperaments to individuals is
the "self." Hence, self is the basis of epistemological, moral, cultural and
social pluralism. Though a product of one's own past and present (and
future too) actions, its subsequent development is not pre-determined
just by these actions. Unlike the body and the *ātman*, which have no history,
the self has nothing but history encompassing several life-spans. Every
individual is uniquely and solely responsible for all s/he is and, hence, has
to work out her/his ultimate spiritual destiny and salvation. So the struggle
of human life is the struggle of the self, through innumerable births and
re-births to become the Self, and to realize that this *ātman* is *Brahman* — to
attain the Ultimate Bliss, to merge into *Brahman* ending the *ātman-Brahman*
duality. So a harmonious move of the universe for this realization is the
ultimate aim of *vyāvahārika* life. Hence, human freedom in the *vyāvahārika*
level of human existential life will be limited as far as Gandhi is concerned
— here morality enters the picture. The limit is wrought by the Ultimate
Truth. This Truth determines our actions. Such a determination is

implications. Every human action, whether self- or other-regarding, affects the collective ethos directly or indirectly. It enriches or diminishes the quality of the prevailing pattern of human relationships: "Rot in one part must inevitably poison the whole system."[127] The rise of one produces a ripple effect of awakening the potentiality of others. On the other hand, if one falls, others fall as well: "I believe that if one man gains spiritually, the whole world gains with him, and if one man falls, the world falls to that extent."[128] Humanity is so intertwined and interdependent that no one could degrade or brutalize another without degrading or brutalizing oneself in the process; no one "takes another down a pit without descending into it himself and sinning into the bargain."[129]

Such a principle of the unity of humankind is not the sentimental moral postulatum but, in Gandhi's language, the very *truth* about human existence. This principle of indivisible human wholeness forms the basis of Gandhi's critique of oppressive and exploitative socio-cultural and politico-economic systems. Hence, the existence of oppression and exploitation degrades and damages not only the victims but also the victimizers and the oppressors. In fact, the latter suffer even more in the process because of their excessive capacity to harden their hearts. Once persons start hardening their hearts, a reversal process of self-transcendence and

---

understood not in the sense that it is Truth (God) that decides every action, but that human actions are always "conforming entities" — conforming to already existing Divine Norms (The Norm is Truth = God, for Gandhi); since "Truth" is that "Divine It" for Gandhi, this "It" prescribes the ultimate *ought* for human endeavours in concrete, practical, existential life. The eternal presence of Truth as truth awaits human acceptance in his/her free choice. See Parekh, *Gandhi's Political Philosophy: A Critical Examination*, pp. 92-95.

127. As quoted by Parekh, *Gandhi's Political Philosophy: A Critical Examination*, p. 89.

128. *Young India*, December 4, 1924.

129. See Parekh, *Gandhi's Political Philosophy: A Critical Examination*, p. 90.

transformation is very difficult, if not impossible, to achieve.

At the same time, the capacity for self-transcendence and transformation is inherent in every human being. Gandhi firmly believed that whatever ideal he could achieve by sheer effort could be achieved by all others as well:

> The ideals that regulate my life are presented for acceptance by mankind in general. I have arrived at them by gradual evolution. . . . I have not the shadow of a doubt that any man or woman can achieve what I have, if he or she would make the same effort and cultivate the same hope and faith.[130]

He continues in the same vein:

> I have been taught from my childhood, and I have tested the truth by experience, that primary virtues of mankind are possible of cultivation by the meanest of human species. It is this undoubted universal possibility that distinguishes the human from the rest of God creation.[131]

Thus he firmly believed in the human potentiality and capacity for growth, transformation, and self-transcendence which make a person "a navigator in the high seas of historical process . . . not as the plaything of circumstances, but gifted with the capacity to control his destiny."[132]

The Mohammedan saying that "Man is not God, but neither is he different from the spark of God," was very dear to Gandhi. Making a clear distinction between the brute force and the indwelling spirit of God within the hearts of every human being Gandhi comments in Harijan, "We are born with brute strength but we are born to realize God who dwells in

---

130. *Harijan,* May, 1936.

131. *Ibid.*

132. Chatterjee, *Gandhi's Religious Thought,* p. 176. Gandhi did not agree with Darwin's notion of human development as the outcome of competitive process. Gandhi believed in the inherent human capacity for growth. Without being a Freudian Gandhi asserted the existence of the variety of latent powers in ordinary masses. Gandhi's effort was to find means and methods for releasing these inherent capacities for personal as well as societal benefit.

us. That indeed is the privilege of man and it distinguishes him from the brute creation."[133] Indeed, God is in the hearts of all.[134] His optimism made him go even to the extent of declaring in 1926, "I refuse to believe that the tendency of human nature is always downward."[135] The following year he wrote, "Men like me cling to their faith in human nature . . . all appearances to the contrary notwithstanding."[136] In 1938 he declared, "Man's nature is not essentially evil. Brute nature has been known to yield to the influence of love. You must never despair of human nature."[137] Hence, the indwelling of God in every individual human person distinguishes the homo from the brute creation and gives dignity to every person.

It is not that Gandhi is offering a Cartesian dualistic view of the human nature. Rather, he believes that a person is neither brute nor God. Though human is bestial in origin, s/he is potentially divine. At the same time, an individual uniquely possesses the power of choice either to re-emphasize the brutalization of her/his nature by embracing violence or to realize and fulfil the innate divine especially by eschewing violence. To realize the divine is to come nearer in thought, feelings and deeds to the whole creation. More concretely, when individuals "act equally toward all and in all circumstances, [they] approach the divine."[138] Thus, physical and the spiritual forces are at work in human beings. Though Gandhi places more emphasis on the spiritual aspect, he is realistic enough not to ignore the influence of the physical and the material on human life. But human uniqueness consists in the capacity of discerning truth and in one's endeavour for spiritual upliftment; therein lies the differences between the

---

133. *Harijan*, April, 1938.
134. *Harijan*, June, 1938.
135. *Young India*, December, 1926.
136. *Young India*, February, 1927.
137. *Harijan*, November, 1938.
138. Diary of Mahadev Desai, July, 1932, p. 247.

human and the brute.

The three categories of "frailty," "impurity" and "depravity" of human nature, as distinguished by Kant in his essay "On the Radical Evil in Human Nature," could better explain Gandhi's rejection of a pessimistic view and his positive assertion of an optimistic view of human nature. According to these Kantian categories, the propensity to do evil is compatible with a view of the intrinsic nature of a person to be good. While weakness of will inevitably causes frailty, even one's own best motives and intentions not fully focused on the highest aspirations and tainted by other considerations bring in impurity. Depravity points to an aberration rather than the inherent evil of human nature itself. At the same time Gandhi cautions us, "It is essential for man to discriminate between what he may consider to be good and what is really good for him."[139]

The above analysis shows that the original inherent "capacity for good" is not without its propensity to evil. Though this propensity to evil is part of human nature, human qua human is capable of transcending evil tendencies and embrace the good. What is to be denounced is the evil actions of a person if one succumbs to the brutal behaviour of which one surely is capable. This is the reason for Gandhi's insistence on the separation of a person's actions and the person himself or herself, and his appeal for interior transformation and the creation of an environment conducive to virtuous actions. And this is why he insists on training the will to form character (akin to Aristotle) in persons. In this light Gandhi could be better understood when he insisted,

> Man and his deed are two distinct things. Whereas a good deed should call forth approbation and a wicked deed disapprobation, the doer of the deed, whether good or wicked, always deserves respect or pity as the case may

139. Pyarelal, *Mahatma Gandhi: The Last Phase*, 2 vols. (Ahmedabad: Navajivan Publishing House, 1956), 1: 348.

be.[140]

Because of this "doctrine of original goodness" humanity cannot be simply divided into good or bad. There are evil acts; but not wholly evil persons. Since a person is intrinsically good, s/he must be capable of developing the good that lies dormant. The intrinsic human goodness enables one to develop the good that lies inert. Though Gandhi does not deny the existence of human shortcomings, (and there are plenty of them in the world of human interactions), he is confident that because the human is essentially a spark of the divine and hence intrinsically good, one is capable of overcoming one's evil tendencies if only one wishes to do so by taking positive steps of adapting the right means and methods conducive to human enrichment. In order to realize the good within and thus to become "what thou art," two conditions are to be fulfilled. First, a person must be conscious of what one is and be aware of the various potentialities; second, a person must have a favourable situation. As a spark of the divine and as a social creature, a person must have proper atmosphere and opportunities to cultivate the good qualities. Hence, the pattern and structure of organization of the human community is very important in Gandhian ethics.

HUMAN INTER-RELATEDNESS

Gandhi's belief in "the essential unity of God and man and for that matter of all that lives,"[141] the indwelling presence of God in each and every individual person made him consider the whole of human race as one large family — that all of us are brothers and sisters.[142] The stoic idea that the universe is a divine whole and that human beings form an essential unity wherein individuals could realize themselves is very dear to Gandhi. Though some may not realize the full dignity

140. Gandhi, *Autobiography*, p. 316.

141. *Young India*, December, 1924.

142. Mahadev Prasad, *The Social Philosophy of Mahatma Gandhi* (Gorakhpur: Vishwavidyalaya Prakashan, 1958), p. 26.

accorded to the human or "some of us do not recognize that status of ours makes no difference except that then we do not get the benefit of the status; . . . it belongs to him nevertheless."[143] That latent human status needs to be actualized. Because of such an intrinsic worth everyone, irrespective of socio-economic status (whether poor or rich, destitute or delinquent), is entitled to dignity commanding respect from others. Hence, it is below human dignity to be treated as a mere cog in the machine. In Gandhi's personal behaviour and dealings this principle was so evident that Louis Fisher remarked, "next to God Gandhi's supreme being was man, the individual."[144]

Since God is in everyone, His "divine music is incessantly going on within ourselves, (though the) loud senses drown the delicate music, which is unlike and infinitely superior to anything we can perceive or hear with our senses."[145] This God within can rule and transform the heart of everyone in terms of loyalties, dispositions, intentions, motifs and attitudes. Faith in God can and ought to make a difference in the orientation and direction of one's life. One can definitely feel this God "if we will but withdraw ourselves from the senses."[146]

A real experience of the God who/that "is in us and yet beyond us," the one who/that "leaves us 'unfettered' to make our own choice between evil and good,"[147] and "alone is . . . (and) is Life, Truth, Light (and) Love . . . Supreme,"[148] makes a person restless within oneself. Such an inner restlessness as felt by Augustine and expressed in his *Confessions* "My soul is restless until it rest in Thee, My Lord," was Gandhi's

---

143. *Young India,* December, 1924.

144. Louis Fisher, *The Life of Mahatma Gandhi* (London: Jonathan Cape, 1952), p. 356.

145. R.K. Prabhu and U.R. Rao, comp., *The Mind of Mahatma Gandhi* (Bombay: Oxford University Press, 1960), pp. 22-23.

146. *Ibid.*

147. Pyarelal, *Mahatma Gandhi: The Last Phase,* 1: 421-22.

experience too. While Augustine's restlessness makes him long for an individual "rest" in the Lord, Gandhi's "restlessness" for having a merger with the divine takes on a practical expression of an identification with the whole of humankind. One who aspires to see and realize this universal and all-pervading Spirit of Truth cannot afford to keep out of any field of life, including politics.[149] This is why Gandhi's religious quest for Truth found practical expression in his involvement in politics. When politics becomes more and more a way of life, more and more one cannot run away from political arena, as John Courtney Murray emphasized.[150] What Gandhi told to a group of missionaries in 1938 makes this amply clear:

> I could not be leading a religious life unless I identified myself with the whole of mankind and that I could not do unless I took part in politics. The whole gamut of man's activities today constitutes an indivisible whole. . . . I do not know of any religion apart from activity. It provides moral basis to all other activities.[151]

Thus, Gandhi attempts to provide guidance for human action within the context of an ultimate reality that always seeks to will the good of creation and promises to sustain it. Like H.R. Niebuhr, Gandhi understands the ever-present creative and sustaining power of God's gracious activity to be liberating and transforming the human. Faith in God can and ought to make a difference in the orientation and direction of one's life and in one's social interactions.

THEOLOGICAL ORIGIN OF GANDHIAN SOCIO-POLITICAL ACTION

The above analysis of Gandhian theology and theological anthropology helps us understand the religious origin and theological foundation of Gandhian socio-political action. It is

---

148. Prabhu & Rao, *op.cit.*

149. See Gandhi, *Autobiography*, p. viii.

150. See John Courtney Murray, *We Hold These Truths: Catholic Reflections on the American Proposition* (New York: Sheed and Ward, 1960).

151. *Harijan*, December, 1938.

more correct to say that Gandhi's politics is based on and originated in his theo-centrism than to suggest, as Jesudasan does, "the political origin of Gandhi's theology."[152] Gandhi's notion of politics and his rules to "play" politics are in direct opposition to the Machiavellian approach.[153] Gandhi fought vehemently against the manipulative power of political entities and strongly insisted on good faith and truth in political arena.

For Gandhi, ethical and/or moral life gives significant *religious* seriousness and underpinnings to all spheres of life including politics. As one "who introduced into human politics the strongest religious impetus of the last two thousand

---

152. See Jesudasan, *A Gandhian Theology of Liberation*, p. 66.

153. The vigorous indictment of Machiavellian political ideas by the Jesuit writer Suarez would be strongly endorsed by Gandhi. Gandhi would agree with Suarez's natural law approach that we humans possess "an inherent justice" which enables us to apprehend the laws of God and employ them in the conduct of our lives. Concerning the obligatory force of human laws Suarez insists in Book III of *The Laws and God the Lawgiver*, that "It is not possible for anything to be a precept of the civil law which is not a precept of the law of nature" (see Skinner 1: 237). Suarez reiterates that Machiavelli is blind to the crucial fact that "the civil law must only be constructed out of honest materials," and must be "limited by the claims of justice," never simply by the claims of political expediency (Skinner, 1: 197). The dictates of natural justice "form the only possible materials for true civil law," so that "there must be nothing in the law which directly overturns equity or natural justice" (Skinner, 1: 176). Gandhi's insistence on good faith and truth in the political arena is already echoed in the Jesuit counter-reformation theorist, Mariana who, like his other Jesuit-companions, Possevino, Ribadeneyra and Suarez, positively rejected Machiavelli's image of the hypocrite prince on pragmatic and moral grounds and reiterated in his *The King and the Education of the King*, that "the principles of good government depend especially on good faith and truth." (Cf. Skinner, 1: 173). The Machiavellian argument that "the interests of the commonwealth demand that the prince practice deceit and prevarication" is refuted even on pure pragmatic consideration that "there is more harm than advantage" to be gained by them (says Mariana) and further, that "the doctrine of these *politiques* (*politici*) is not in fact of any value for the maintenance of a temporal republic or kingdom," simply

years,"[154] Gandhi integrated "mysticism with humanism."[155]
Such an integration helped him view politics, economics,
culture, religion, nay the whole of civilization as part of a
continuum whose final goal is God-realization in and through
the process of self-realization. Thus it is obvious that his socio-
economic and political views, including his indictment of
modern civilization, spring from a foundational belief-system
that included God, human nature, human perfectibility, person-
to-person and person-to-God relationships. The deep respect
with which Gandhi held the human person stands out as the
most salient feature of his belief-system. Given his conviction
about the essence of human nature and the possibility of
becoming "what thou art" with respect to and in relation with
himself, with the other and with God, Gandhi could, with
Pauline passion, carry on his *ahiṁsātmaka satyāgraha* in his task
of re-creating of the human with a new relationship of mutual
love and respect, irrespective of socio-economic disparities or
colour, creed and/or religio-cultural differences.[156] In the same
vein, Gandhi's socio-economic and political philosophy was
centred around his notion of the individual — so much so
that "The most salient feature that stands out unmistakable in
every aspect of the social revolution that Gandhi worked out

because, "honesty is in fact of greater power in maintaining peace and
political felicity" than anything else (Skinner, 1: 198).

154. Rolland, *Mahatma Gandhi*, p. 4.

155. Geoffrey Ashe, *Gandhiji, A Study in Revolution* (London:
Heinemann, 1968), p. 389.

156. In this respect Gandhi's ideas, life and actions stand in continuity
with other great thinkers history has witnessed. Practically all the political
or social theory propounded so far in history, either implicitly or explicitly,
begin with a concept of the human person — human self-understanding,
human psychology, relation to the other and to God. Though sociologists
like Durkheim might not agree with this proposition, the more
fundamental questions raised by moral and political philosophers and
theologians down the centuries from Plato, Aristotle, Śaṅkara, Rāmānuja,
Madhva, Hobbes, Locke, Mill, Aquinas, Kant, Vivekananada, John Rawls,
Radhakrishnan, Niebuhr, Tillich, Rahner, Häring, Gustafson, involve an

in India, is the deep respect with which he held (hu)man. . . .
For in truth it was this conviction about the inviolable dignity
that he attached to every single person that proved to be his
spring of action."[157]

In his life of relentless action, Gandhi was constantly
protesting against all that made for fragmentation of life within
the individual and in society. He was adamant in not separating
economics and politics from religion, morality and spirituality.
He was so much convinced of the non-separation of the sacred
and the profane that he consistently emphasized upon the
sacredness of the secular. He did not make a distinction
between phases of activity now political, now secular, now

anthropology. Though these thinkers differ in their understanding of the
nature and dignity accorded to the human, one finds that any socio-political,
economic or moral philosophy involves a serious search for the "definition
of man" both in descriptive and prescriptive categories. In his earlier
philosophical writings, Karl Marx too attempted to query about human
nature, "but he entirely ignored them in his later works in which Marxism,
as a system, was elaborated." (Iyer, *The Moral and Political Thought of
Mahatma Gandhi*, p. 88) Underlying Hobbes' mechanistic, authoritarian
state there is an understanding of human beings at war with each other.
On the assumption that the human is naturally harmless and self-
improving, Locke and Mill advocated a minimal role for governments.
Even for Hume, who did not believe in a natural law or transcendental
order, there are "the constant and universal principles of human nature."
(Cf. Iyer, *op. cit.*, p. 89). Understanding the human as a microcosm of the
macrocosm was prevalent in Vedic India and Pythagorean Greece. For
Feuerbach, the human as an observer and an active agent (both standing
outside the world and influencing it from within) affecting and affected by
the world, is different from brute and God or Nature. (See Iyer, *op. cit.*, p.
90; also cf. Gilbert Ryle, *Dilemmas* (London: Cambridge University Press,
1954), pp. 64-65.

    157. V. Tellis-Nayak, "Gandhi on the dignity of the Human Person,"
Gandhi Marg, 7 (January 1963), p. 40. Gandhian scholars agree unanimously
on this point. Jayaprakash Narayan, a Gandhian disciple, points out that
"the Gandhian starting-point, . . . is man himself." *Research on Gandhian
Thought* (Bombay: Round Table on Research Programme on Gandhian
Thought, 14th-15th June, 1969. Papers and proceedings. December, 1970),
p. 19.

sacred: "You cannot divide social, economic, political and purely religious work into watertight compartments."[158] Hence it could be authentically said about Gandhian thought that it was his notion of God as Truth and the corresponding theological anthropology that formed the springboard of his beliefs and actions. The sacredness of the human person stands out as the *antaryāmin* of his whole belief-system.[159] The sacred reverence for every single individual (whether living in the Siberian desert, Alaskan snowbelt, Australian jungles or the Himālayan mountains) implies the possibility and the actuality of realizing one's spiritual dignity and significance in freedom.

This implies that there is a Gandhian "integral humanism" (to borrow a phrase from Jacques Maritain) at work in his understanding of liberative transformation.[160] We should keep in mind that the integral humanism of Gandhi has a transcendental dimension because it rests on the horizon of an Absolute, that is, God as Truth. Though the immediate focus is human and the world of human affairs, the focus is not independent of the God of human search.

---

158. Gandhi protested against the compartmentalization of human life that had been brought about in the name of separation of religion and politics. Cf. Tendulkar, *Mahatma: Life of Mohandas Karamchand Gandhi*, 7: 314.

159. *Antaryāmin* is one of the qualities attributed to *Brahman* (God) in Hindu philosophy. A Sanskrit word means the inner controller which directs the life of a being. I have used this word in the sense of "that inner force," "that underlying entity," which gives meaning and existence to life and is the *raison d'être* of Gandhian theology as such.

160. As Jacques Maritain suggests, the word "humanism" is an ambiguous term. Every individual human being is called to more than a purely human life. Hence the philosopher's remark would be very meaningful and acceptable to Gandhi as it sounds metaphysic. To propose to a person only the human, what is just humanly possible, is to betray personhood and to wish misfortune because the principal part of a person is the spirit (according to Aristotle and Gandhi), and the vocation of a person is to something beyond a purely human life. The invocation of this word brings into play an entire metaphysic and a life of transcendence,

At the same time, throwing overboard a world-negating metaphysical world-view and seeking a meaning for individual humans and collective human existence in terms that are not repugnant to reason, Gandhian humanism and theological anthropology sought to revive the past Indian experience in order to find a foundational basis for his search and experiments.[161]

Since the universe including the world of humans is in God and not outside Him as a mere epiphenomenon, human condition and human station in society cannot be overlooked. The human is a sacred entity. When a medieval poet of Bengal exclaimed: "Listen, O brother man! above all is the truth of man; there is none higher than this,"[162] it was not an effort at banishing God and replacing Him with the present deified homo. Elevation of the human as a sacred entity enables the

---

and as Maritain suggests, it "tends essentially to render man more truly human, and to manifest his original greatness by having him participate in all that which can enrich him in nature and in history," demanding at once that a person develops "the virtualities contained within him, his creative forces and the life of reason, and work to make the forces of the physical world instruments of his freedom." [See Jacques Maritain, *Integral Humanism: Temporal and Spiritual Problems of a New Christendom*, tr. Joseph W. Evans (Notre Dame: Indiana University of Notre Dame Press, 1973), p. 2]. Hence I am using humanism here in a sense beyond the articulation of B.N. Ganguli who uses it as "the ideal of man's endeavour to reconstitute himself as a free individual by shifting his attention to man and human affairs as the focus of interest, on the assumption that man's spiritual life can have meaning only in terms of a rational philosophy and sound social institutions and that the human "existence" can be understood and fulfilled in terms of such a meaning." [Cf. B.N. Ganguli, *Gandhi's Social Philosophy: Perspective and Relevance* (Delhi: Vikas Publishing House, Pvt. Ltd., 1973), p. 120].

161. I am not going into the various nuances nor the *mīmāṁsā* or *bhakti* roots of Gandhian humanism here. For an adequate treatment of this see Ganguli, *Gandhi's Social Philosophy: Perspective and Relevance*, Chapter VI, pp. 120-42.

162. As quoted in Ganguli, *Gandhi's Social Philosophy: Perspective and Relevance*, p. 122.

development of a social ethic wherein human poverty or human negativity of whatever nature could be condemned and eliminated and liberative transformation could be affirmed and placed on a deeper foundational base. In fact, the concept of God as *daridra-nārāyana* shows the possibility of such an ethic. He is Nārāyana (the Lord) who has assumed the role of the *daridra*, the poor, the lowly and the downtrodden. Hence, to serve the *daridra* is to serve the Nārāyana. One should note here that etymologically the word Nārāyana (a name of the Lord) is connected to *nara*, i.e., the human being. Such a human-God identity is not pure Monism or Monistic theism. Gandhi's embrace of *carkhā* (spinning wheel) as the symbol and means by which Indian mass poverty could be alleviated is precisely because *carkhā* symbolized to him the image of *daridra-nārāyana*.[163] This is clear from what he said in 1926: "For better or for worse I have staked my all on the *charkha*, for it represents to me *Daridra-Narayana* — God *of*, and *in*, the poor and the downtrodden."[164]

As against a world-negating metaphysical world-view, Gandhi has actively advocated a liberating force of humanism linking it to a theo-centric ethic, wherein God as Truth expropriates the primacy in human undertakings and valuation. Since this God is omnipresent,

> The best and most understandable place where He can be worshipped is a living creature. The service of the distressed, the crippled and the helpless among living things constitutes worship of God. The repetition of *Rāmanama* is also meant to help us learn to do so. If *Rāmanama* does not thus result in service, it is both futile and a sort of bondage.[165]

Rigorous ethical activism in a pluralistic and conflictual world of human interaction and human dissension, must lead

---

163. See Ganguli, *Gandhi's Social Philosophy: Perspective and Relevance*, p. 123.

164. As quoted by Ganguli, *Gandhi's Social Philosophy: Perspective and Relevance*, p. 123.

165. *Navajivan*, May 6, 1928; Iyer 1: 582.

to an enlightened integral humanism where "religious life" may help us in the process of identification of the self with the whole of human race incarnating oneself in all fields of human activities including political and economic.

CONCLUSION

It is clear that Gandhi's religious faith led him to politics. His theological convictions gave the motif-force for his theo-political theory of action, viz., *satyāgraha,* and for his continuous effort of achieving a situation of healthy and transformed human relationship through the means of *ahiṁsā.* His relentless search and thirst for truth made him embrace a spirituality (of absolute non-violent resistance) whereby various fields of human interaction — political, economic, social, spiritual, and/ or religious — would usher in a harmonious unitive wholesomeness without dichotomizing different areas of interaction, specifically of religion and politics.

Having had such a firm religious conviction that surpassed particular religious tenets, Gandhi devoted his entire life to a process of liberative transformation by embracing *ahiṁsātmaka satyāgraha* in order to expedite a transformed kingdom of human relationship which he named as *Rāmarājya.* The ultimate Gandhian goal of *Rāmarājya* and the means of attaining the goal, viz., *ahiṁsā* will be taken up later.

Foundational Basis of Liberation According to Gutiérrez

A PARADIGM SHIFT

In order to understand the foundational basis of Liberation Theology, as propounded by Gutiérrez, two basic insights that form its "backbone" need clear articulation. "From the beginning, the theology of liberation had two fundamental insights. . . . I am referring to its theological method and its perspective of the poor."[166] The first act is involvement in the liberation process, and that theology comes afterward, as a second act. Critical reflection from within and upon concrete

166. Gutiérrez, *The Power of the Poor,* p. 200.

historical praxis in the confrontational light of the word of the Lord as lived and accepted in faith, form the theological moment — the *kairos*. Gutiérrez attempts "to situate the work of theology within the complex and proliferous context of the relationship between practice and theory."[167] The second insight was the decisions to work from the perspective of the poor — the exploited classes, marginalized ethnic groups, and scorned cultures — and it led it to take up the great theme of poverty and the poor in the Bible. As a result, the poor appear within the theology of Gutiérrez as the key to an understanding of the meaning of liberation and of the meaning of the revelation of a liberating God.

Historically, the Christian theologian Dietrich Bonhoeffer, who died in the Nazi extermination camp in Flossenburg in 1945, sought to locate God at the very heart and centre of human life and had begun to move forward in the perspective of "those beneath" — those on the "under-side of history," and hence, foreshadows Gutiérrez.[168]

Picking up a theological quarrel Gutiérrez argues that none of the mighty trio of twentieth-century theologians (Barth, Bultmann, and Tillich — and for that matter even Bonhoeffer who objected to their theology, and sought to locate God at the very heart and centre of human life as mentioned above) made an effort, in their critique of the Enlightenment and response to the challenges of the modern world, to criticise it in its economic bases, as much as on its social and ideological levels. For Gutiérrez this is because they never "vanquished the modern, bourgeois mentality while remaining at its heart."[169] Beginning "from above," — from the Trinity, from revelation — Barth descends to the human being. For

---

167. Gutiérrez, *The Power of the Poor*, p. 200.

168. *Ibid.*, p. 231. Mention must be made here of the efforts of Bartholomew de la casas, who could very well be termed as the "grandfather" of liberation theology.

169. Gutiérrez, *The Power of the Poor*, p. 223.

Bonhoeffer the question that ultimately facing us is not "What is the modern spirit and what can it accept in the Christian faith?" The fundamental question, charged with force and power demanding our answer in a much more radical way is: "Who is God?" and "What does it mean to be a Christian?"[170] Bonhoeffer's questions enabled him to point to a new way of understanding God. But today, according to Gutiérrez "he will need a new way of understanding God's presence in history. And here there is a fork in the road, and it is for us to make the choice."[171] This new mode of understanding the presence of God in history is what is seminal in the insightful discovery of Gutiérrez.

The emphasis of Gutiérrez is on the covenantal God of liberation taking side with the "underside" of history. The viewing of theology from the underside of history and his insertion into the world of the poor, his concrete option for the poor, made him see the God of the Bible as a liberating God. And it is Gutiérrez's sense of the God of the Bible, who was revealed in Jesus Christ, who "made himself poor though he was rich"(2 Cor 8,9), that leads him to a perception of what it really involves to read reality from the viewpoint of the poor. The specific reading of the God of the Bible and the fashioning of the theological insight take place in a dialectical manner. A reflection on the historico-salvific manifestation of God (*Mysterium Liberationis*) — a salvation that is first and foremost offered as good news to the poor (Lk 4,18) — led Gutiérrez to hold firmly that the God of the Biblical revelation is the God of the poor. In

---

170. The answer of Bonhoeffer as understood by Gutiérrez is that "God is the God of Jesus Christ. That is, God is a God who saves us not through his domination but through his suffering. Here we have Bonhoeffer's famous thesis of *God's weakness*. It will make its mark in theology after he is gone. It is of this God, and only of this God, that the Bible tells us. And it is thus that the Cross acquires its tremendous revelatory potential with respect to God's weakness as an expression of his love for a world come of age." *Ibid.*, p. 230.

171. Gutiérrez, *The Power of the Poor*, p. 231.

his search to hermenutically understand the revealed word in the light of the contemporary experience of the reality of the poor, the mystery of God itself is encountered and understood at a deeper level taking a novel path where Bonhoeffer took leave at the point where the "fork in the road" began.

Hence it is not just viewing the mystery of God from the "anti-history of the downtrodden," as Victor Araya suggests in his *God of the Poor: The Mystery of God in Latin American Liberation Theology,* that Gutiérrez is after. His discovery of the God of the Bible as the God of the poor is what is innovative in Gutiérrez.

So in his theology of liberation Gutiérrez is not just attempting to offer a new way of "talking about" the world, remaining just at the level of reflection, but rather he seeks a theological methodology for the discernment of the presence or absence of God in history and tries to give a response to God's contemporary ever new manifestations at the heart of reality, becoming a part of the process through which the world is transformed into "a new, just, and fraternal society — the gift of the Kingdom of God."[172] When H. Richard Niebuhr asks "What is God doing in War ?" in the midst of a war torn world of human conflict, Gutiérrez sets out to search for his God in a historical reality of oppression and suffering. Gutiérrez's insight into the mystery of God and human encounter with this Reality and what that entails in terms of prescriptions for action, form the aim of my treatment in the following pages.

THE GOD OF GUTIÉRREZ

Standing before the ultimate foundation of our Christian faith and our being, we "touch bottom" in our reflection on God: "In speaking of God we are touching the very nerve of our Theology. Ultimately all theology is a reflection on God."[173]

---

172. Gutiérrez, *A Theology of Liberation,* p. 15.

173. Gutiérrez, "Communidades," p. 35. As quoted by Araya, *God of*

This ultimateness of God is a recurring theme in Gutiérrez.[174] He refers to the mystery of God in a number of ways and his reflections need synthesized articulation.

God of Life

Faced with a Latin American situation of "death"[175] that is alien to the basic requirement of the Gospel message and contrary to the Kingdom of life proclaimed by the Lord, God as the God of Life profoundly appeals to Gutiérrez. The recognition of the God of life is based on the existential experience of the poor in Latin America. "Poverty means death." It is this God that is discovered at the core of commitment to the poor and forms the very notion of the commitment to solidarity with the poor:

> The ultimate reason behind our option for the poor and our solidarity with their struggles is the God in whom we believe.

---

the Poor, footnote 17, p. 156. In *El Dios De La Vida*, where Gutiérrez is at his best in his reflection on God, he expresses God as the foundational structure of our faith and being.

174. What gives ultimate meaning to our life and actions is finally God: "In speaking of God, we "touch bottom." We stand before the ultimate foundation of our faith and our being. We face our options of every sort — personal, evangelical, spiritual, political, and so on. In speaking of God we are speaking of what gives meaning to the whole of our personal and collective life." *El Dios de la vida*, p. 5, as quoted by Araya, *God of the Poor*, p. 4. Also see Gutiérrez, "Communidades," p. 14; *The Power of the Poor*, pp. 77-90.

175. Gutiérrez emphasizes "Poverty means death . . . death through hunger or sickness, or from the repressive methods of those who see their privileges endangered by every attempt to liberate the oppressed. To this physical death can be added a cultural death, since the dominator seeks to annihilate all that gives unity and strength to the dispossessed of this world so as to make them fall an easy prey to the machinery of oppression. This is the setting for the social analysis that forms part of our theological endeavor, helping us to understand what particular forms this reality of death takes in Latin America. . . . What we have here is something contrary to the Kingdom of life proclaimed by the Lord." "Speaking about God," *Concilium* 171 (1/1984): 29.

There may well be other reasons for this privileged commitment. For the follower of Christ, however, this solidarity is ultimately rooted in our faith in the God of life.[176]

An option for this God of life implies preferential option for the poor in their struggle to overcome death.

God in and of History

God is present and acts in history. God's presence and activity cannot be contained in just historical occurrences and historical places. Thus, we cannot fix limits to God's presence and activity. Gutiérrez puts it so remarkably well in his El Dios de la vida, which, perhaps, reveals Gutiérrez at his best:

> Neither the mountain, nor the ark, nor the temple, nor any single reality or social dimension, nor indeed any experience or historical occurrence can set limits to the presence of God. This is one reason for the Old Testament opposition to the fashioning of images: they cannot depict God. And so, at the very moment when the Jewish people, having recalled the presence of the Lord on the mountain and the experience of God's company in the wilderness, built a temple, a fixed place for God to dwell, the prophets had to engage in a bit of mind-stretching. Standing before the beautiful temple, fashioned of cedar of Lebanon, the prophets retort: God's dwelling is the heavens. 'Listen to the potions of your servant,' they cry to the Lord, 'and of your people Israel which they offer in this place. Listen from your heavenly dwelling and grant pardon' (1 Kings 8: 30). . . . (God) abides above any attempt to limit the scope of the divine presence, as happens with the establishment of an immovable, unequivocal place of residence for God.[177]

And the concrete locus of our encounter with the Father of Jesus Christ is human history: "History, concrete history, is the place where God reveals the mystery of God's personhood. God's word comes to us in proportion to our involvement in

---

176. Gutiérrez, "Reflections from Latin American Perspective," in Virginia Fabella M. M. and Sergio Torres, eds., *Irruption of the Third World: Challenge to Theology* (New York: Orbis Books, 1983), p. 233.

historical becoming."[178] Since this history is a conflictual one, "a history of conflicts of interest, of struggles for greater justice, a history of the marginalization and exploitation of human beings, of aspirations for liberation,"[179] by getting involved in this disharmonious historical process in an option, ultimately an option for Christ's cross, one receives the gift of filiation, receiving the authority to call God, "Abba." The manner of receiving the free gift of filiation, then, is

> to make an option for the poor, for the exploited classes, to identify with their lot and share their fate, to seek to make this history that of an authentic community of brothers and sisters. There is no other way to receive the free gift of filiation, of the status of children of God. It is an option for Christ's cross, in the hope of his resurrection.[180]

At the same time there is the urgent necessity of re-reading history: "History, where God reveals himself and where we proclaim him, must be re-read from the side of the poor." Since history's losers have an outlook different from that of the dominators, "history must be read from a point of departure in their struggles, their resistance, their hopes."[181]

A God Hidden, Present, Active and Acting

Gutiérrez affirms the mystery of a hidden God, a Deus Absconditus:

> The God of the Bible is a God who is revealed, who is discovered, who comes to evidence, without ceasing to be a hidden God, and a God who is revealed in what is new. 'See, I make all things new!' (Rev. 21:5). God is the one who has been, who is, and who will be.[182]

---

177. Gutiérrez, *El Dios de la vida*, pp. 53-54. As quoted by Araya, *God of the Poor*, Footnote 11, pp. 171-72.

178. Gutiérrez, *The Power of the Poor*, p. 52; see also Ibid., p. 201.

179. Gutiérrez, *The Power of the Poor*, p. 52.

180. *Ibid.*

181. *Ibid.* p. 201.

182. Gutiérrez, *El Dios de la vida*, pp. 60-61. Cf. Araya, *God of the Poor*, p. 170.

Such a hidden presence of God in loving solidarity with the poor (on the side of the poor), is at the very heart of history, and "is most accessible from the most negative element in that history: its conflictuality, its sin, its injustice."[183] Hence though hidden, God reveals his presence in history in the dying, the living, in the struggles, sufferings, the deaths, and negations of individual human beings. Gutiérrez, thus, does not agree with the Aristotelian view of God as primum movens, who in the words of Moltmann pulls "history to its future, but without being involved in history."[184]

Though self-revealed at the heart of history, the Divine presence therein is concealed:

> God often performs a deed of justice, of liberation, of salvation, in a hidden manner. The indwelling of God in history is not effected in a simple and obvious fashion, so that anyone going in search of God will find God quickly, directly, or unequivocally. God is within human history, yes, in its tensions, advances, and conflicts. But to find God one has to look, one has to search. This search is a deep spiritual theme in any treatment of the journey to God, any reflection on unprecedented modes of access to this hidden God whose salvific work more often than not travels ways that are not our ways, as we read in Isaiah (55: 8).[185]

The indwelling God who acts in a hidden manner awaits human disclosure:

> The poor person, the other, becomes the revealer of the Utterly Other. Life in this involvement is a life in the presence of the Lord at the heart of political activity, with all its conflict and with all its demand for scientific reasoning. It is the life of — to paraphrase a well-known expression — contemplatives in political action.[186]

---

183. Araya, *God of the Poor*, p. 50.

184. Gutiérrez, *A Theology of Liberation*, p. 217.

185. Gutiérrez, *El Dios de la vida*, pp. 55-56. As quoted by Araya, *God of the Poor*, p. 51.

186. Gutiérrez, *The Power of the Poor*, p. 52.

If God is active and present in history, God can be and is encountered in history; God can be experienced in historical encounters. Through the mystery of the incarnation, the presence of the hidden God is manifestly bestowed first and foremost on the lowly, the poor, the oppressed, the marginalized, and those humiliated by historical processes:

> God's smallness and hiddenness is underscored in the fact of revelation through the poor. We are familiar with the straightforwardness of Mathew 25 in speaking of the Last Judgment. The true relationship with the Lord is a relationship with the hidden Lord. "When did we feed you? When did we give you to drink ? when did we visit you when you were ill or in prison ?" These are the perplexed questions asked by the just. "When did we see you hungry or thirsty or away from home or naked or ill or in prison and not attend you in your needs ?" This is the question asked by those being rejected from the reign of God. "Sticking fast to God" — to borrow an expression from the Book of Deuteronomy — is therefore the establishment of a relationship with the hidden God, which calls for decision, process, search, journey.[187]

The hidden God is, thus, encountered in history, especially in the poor. Agreeing with Von Rad that "it is in history that God reveals the secret of his person," and responding with approval to Andre Dumas' recapitulation of Dietrich Bonhoeffer, that "The space of God is the world; the secret of the world is the hidden presence of God. Jesus Christ is the structuralization of this space and the name of this secret," Gutiérrez asserts that "Human history, then, is the location of our encounter with him, in Christ."[188] This divine hiddenness can be known, as Langdon Gilkey asserts, "in the void of insecurity, despair, doubt, guilt, and death, which every

187. Gutiérrez, *El Dios de la vida*, p. 57; see also *A Theology of Liberation*, pp. 196-203.

188. Gutiérrez, *A Theology of Liberation*. p. 189; also see Ibid., footnote 3, p. 208.

human faces — even Jesus himself in his cry from the cross."[189]

This revealing and Hidden God is liberative indeed. As Dios Mayor, God is the Lord of truth and freedom, and thus, beyond any measure of human manipulation and outside the inventions of human interests. Hidden in history, Gutiérrez's biblical God acts in history and therefore is present to history. God continues to be manifest in the midst of history. In Jesus, God becomes the Liberation God Incarnate. The most important and definitive self-manifestation of the Mystery of God in history is Jesus of Nazareth. As the definitive path to the mystery of God's Truth, Jesus becomes the manifestation of the Father's truth, and thus becomes the definitive

---

189. Langdon Gilkey, *Naming the Whirlwind: The Renewal of God-Language*, third Printing (New York: The Bobbs-Merrill Company, Inc., 1969), p. 469. Both Gutiérrez and Gilkey agree that God is the divine ground of our existence and operation, the hidden presence of God in history, and human relatedness to God in our worldly affairs: "To talk meaningfully of God is to talk of our existence in contingency and freedom in relation to its divine ground, Judge, and redeeming source, understood symbolically in the terms of our community's life. . . . This dialectic of immanence and transcendence, of hidden presence to all of life and of absence from it when we look for him is, of course not all of God that we can know, or that the Christian community has believed itself to know. It is only a beginning. "God" here remains perhaps real, deep, but vague and elusive — the mysterious, sacral power from which life comes and which rules our destiny, and the eternity from which we are now separated. . . . When Christian experience and thought move beyond this point, and in the light of those more personal and moral questions raised by our freedom and by our relations to others in community and in history, begin to know the love and acceptance of God in his long relation to his people and especially in the figure of Jesus, then we can say we begin to know the sacred more directly as it is, we begin to know "God." . . . But that presence of God is real in secular life, and that our dependence on him makes us search for him even in our most worldly affairs, is true, and thus begins the possibility of knowing the reality of God and of speaking of him in a secular age. Our Biblical symbols, the treasured vehicles of our community's life and faith, can be understood as meaningful and asserted as valid as forthrightly in our secular existence as in any other age — but only if we retain, both in our thought and in our existence, a lively sense of

hermeneutic principle of our faith and of all powers.[190]

At the same time God's presence and activity cannot just be "contained" in historicity. Being "u-topic," no historical place or occurrence is capable of fixing limits to God's activity or presence.[191]

God of Communion and Commitment

Of course God is Mystery. Yet main aspect of the mystery of God is that of the divine self-revelation in history and its salvation. Being present to history, God's otherness is not an inaccessible mystery. By divine initiative God's self-manifestation oozes through the otherness. The Biblical God is close to the humans — a God of communion with and commitment to the human beings.[192] Gutiérrez often emphasizes the active presence of God, a God who pitches his tent (Shekinah) with his people. The promise of God's active presence, fulfilled in different ways all throughout history — the mountain (Exodus 19; I Kings 20: 28); the tent (Exod. 33: 7-11; Num. 11: 16, 24-26; Deut. 31: 14)), the Ark of the Covenant (Num. 1: 1; Num. 10: 35-36; Josh. 4: 5, 13; 1 Sam. 4: 17) — reached its fullness surpassing all human expectations, when God became man. In the *Verbum Caro factum est* "God's presence became both more universal and more complete."[193]

At the same time, the full strength of God's universality and transcendence takes Gutiérrez's Biblical God beyond the

their relatedness to our ordinary secular life." Gilkey, *Naming the Whirlwind*, pp. 468-70.

190. Gutiérrez, *The Power of the Poor*, pp. 60-61.

191. A clarification should be added here to understand Gutiérrez properly: "It would be erroneous, surely, to state that nothing contains God, not even Jesus, Son of God in person. Thus the New Testament, in speaking of Christ, speaks of the coming of the fullness of time, or the moment of God's total habitation." See Gutiérrez, *El Dios de la vida*, pp. 55-56.

192. Gutiérrez, *A Theology of Liberation*, pp. 190-94.

193. Gutiérrez, *A Theology of Liberation*, p. 190.

confines of place, tent, mountain, ark or temple (2 Sam. 7) to the heavens and beyond (Gen. 11: 5; 18: 21; 28: 12; Exod. 19: 11; Deut. 4: 36; Ps. 2: 4). God dwells everywhere.[194] Harsh prophetic criticism of purely external worship, and its censure of people's attitude of confining God to places of worship (to buildings of stone and gold — Jer. 3: 16; Isa. 66: 1-2), are manifest indications for Gutiérrez that "God's presence is not bound to a material structure, to a building of stone and gold," but positively, "Yahweh's preference is for a profound interior attitude."[195] Yahweh's proclamation of the new covenant, that "I will take the heart of stone from your body and give you a heart of flesh. I will put my spirit into you and make you conform to my statutes, keep my laws and live by them" (Ezek. 36: 26-27; Also cf. Jer. 31: 33), is the clearest manifestation for Gutiérrez that God is and will be present in the heart of every person.

God of Love

As mentioned above, Gutiérrez's' God is a God related to history and to the concrete world of human action and interaction. Further, God is a God of love. The love that God manifests is gratuitous. God's love, especially for the poor, is not based on a moral superiority or special openness to Him. God's preferential love is not merited. He loved us into existence; and continues to love us in our existence. It is the Father "who loved us first, without any merit of our own, and who fills our life with love and largess. Love is at the very wellspring of our existence. . . . God loves us by establishing justice and right in this conflict-charged history of ours."[196] If we courageously and unflinchingly take the gospel statements at their face value without "spiritualizing"[197]

194. See *Ibid.*, p. 192.

195. Gutiérrez, *A Theology of Liberation*, p. 192.

196. Gutiérrez, *The Power of the Poor*, p. 20.

197. If we fall into the temptation to spiritualize the poor we would be robbing God of His gratuitous love and preferential seeking: "If we

poverty "what we have is God's love for the poor first and
foremost simply because they are poor, simply because they
are literally and materially poor."[198] Gutiérrez emphasizes this
again when he reiterates

> God loves the poor just because they are poor, and not
> necessarily, or even primarily, because they are better
> believers than others, or morally firmer than others. God
> loves them simply because they are poor, because they are
> hungry, because they are persecuted.[199]

God's love for them cannot be grounded on any
presumption of moral superiority or greater openness to God:

> God loves the poor with all freedom and gratuity — and
> that God does so not because the poor are good, or better
> than others, but just because they are poor.[200]

The gratuitous character of God's love is very clearly
presented in Gutiérrez's analysis of the Beatitudes. He claims
that "the Beatitudes are less a revelation about the poor than
they are a revelation about God. They tell us who God is."[201]
Irreducible to our mode of thinking, the mystery of God tells
us that "God is God" and that the "privilege of the poor . . .
has its theological basis in God."[202] As the proclamation of

---

'spiritualize' the poor too early, before the proper moment in the dialectic,
we 'humanize' God. We make him more accessible to human
understanding by attempting to fit him into bourgeois categories and a
middle class mentality. But the theology of the Beatitudes must always
come before their anthropology. God, one could think, would surely
have a preferential love for the good. After all, the good have more
merits. But if instead we maintain that God prefers the poor just because
they are poor (again, materially poor) — then we may be flying in the face
of logic, but we are standing pointblank before the mystery of God's
revelation and the gratuitous gift of his kingdom of love and justice."
Gutiérrez, *The Power of the Poor*, p. 141.

198. *Ibid.*, p. 95.

199. *Ibid.*, p. 95.

200. *Ibid.*, p. 140.

201. Gutiérrez, *The Power of the Poor*, p. 95; see also *ibid.*, pp. 140-41.

202. Gutiérrez, *The Power of the Poor*, p. 141.

Jesus' central message ("the kingdom of God is at hand"), the beatitudes have two complementary aspects, viz., theological and anthropological. The theological character tells us who God is; the anthropological emphasizes the importance and significance of spiritual dispositions in those who hear the word. The former aspect reveals that

> God is God and that God loves the poor with all freedom and gratuity — and that God does so not because the poor are good, or better than others, but just because they are poor. That is, they are afflicted, they are hungry, and this situation is a slap in the face of God's sovereignty, God's being the Go'el ("Savior, Redeemer"), the Defender of the poor, the "Avenger of the lowly."[203]

The "blessedness" of the poor is because of the fact that "the God of the Bible is a God of justice, and hence a God of the poor," and, once we appreciate the primary theological notion, the second, anthropological, follows:

> Spiritual poverty — that is, spiritual childlikeness — is the condition for being able to hear the revelation of the kingdom. At the same time it remains clear that if we forget that the Beatitudes are talking about the materially poor, and therefore are talking about God, we will not understand what they tell us about the spiritually poor, the "poor in spirit".[204]

A God of Preferential Love

The above analysis helps us to understand Gutiérrez's God as a God of special relationship with the poor. This relationship takes the form of a "preferential love" toward the poor and the oppressed. Such a theological understanding has serious anthropological implications. God's preferential love will not leave a committed Christian with any other option than the radical "preferential option for the poor." Gutiérrez's contribution to the theologizing process in the Latin American

203. Gutiérrez, *The Power of the Poor,* p. 140.
204. *Ibid.,* p. 141.

context lies in his insightful articulation of the radical demands that option entails to committed Christians: "A living love is an affirmation of God. Belief in God does not mean simply maintaining that he exists. Belief in God means commitment of one's life to him and to all women and men."[205] The foundational basis underlying such a preferential option for the poor is clearly articulated in the very description of theology as given by Gutiérrez:

> Theology in Latin America today will be a reflection in, and on, faith as liberation praxis. It will be an understanding of the faith from an option and commitment. It will be an understanding of the faith from a point of departure in real, effective solidarity with the exploited classes, oppressed ethnic groups, and despised cultures of Latin America, and from within their world. It will be a reflection that starts out from a commitment to create a just society, a community of sisters and brothers, and that ought to see that this commitment grows more radical and complete. It will be a theological reflection that becomes true, verified, in real and fruitful involvement in the liberation process.[206]

Quoting with approval the Pueblo statement that "the poor merit preferential attention, whatever may be the moral or personal situation in which they find themselves" (# 1142), Gutiérrez argues that "The preference for the poor is based on the fact that God, as Christ shows us, loves them for their concrete, real condition of poverty," whatever may be "their moral or spiritual disposition" and with remarkable tenacity Gutiérrez reiterates the theological affirmation of the Peruvian episcopate as unmistakable:

> (T)he privilege of the poor, then, has its theological basis in God. The poor are "blessed" not because of the mere fact that they are poor, but because the kingdom of God is expressed in the manifestation of his justice and love in their favor.[207]

---

205. Gutiérrez, *The Power of the Poor*, p. 59.

206. *Ibid.*, p. 60.

207. Gutiérrez, *The Power of the Poor*, p. 138.

Hence he asserts:

The preferential option is for the poor as such, the poor as poor. The value of their attitude of openness toward God is not neglected. . . . But this does not constitute the primary motive of the privilege of the poor[208]

Hence we can conclude that Gutiérrez's call for a preferential option for the poor is just because they are "God's favourites." This mystery of the hidden God, abiding in loving solidarity with the poor, at the very heart of history is most accessible from negative elements of that history — sin, injustice, conflicts and sufferings. Therefore, at this historic juncture, "we stand before a God who is a challenge, a God who overturns our human categories, a God who will not be reduced to our mode of thinking, and who judges us on the basis of our concrete, historical actions toward the poor."[209] All of us stand before such a challenging God who, overturning our human categories of thinking and acting, stands in judgement upon us on the basis of our concrete, historical actions toward the poor and the oppressed.

Jesus Christ The Liberator

Christ is the fulfilment of the promise of the Father. The complete fulfilment of Yahweh's covenant-proclamation took place in the Incarnation of the Son of God: the word became flesh; he came to dwell (pitch his tent) among us" (John 1: 14). Being the temple of God (Jn. 4: 21-23; Jn. 2: 19, 20), it is in Christ that the complete reality of the Godhead dwells (Col. 2: 9; cf. Eph. 2: 20-22; 1 Pet. 2: 4-8). Hence "God manifests himself visibly in the humanity of Christ, the God-Man, irreversibly committed to human history."[210] Jesus Christ is the full manifestation of the God who is love. He is the fulfilment and the new departure of the promise of love.[211] In

---

208. Gutiérrez, *The Power of the Poor*, p. 138.

209. *Ibid.*, p. 95.

210. Gutiérrez, *A Theology of Liberation*, p. 192.

211. See Gutiérrez, *The Power of the Poor*, pp. 12-13.

Jesus God not only reveals himself in history, he becomes history. He "pitches his tent" in the midst of history (John 1: 14). Jesus Christ is precisely *God become poor*.[212] Hence "this is the place where Jesus dwells: the tent he has pitched in the midst of us, at the centre of history. Jesus lives in his task of proclaiming the gospel, for that is where his Father's business is located (Luke 2: 49)."[213] The self-revelation of the Mystery of God hidden in history and present to history acquires its most concrete form in Jesus of Nazareth. With the incarnation of the Son of God, "The Word became flesh and dwelt (pitched his tent) among us." (Jn. 1: 14). As far as Gutiérrez is concerned the above-mentioned proclamation of Yahweh was completely fulfilled with the Incarnation. The place where God had deigned to pitch his tent, namely, "in the midst of us, at the centre of history," is the location of the business of the Father. Therein Jesus dwells; therein He lives in his task of proclaiming the gospel.[214] In Christ, the God-Man, one encounters God and the individual human being: "In Christ man gives God a human countenance and God gives man a divine countenance."[215] This takes us to Gutiérrez's notion of human beings and his understanding of the nature of encounter between God and human beings.

GUTIÉRREZ'S HOMO

Gutiérrez has recourse to St. Paul 1 Cor. 3: 16-17 and 1 Cor 6: 19 to positively establish that "The Spirit sent by the Father and the Son to carry the work of salvation to its fulfilment dwells in every man — in men who form part of a very specific fabric of human relationships, in men who are in concrete historical situations."[216] Gutiérrez goes beyond Paul in his extension of the dwelling of the spirit, and claims correctly:

212. See Gutiérrez, *The Power of the Poor*, p. 13.
213. Gutiérrez, *We Drink From Our Own Wells*, p. 41.
214. *Ibid.*
215. Gutiérrez, *A Theology of Liberation*, p. 206.
216. Gutiérrez, *A Theology of Liberation*, p. 193.

Furthermore, not only is the Christian a temple of God; every man is. The episode with Cornelius proves that the Jews "were astonished that the gift of the Holy Spirit should have been poured out even on Gentiles." Peter draws the conclusion: "Is anyone prepared to withhold the water for baptism from these persons, who have received the Holy Spirit just as we did ourselves?" (Acts 10: 45, 47; cf. 11: 16-18 and 15: 8). For this reason the words of Christ apply to every man: "Anyone who loves me will heed what I say; then my Father will love him, and we will come to him and make our dwelling with him (John 14: 28).[217]

Gutiérrez discerns a twofold process here. First of all the "presence" of God is universalized. It is extended to all the peoples of the earth breaking away from the narrow understanding of it being localized and linked to a particular people (Amos 9: 7; Isa. 41: 1-7; 45: 20-25; 51: 4; and the entire Book of Jonah). Secondly, there is an aspect of internalization. It is a process of integration of the presence. This presence is transferred from places of worship to the heart of history, embracing the human as a whole.[218] Christ becomes the converging point of both developments. In the personal uniqueness of Christ, transcending the particular, the universal becomes concrete. In him, in his Incarnation, what is personal and internal becomes visible. Henceforth, this will be true, in one way or another, of every human being. In God's becoming man, humanity — every individual human being — as well as history, has become the living temple of God. The "pro-fane" (that which is outside the temple) does not exist any longer.[219] Such a line of theologizing gives the basis for asserting that God is present and active in every individual person.

The nature and form of our encounter with God manifests the modes of God's presence in the individuals and in history. If each human being is the living temple of God, then in our

217. Gutiérrez, *A Theology of Liberation*, p. 193.

218. *Ibid.*

219. Gutiérrez, *A Theology of Liberation*, pp. 193-94.

encounter with any other we meet God; we encounter God in our commitment to history and the historical process of humankind. Such a close relatedness of the God of the Bible to humanity brings in the dimension of mutual respect and responsibility, of mutuality and justice:

To despise one's neighbour (Prov. 14: 21), to exploit the humble and poor worker, and to delay the payment of wages are to offend God:

> You shall not keep back the wages of a man who is poor and needy, whether a fellow-countryman or an alien living in your country in one of your settlements. Pay him his wages on the same day before sunset, for he is poor and his heart is set on them: he may appeal to the Lord against you, and you will be guilt of sin" (Deut. 24: 14-15; cf. Exod. 22: 21-23)

This explains why "a man who sneers at the poor insults his maker" (Prov. 17: 5).[220]

Further, to know such a God of relationship is to do justice to the poor and oppressed. Gutiérrez asserts emphatically that "Where there is justice and righteousness, there is knowledge of Yahweh; when these are lacking, it is absent. . . . To know Yahweh, which in Biblical language is equivalent to saying to love Yahweh, is to establish just relationships among men, it is to recognize the rights of the poor."[221]

Created in the Image and Likeness of God

There is a reaffirmation of the human in Gutiérrez's liberation agenda. Every person is a child of God. Created in the image and likeness of God, a person receives dignity in the very fact of being a child of God and redeemed by the blood of Jesus on the Cross. Revelation itself emphasizes the value and

220. Gutiérrez, *A Theology of Liberation*, p. 194.

221. *Ibid.*, p. 195. Gutiérrez quotes with approval Jeremiah's insight of what knowing God entails: "Shame on the man who builds his house by unjust means, and completes its roof-chambers by fraud, making his countrymen work without payment, giving them no wage for their labor!

dignity of human beings as created in the image and likeness of God.[222]

Humans are destined to total communion with God and to the fullest fellowship with one another. Rejection of such a communion is a rejection of the very meaning of human existence.[223] Mutual acceptance is the manifestation of communion and fellowship among all peoples. And we will definitely be judged by our "capacity to create brotherly conditions of life."[224] Gutiérrez puts emphasis on communion as the ultimate meaning of human life itself. This communion is manifested through concrete actions of love: "doing" favoured over simple "knowing." Even the freedom to which we are called is not an end in itself, but must be ordered to love and service.[225] Further, freedom "presupposes the going out of oneself, the breaking down of our selfishness and of all the structures that support our selfishness; the foundation of this freedom is openness to others. The fullness of liberation — a free gift from Christ — is communion with God and with other human beings."[226]

The Fact of Sin

Though humans are called to communion and fellowship with God and with one another, there is the existential fact of their rupturing that fellowship. This is the meaning of sin. By the

Shame on the man who says, 'I will build a spacious house with airy roof-chambers, set windows in it, panel it with cedar, and paint it with vermilion'! If your cedar is more splendid, does that prove you are a king? Think of your father: he ate and drank, dealt justly and fairly; all went well with him. He dispensed justice to the cause of the lowly and poor; did this not show he knew me? says the Lord" (Jer. 22: 13-16). Further, he refers to Hosea 4: 1-2 to prove his point that the knowledge of Yahweh entails justice and righteousness. See *A Theology of Liberation*, p. 195.

222. See Gutiérrez, *The Truth Shall Make You Free*, p. 35.

223. Gutiérrez, *A Theology of Liberation*, p. 198.

224. *Ibid.*, p. 199.

225. Gutiérrez, *The Truth Shall Make You Free*, p. 139.

226. Gutiérrez, *A Theology of Liberation*, 15th Anniversay edn., p. 24.

action of free will human beings are capable of rejecting the gift of God's love, of breaking friendship with God and with others. Sin is the rejection of the gift of God's love. As a personal and free act, sin "is the refusal to accept God as Father and to love others as the Lord loves us,"[227] and it "is the ultimate root of all disruption of friendship and of all injustice and oppression."[228] It is the root of all divisions among human beings. Behind every unjust social structure there is a personal or collective will responsible for rejecting God and neighbour.[229] This implies that "social transformation, no matter how radical it may be, does not automatically achieve the suppression of all evil."[230] Personal transformatory conversion is essential for achieving harmony and communion. Hence, self-centeredness that prevents human beings from going out of themselves is sin. Further, "because sin is a personal and social intrahistorical reality, a part of the daily events of human life, it is also, and above all, an obstacle to life's reaching the fullness we call salvation."[231] In fine, "sin is regarded as a social, historical fact, the absence of fellowship and love in relationships among persons, a breach of friendship with God and with other persons, and therefore, an interior, personal fracture."[232] Locating the structural presence of sin, Gutiérrez argues,

> sin is evident in oppressive structures, in the exploitation of humans by humans, in the domination and slavery of peoples, races, and social classes. Sin appears, therefore, as the fundamental alienation, the root of situation of injustice and exploitation. It cannot be encountered in itself, but only

227. Gutiérrez, *The Truth Shall Make You Free*, p. 136.

228. Gutiérrez, *A Theology of Liberation*, p. 37.

229. See Gutiérrez, *The Truth Shall Make You Free*, p. 137. See also *A Theology of Liberation*, p. 35.

230. Gutiérrez, *A Theology of Liberation*, p. 35.

231. *Ibid.*, 15th Anniversary edn., p. 85.

232. *Ibid.*, 15th Anniversary edn., pp. 102-103; see also *The Truth Shall Make You Free*, p. 137.

in concrete instances, in particular alienations. It is impossible to understand the concrete manifestations without understanding the underlying basis and vice versa. Sin demands a radical liberation, which in turn necessarily implies a political liberation. Only by participating in the historical process of liberation will it be possible to show the fundamental alienation present in every partial alienation.[233]

Saving Action of God

Precisely because sin is a breaking of friendship with God and others and since it is the ultimate root of all injustice, oppression, and all division among human beings, God's gratuitous grace alone can overcome it. It is Christ who makes humankind truly free, enabling us to live in communion with him and with one another: "It is the grace of Christ that liberates us from sin and enables us to live in communion."[234] Responsible pursuit of the human task in history is a positive manifestation of the gratuitous love of God; and "passivity or quietism is not only not a real acknowledgement of the gratuitous love of God, but even denies or at least deforms it."[235] While the saving love of God is a free, gratuitous gift, its acceptance entails a commitment to one's neighbour. Thus Christian life is located between the gratuitous gift of God and the obligation that is entailed in such a gift.

The gift of filiation is gratuitously given to every human being in the sonship of the Son. The third level of liberation, namely, the liberation from sin and the resultant communion with God and with one another, is an unmerited gift of the Father in his incarnate son, Jesus made man. If liberation from sin is unmerited, then what is the role of human action in historical praxis? There is no Pelagian heresy involved in the affirmation of God's saving grace and of responsible human

233. Gutiérrez, *A Theology of Liberation*, 15th Anniversary edn., p. 103.
234. Gutiérrez, *The Truth Shall Make You Free*, p. 136.
235. *Ibid.*, p. 35.

action. According to Gutiérrez, there is not only no
contradiction between the two but also the acceptance of the
gift of the kingdom calls for a commitment to the other,
especially the poorest and the most helpless.[236] God's
gratuitousness entails an obligation:

> The saving love of God is a gift, but its acceptance entails a
> commitment to one's neighbour. Christian life is located
> between the gratuitous gift and the obligation . . . to create
> brotherly and sisterly relations among human beings.[237]

Human Responsibility

Since human beings are capable of falling short of the fullness
of human life to which they are called, they have to understand
clearly that "the saving action of God does not do away with
human responsibility and the human task in history."[238] This
is why discussion on gratuitousness is not a flight from the
reality of the human world and from concrete efforts within
human history. Gutiérrez goes on to say that the critical
reflection on historical praxis is undertaken under the light of
the gift of grace:

> The fundamentals to be preserved are clear: the action of
> God and the action of human beings. St. Augustine gave
> profound expression to their connection when he had God
> say: "I created you without you; I cannot save you without
> you. . . ." The light of faith will be there to show that the
> starting point of everything is to be found in the divine
> initiative.[239]

The critical reflection and judgement on historical praxis
in the light of God's word accepted in faith, will keep historical
praxis from replacing the gift of grace.

Nature of the Human-God Encounter

---

236. Gutiérrez, *The Truth Shall Make You Free*, p. 35.

237. *Ibid.*, p. 36.

238. *Ibid.*, p. 35; see also *Ibid.*, p. 51.

239. Gutiérrez, *The Truth Shall Make You Free*, p. 35.

The true nature of all that is human is illumined in God's encounter with history and the human encounter of God in history: "the Word is not only a word about God and about man: the word is made man. If all that is human is illuminated by the Word, it is precisely because the word reaches us through human history."[240] Quoting with approval the comments of Von Rad that "it is in history that God reveals the secret of his person,"[241] Gutiérrez asserts:

> Human history, then, is the location of our encounter with him, in Christ. Recalling the evolution of the revelation regarding the presence of God in the midst of his people will aid us in clarifying the form this encounter in history takes. Both his presence and our encounter with him lead humanity forward, but we celebrate them in the present in eschatological joy.[242]

Hence, one encounters God in one's concrete actions towards others, especially the poor. Herein lies the privilege of the poor, i.e., to possess the prerogative and the capacity to reveal God more than fully and make God's presence more of a living reality to all those who actively seek out the poor in order to change the oppressive and dehumanizing conditions and work for a more than just humane order of brotherhood and sisterhood. If each and every individual in this world irrespective of sex, colour, creed, nationality, social or professional status, "is the living temple of God, we meet God in our encounter with (wo)men; we encounter him in the commitment to the historical process of mankind."[243] A very distinguishing characteristic of the God of the Bible is such an interrelationship that exists between God and the neighbour. Despising one's neighbour (Prov.14: 21), exploiting the poor and the humble worker, delaying the payment of wages are

240. Gutiérrez, *The Truth Shall Make You Free*, p. 189.

241. Gerhard von Rad, *Old Testament Theology*, tr. D.M.G. Stalker, vol. II (New York: Harper & Row, Publishers, 1965), p. 238.

242. Gutiérrez, *A Theology of Liberation*, p.189.

243. Gutiérrez, *A Theology of Liberation*, p. 194.

positively offences against the God of such relationship.[244] The advice of the prophets, especially, Jeremiah, Hosea and Isaiah (Cf. Jer. 22: 13-16; Hos. 4: 1-2; Isa.1, Is. 1: 6-17) bear witness to this position of Gutiérrez.[245]

By the Incarnation of the Word the bond between the neighbour and God is changed, deepened, and universalized. A clear and thorough exegesis of the parable of the final judgement as given in Mathew 25: 31-45, makes Gutiérrez emphasize three points: the emphasis on communion and fellowship (brotherhood/sisterhood) as the ultimate meaning of human life; the insistence on love which is manifested in concrete historic actions, in "doing" rather than "knowing;" and the revelation of the human mediation necessary to reach the Lord.[246] Hence Gutiérrez concludes that every human is ultimately destined to "total communion with God and to the fullest brotherhood with all men."[247]

Rich in ramifications, the idea of God's presence in humanity, in each and every human being, that is implicit in the notion of *Shekhina*, vividly suggests to Gutiérrez that

---

244. The Deuteronomic code is very clear in this regard: "You shall not keep back the wages of a man who is poor and needy, whether a fellow-countryman or an alien living in your country in one of your settlements. Pay him his wages on the same day before sunset, for he is poor and his heart is set on them: he may appeal to the Lord against you, and you will be guilty of sin" (Deut. 24: 14-15; cf Exod. 22: 21-23). This is why "a man who sneers at the poor insults his maker" (Prov. 17: 5). To know and thus to love Yahweh "is to establish just relationships among men, it is to recognize the rights of the poor." Cf. Gutiérrez, *A Theology of Liberation*, p. 195.

245. The prophetic denunciation of Jeremiah quoted above is worth listening again: Jer. 22: 13-16. Hosea is equally strong in his condemnation: "there is no good faith or mutual trust, no knowledge of God in the land, oaths are imposed and broken they kill and rob; there is nothing but adultery and license, one deed of blood after another" (Hos. 4: 1-2).

246. Gutiérrez, *A Theology of Liberation*, p. 198. Gutiérrez takes extreme care to explain these three notions in pages 198-203 of his seminal work.

247. Gutiérrez, *A Theology of Liberation*, p. 198, See also 1 John 4: 7-8.

God's temple is human history; the "sacred" transcends the narrow limits of the places of worship. We find the Lord in our encounters with men, especially the poor, marginated, and exploited ones. An act of love towards them is an act of love towards God.[248]

In our encounter with those "whose human features have been disfigured by oppression, despoliation, and alienation" we encounter the Lord.[249]

So it is from the outlook of the poor that we can sense God's activity more deeply. Here is where "We shall meet the Lord" says Gutiérrez.[250] Deeds of love and solidarity make our encounter with the exploited one effective. In that person we encounter Christ as well. Thus "the poor person, the other, becomes the revealer of the Utterly Other," and a life of involvement in the political arena with all its conflictual character and its demand for scientific reasoning, is a life of "contemplatives in political action," a life in the presence of the Lord.[251] Hence our involvement in this hour of history with a spirituality of action fighting for the most elemental rights of an oppressed social class and for the construction of a society in which persons can live as human beings makes us really encounter the Lord. Transforming our socio-economic, political, and cultural milieu, the authentic spiritual experience, an encounter with Christ in the poor takes place. Such an encounter with Christ in the poor person constitutes an authentic spiritual experience of living in the Spirit. Such a life "is a life in the Spirit, the bond of love between Father and Son, between God and human being, and between human being and human being."[252]

And such a profound communion necessitates an involvement in concrete historical liberation praxis "in a love

---

248. *Ibid.*, p. 201.

249. *Ibid.*, p. 202.

250. See Gutiérrez, *The Power of the Poor*, pp. 53, 199-200.

251. *Ibid.*, p. 52.

252. See Gutiérrez, *The Power of the Poor*, p. 53.

for Christ in solidarity with the poor, in faith in our status as
children of the Father as we forge a society of sisters and
brothers, and in the hope of Christ's salvation in a commitment
to the liberation of the oppressed."[253]

Thus the poor are the key to an understanding of the
meaning of the revelation of a liberating God.[254] The
fundamental basis of the liberation agenda of Gutiérrez is,
then, the God of love whose active presence, communion, and
encounter with every human being in historical praxis which
culminated in the Word made flesh in Jesus Christ, and
necessitates a spirituality of brotherhood and sisterhood of
every human being. The love of God requires committed
followers to make a preferential option for the underside of
history. Hence to view reality from the foundational basis as
propounded by Gutiérrez implies a call to an authentic
spirituality, to an integrated approach to theology and
spirituality, (a spiritual-theology) of *imitatio Christi.*[255]

Thus we see that the foundational basis of Christian praxis
for Gutiérrez is ultimately the Biblical God understood as one
who finally and fully revealed in Jesus Christ and thus pitched
His tent in the heart of human history as one who has a
preferred love for the poor and the oppressed. Taking
inspiration from Biblical scriptures, Gutiérrez makes the faith-
assertion that the locus of verification of our Christian faith in
such a revealed God of Jesus Christ is in the praxis of love
and justice, and that faith in that God consists not in mere
verbal, reflective, cerebral assertion of His existence but in
acting as God does.[256]

Besides, such a "praxis secundum Deum" is also the ground
of verification of a true Christian life in Jesus Christ. Thus the

---

253. Gutiérrez, *The Power of the Poor*, p. 53.

254. *Ibid.*, p. 200.

255. Gutiérrez, *We Drink from Our Own Wells*, p. 36.

256. In his letter St. James asserts that "the faith that does nothing in
practice . . . is thoroughly lifeless." (James 2, 17; Also see James 2, 14-26).

only faith-life is the one Scriptures call "witness," a witness borne in action. The Pauline notion of the actualization of faith (Gal. 5, 6) by means of love and Johannine linking of the knowledge of God with love for concrete human persons (1 Jn. 3, 18-19) underlie Gutiérrez's assertion "(T)o believe is to practice,"[257]and "God is practiced."[258]

So faith is not just a nostic phenomenon. Belief has to be manifested through a living process. A mere doctrinal acceptance of a truth is not a necessary indication of a commitment to concrete transformation and conversion and action-process. Transcending mere verbal assertions and wordy confessions, faith must manifest its affirmation in the reality of the personal and societal process of living.

The liberation theology of Gutiérrez, thus, seeks to be liberative in the manner of what Victorio Araya has termed as theo-praxis (*praxis secundum Deum*). There is an urgency in the action of love to be a preferred love opting for the poor. Being-neighbour implies a becoming-neighbour, indicating that in the "becoming" process "being" gets its full meaning. The means involved in this theo-praxis that are necessary for the "becoming process" need further analytical evaluation. I shall take it up in the next chapter.

---

257. Gutiérrez, *Power of the Poor*, p. 17.
258. Gutiérrez, *El Dios de la vida*, p. 6. See Araya God of the Poor, p. 79.

4

A Spirituality of Liberative Transformation

Introduction

It has been mentioned earlier that a spirituality of action has sprung forth from the respective foundational basis of faith in both Gandhi and Gutiérrez. Though non-violence has been largely preached and proclaimed by some religious figures, mystics, and prophets as a cardinal moral virtue, political pundits, philosophers and theologians, and, *a fortiori*, many statesmen, have generally focused on the justification and exercise of power and force to resolve conflicts and settle political problems. With the advent of Gandhi on the Indian political scene a radical change has taken place in the socio-political arena. It has been rightly pointed out that "Gandhi will be remembered as one of the very few who have set the stamp of an idea on an epoch. That idea is Non-violence."[1] Gandhi introduced a novel method of socio-political transformation and adamantly insisted on means consonant with the final goal of human aspiration.[2]

1. Edward Thompson in *Mahatma Gandhi: Essays and Reflectios on His Life and Work*, ed. S. Radhakrishnan, 2nd edn. (London: Allen and Unwin, 1949), p. 298. See Iyer, *Moral and Political Writings of Gandhi*, p. 178.

2. Reflections on the doctrine of non-violence and the insightful

The subtitle of Gutiérrez's important work, *We Drink from Our Own Wells: The spiritual journey of a people* is indicative of his attempt to build a spirituality into his theology and to translate his theology into a spirituality of contemplative-action. Going beyond particular areas of Christian existence, he wants to propose a "new style of life," a "new mode of being" a Christian — the *spiritual journey of a people*. The nature of these two spiritualities of means in terms of concrete prescriptions for action need further analysis. I shall look at the means which both of them advocate for the liberative transformation process and try to see how they have sprung up from their respective foundational bases. This is my task in the present chapter.

---

understanding of the force of truth in human encounters are not just a Gandhian contribution. A quick glance through the pages of history will reveal that the fundamental concepts of *satya* and *ahiṁsā* may be found in the world's major religious, philosophical and theological traditions and thinkers. According to Zeno, it is *harmonoia* (harmony) that binds the universe. Tiberius even dedicated a temple to its Latin equivalent *concordia*.

From very ancient times, long before the Christian era, the Hindus chanted hymns about human concord praising the spiritual oneness of all reality. The ideal for Jainism is *ahiṁsā*. More than five hundred years before the birth of Christ, Gautama the Buddha told his friends, "If a man speaks or acts with a pure thought, happiness follows him, like shadow that never leaves him. . . . Hatred does not cease by hatred at any time: hatred ceases by love. Let a man overcome anger by love, let him overcome evil by good; let him overcome the greedy by liberality, the liar by truth! Speak the truth, do not yield to anger; give, if thou are asked for little; by these three steps thou wilt go near the gods." (from the *Dhammapad*, see Robert O. Ballou, ed., *World Bible* (New York: Viking Press, 1944), p. 135.

The ancient Far East tradition of Taoism too expresses a non-violent approach to life. Seeing the corruption of Chinese civilization, the "Old Philosopher," Lao Tzu (as he is affectionaly called), finds his own "Walden" beyond the walls of the state. The document he wrote, the *Tao-Te-King*, became the basic scripture of Taoism. The divine harmonious principle of the universe, Tao, is innate in all humans. The *Tao* — the way of harmony — and the *Te* — the power — enables the human to return love for hatred:

Gandhian Novelty and Contribution

It has been rightly claimed that *satyāgraha* (search for truth and truth in action via active non-violence) and *sarvodaya* (welfare of all) are the two most significant contributions of Gandhi to contemporary political thought and action. These two doctrines were both the logical corollaries of his fundamental premises about God as Truth, human-God

"Return love for great hatred.
Otherwise, when a great hatred is reconciled, some of it will surely remain.
How can this end in goodness?
Therefore the sage holds to the left half of an agreement but does not exact what the other holder ought to do.
The virtuous resort to agreement;
the virtueless resort to exaction.
The Tao of heaven shows no partiality;
It abides always with good me."
                              — from the *Tao-Te-King*. Cf. *World Bible*, pp. 551-52.

The Stoic notion of human duty of enduring the consequence of violence without anger or resentment, and the Jewish concept of the Suffering Servant were passed on to Christianity. Early Christianity had even rejected the obligation of military services in the Roman army. Though the early Fathers of the Church such as Ireneus, Clement of Alexandria and Origen had argued for the ideal of martyrdom, we see in Augustine of Hippo a defense of the doctrine of just war and the inevitable necessity of bearing the sword to secure justice in spite of his emphasis on "inward disposition" (see St. Augustine's *Reply to Faustus*). In the middle ages Thomas Aquinas systematically reflected on the notion of just war theory. The extreme position of the early Fathers of the Church, and the more moderate and flexible positions of Sts. Augustine and Aquinas with respect to the use of force are mirrored after the middle ages. Take Erasmus and Grotius for instance. For Erasmus perfect harmony is the order of reality Instead of being at war with oneself and with one another, as Hobbes would propose later on, human beings can, given correct and right choices, live in mutual concord and peace (see *The Complaint of Peace*). Grotius, on the other hand, considered the right of defense and the place of punishment in human society. At the same time he holds (as he does in his *De Jure Belli ac Pacis*) that whatever contradicts the hope for order is antagonistic to human nature and the law of nature. Immanuel Kant has categorically held the conditional duty of sustaining one's life with the relationship, human nature and perfectibility, and the ultimate results of his continuous experiments in socio-political and economic transformatory process.[3] They were based on his fundamental notion of *satya* and the supreme means *ahiṁsā* that spring forth from his foundational basis as concrete means to the attainment of the goal.

Though the two fundamental concepts of *satya* and *ahiṁsā* (truth and non-violence) can be found in all major religious,

---

unconditional duty of not taking the life of another. While De Maistre challenged the assumptions of the Enlightenment and postulated that there is nothing but violence in the universe, we see, the French social philosopher, Saint-Simon advocating the view that in the type of society that he had in mind (ratioally planned in a manner advantageous to all) there would be little or no need of force to coerce obedience to law. Auguste Compte asserted that love is the very basic principle of human society and that only self-sacrificial acts regardless of personal reward can sustain a society. The English political philosopher, William Godwin, maintained that every form of coercion is evil (see his *Political Justice*). Condemning vehemently Sorel's flamboyant justification of the ethic of violence, Leo Tolstoy made a positive commitment to the ethic of non-violence as the only permissible ethic in society (see particularly his essays, "The Law of Violence and the Law of Love" (1908) and "The Only Commandment" (1909). In his famous letter to Einstein entitled "Why War?" written in 1932 Freud, in prophetic anger, argues for a "constitutional intolerance" to moral flabbiness and the violence of war. Holding *ahiṁsā* as the law of our species, Gandhi would absolutely disagree with Karl Marx's assumption that violence could be tolerated in history and only in that process can the fog of "moral pretensions" and "hypocritical dialogue" be eliminated from the face of history. Gandhi wouldn't agree with Edmund Burke either, when the British statesman and political philosopher suggests that "the dreadful exigence in which morality submits to the suspension of its own rules in favour of its own priciples." For a rather detailed description of the same see Iyer, *The Moral and Political Thought of Mahatma Gandhi*, pp. 218-22 (To these pages of Iyer I am very much indebted for this footnote). Also see Ballou, ed., *World Bible.*

3. See Iyer, *The Moral and Political writings of Mahatma Gandhi*, 3: 1. Iyer suggests that Gandhi's "concept of *satya*, with *ahiṁsā* as the means, determined his doctrine of *satyagraha* or active resistance to authority, while the concept of *ahiṁsā*, with *satya* as the common end, enabled him to formulate his doctrine of *sarvodaya* or nonviolent socialism." *The Moral and*

theological and philosophical traditions that humankind has witnessed, the unique Gandhian contribution lies

1. in his fusion of the two into a viable theory of what I have called *ahiṁsātmaka satyāgraha*, evolved as a unique and an all encompassing system of conflict resolution in and through his application of the concepts of *satya* and *ahiṁsā* to the process of achieving *swarāj*, *Rāmarājya*, and, ultimately, *mokṣa* itself, and[4]

2. in the application of the same to personal, socio-political and economic transformatory process and the resolution of conflicts arising in any growth process.

In such a fusion, *satya* and *ahiṁsā* are two interdependent dimensions of the Gandhian *satyāgraha*.

Satya and Ahiṁsā

For Gandhi *satya* has much wider meaning and connotation than its narrow epistemological sense in common usage as veracity, or even the Hegelian and Kantian correspondence between the objective notion (*Begriff*) and the thing in itself (*Sache*). *Ahiṁsā* is usually translated as non-violence. Though, in spite of Gandhi's statements at different times, the doctrine of *ahiṁsā* is not free from ambiguities, he has evolved a subtle and nuanced doctrine that cannot be easily grasped or lightly dismissed.[5]

Political Thought of Mahatma Gandhi, p. 252.

4. I do not think Gandhi has used the phrase *"ahiṁsātmaka satyāgraha"* as such in his writings. Holding on to truth non-violently is a constitutive element of Gandhian *satyāgraha*. *Satya* and *ahiṁsā* are the two sides of the same coin in Gandhian approach. So it is more appropriate to phrase Gandhian non-violent approach as *ahiṁsātmaka satyāgraha* than just name it as *satyāgraha*. Its literal meaning is holding on to the forces of truth in a non-violent manner.

5. See Iyer, *The Moral and Political Thought of Gandhi*, pp. 178-80. *Ahiṁsā* literally means non-injury. In its narrowest sense it implies non-killing. In its wider sense it implies the renunciation of the will to kill and even of the intent to hurt any living thing, abstention from adverse thought, word

For Gandhi truth is not just the object of reason, or simply something to be created as a product of human decision. As the Eternal Law of Nature it must be pursued; once discovered, it must be acted upon. Hence, truth must be both discovered and manifestly enacted. Once discovered, truth awaits human creative enactment in freedom. Thus it is not just enough for human thought to be based upon truth, but human actions must visibly represent it in concrete terms. There are objective moral truths awaiting human discovery. Their truth content does not depend on human validity or even human enactment. All the same, Gandhi stressed that one could lay no claim to independent truth unless one's daily life manifests this truth

and deed (see Monier-Williams, *Sanskrit-English Dictionary*, Oxford, 1899). In the Hindu, Buddhist and Jain traditions, *ahiṁsā* is highlighted in many ways, and is given both a minimal and maximal meaning and interpretation. It is even regarded as akin to dharma (the Moral Law). Invoking *ahiṁsā*, *Mahābhārata* condemns cruel practices. Gandhian innovation consists in his desire to give it a social rather than a mystical meaning. See Iyer, *The Moral and Political Thought of Mahatma Gandhi*, pp. 178-79.

The idea of non-violence, originally found even in the crude Indo-Arian notion of sacrifice, underwent an intellectual refinement in the Upaniṣads and a humanistic tranfusion from the two off-shoots of Hinduism, viz., Jainism and Buddhism, until it reached the Gandhian imagination. The Hindu scriptures look upon *ahiṁsā* as the highest virtue, (see *Mahābhārata* Anuśāsana Parva, Ch. IV. 125), which many consider to be India's greatest contribution to the world and to the history of ideas and thought. See Radhakrishnan, S., *Religion and Society* (London: George Allen & Unwin Ltd., 1947).

Gandhi's contact with Tolstoy and Ruskin among others along with his reading of the *Gītā* (among other writings) helped him concretize the notion of nonviolence. This principle as applied to social problems is found in Tolstoy's conviction that a spiritual force manifesting a higher moral standard of a people as a whole and expressed in public opinion is the only force by which the real progress is made: "The sole guide which directs men and nations has always been and is the unseen, intangible, underlying force, the resultant of all the spiritual forces of a certain people, or of all humanity, which finds its outward expression in public opinion." Leo Tolstoy, *The Kingdom of God is Within You* translated by Constance Garnett

in a visible manner. Here Gandhi is at variance with Nietzsche who, rejecting the Socratic notion of truth, holds that truth is something to be created, not discovered.[6]

Truth is an all-inclusive principle to Gandhi. It is logically prior to all the other human virtues and excellences. A human can be fully alive only to the extent that s/he is truthful:

> You feel vitality in you when you have got truth in you. . . .
> It is a permanent thing of which you cannot be robbed. You
> may be sent to the gallows or put to torture; but if you have
> truth in you, you will experience an inner joy.[7]

Truth is the substance of all morality.[8] Universal values like truth (in the realm of knowledge), righteousness (in the sphere of conduct), and justice (in the domain of social relations) derive their origin from *satya*, which itself is derived from *sat*, the One omnipotent Reality. Truth as truth (veracity) in the epistemological realm is only a part of its wider meaning. Truth, the most important and all inclusive principle, is also logically prior to all the other human virtues and excellences, "a million times more intense than that of the sun, it is the very breath of life."[9]

It is clear that Gandhi's notion of *ahiṁsā* has sprung forth from his foundational belief system. He has succeeded in bringing this ancient Indian concept from the mystical level of

------

(Lincoln: University of Nebraska Press, 1984), p. 259.

The important sources of Gandhi's concept of non-violence is well documented in V.P. Gaur, *Mahatma Gandhi: A Study of his Message of Non-Violence* (New Delhi: Sterling Publishers Private Limited, 1977), Chapter 2. Also See Chatterjee, *Gandhi's Religious Thought* and Green, *Origins of Nonviolence: Tolstory and Gandhi in Their Historical Setting.*

6. For Gandhi truth had to be realized in action, "truth in action," which put context and circumstances at the center of knowing the truth and of realizing it.

7. *Collected Works*, p. 36.

8. *From Yeravda Mandir*, Ch. 1.

9. *Ibid.*, p. 2.

the sages and the saints to the social realm of ordinary humans. Gandhi converts the age-old concept of the virtue of *ahiṁsā* into a collective moral force against a structural evil (for example, modern civilization as depicted in his *Hind Swaraj*) present in socio-political situations. For Gandhi non-violence was not just a strategic policy or a matter of convenient political tactic, but a *creed* born out of his conviction of what the human is and what the inter-human relationships demand in a life of relentless pursuit of God as Truth.

On a superficial glance *ahiṁsā* seems to be a negative principle, implying absence or avoidance of *hiṁsā* (violence) or avoidance of injury to any living being. For Gandhi it is not just "a negative state of harmlessness," but, on the contrary, "it is a positive state of love, of doing good even to the evil-doer."[10] Further, it does not mean "mere non-killing. A person who remains smugly satisfied with the non-killing of noxious life, but has no love in his heart for all that lives, will be counted as least in the Kingdom of Heaven."[11] Not to hurt any living thing is only a part of *ahiṁsā*; in fact, it is only its "least expression." The canon of *ahiṁsā* "is hurt by every evil thought, by undue haste, by lying, by hatred, by wishing ill to anybody. It is also violated by our holding on to what the world needs."[12]

It is more than mere external restraint or moderation from violence. It is the emancipation of the individual from enslavement to the merely physical. As the root of *hiṁsā* (violence) is deeply inherent in the heart and soul of an individual, mere abstention from external violence does not facilitate individual humans awakening to the inner spirit. First and foremost, the heart and soul, the inner core of a person, has to be purged of its potentiality for violence. An interior transformation and an orientation to the potency of the spirit

---

10. *Young India*, August 25, 1920.

11. *Young India*, September 20, 1928.

12. *From Yeravda Mandir*, p. 7.

within need to be achieved before one thinks of external
restraint from violence and physical coercion.[13]

Verily, then, *ahiṁsā* is a natural capacity of the soul. As a
positive virtue, *ahiṁsā* is the "soul-force or the power of the
Godhead within us."[14] It is the soul's capacity for love and
forgiveness. As the law of our species,[15] it distinguishes the
human from the brute. The hallmark of its success is the
reciprocation of ill-will with love. Non-violence implies love
and is the way of loving service instead of the modern
"virtues" of expediency, competition, taking undue advantage
of opportunities of the weakness, vulnerability and/or
helplessness of others. Coercion, indeed, would violate the
very spirit of *ahiṁsā*.

The root of *hiṁsā* (violence) lies deep in the heart and soul
of an individual and mere external restraint or moderation
from violence cannot be considered as true *ahiṁsā*. Drawing
power from the spiritual resources of the human, *ahiṁsā*
emancipates the individual from enslavement to the physical.
It facilitates the human awareness that the "spirit" and the
"spiritual" in the human are more important than desires for
material and physical satisfaction, and that it further helps
the human awakening to the oneness of reality and the oneness
of being and oneness of human family — the unity of humans.

In its widest sense *ahiṁsā* means the willingness to consider
everyone as oneself. It is not just an other-regarding love, but
a love that considers the other as part of the self. Since all
beings are one, there is a universal imperative to move towards

---

13. Gandhi is categorical in his assertion of the need for personal
interior conversion to truth and transformation from physical enslavement
(enslavement to the carnal, to the brutish forces within, to the tendency to
hiṁsā) to the power of the spirit of *satya* and *ahiṁsā*. One can sense a
Pauline passion in Gandhi's insistence on the need for individual personal
transformation to expedite the advent of *Rāmarājya*.

14. *The Law of Love*, p. 71.

15. *Young India*, August 11, 1920; *Harijan*, November 4, 1939.

the realization of this oneness through action in resonance with this universal imperative of Truth realization. Thus *ahiṁsā* is identical to striving for Absolute Truth through universal human interaction. It is only in a very limited sense that one speaks of *ahiṁsā* as a repudiation of inflicting positive harm. In its authentic sense *"ahimsa* means the *largest love*, the greatest charity."[16]

One who brings injury to others especially through violence is prevented from seeing one's kinship with others. Since the sum total of all life is God, any denial of life through violence is a denial of God too. Whenever one injures another through mental or physical violence the realization of the unity of human race is smothered, and to that extent, the realization of *Rāmarājya* is thwarted. Violence begets violence. In a climate of spiralling violence, reconciliation among humans becomes all the more difficult.[17]

Further, in its social aspect, *ahiṁsā* is concerned about modalities, organizational principles, and rules of conduct in an organized venture especially of political resistance. Complementing *satyāgraha, ahiṁsā* both limits it and, at the same, makes it something more than an act of simple civil disobedience. *Ahiṁsā* is the necessary and sufficient rule for eliciting and concretizing the truth of *satyāgraha*.

It is clear, then, that there is a very strong interrelationship between *satya* and *ahiṁsā*. In a letter written to Narandas Gandhi, Gandhi makes this abundantly clear:

16. M.K. Gandhi, "On *Ahimsa*: Reply to Lala Lajpat Rai", *Modern Review*, October 1916. See M.K. Gandhi, *Speeches and Writings of Mahatma Gandhi*, 4th edition (Madras: G.A. Natesan, 1933).

17. Many cultures and ethnic groups are victims of such a sad condition in the contemporary world context. Look at the conflict between the Irish and the English, the Hindus and the Muslims, Muslims and Christians, Jews and Palestinians, the conflicts in many parts of Central and South America, the racial tensions in the U.S.A and South Africa — hatred, prejudice and violence appear to be an endless process. See Erikson on pseudo-speciation, in *Gandhi's Truth*.

Ahiṁsā and Truth are so intertwined that it is practically impossible to disentangle and separate them. They are like the two sides of a coin, or rather of a smooth unstamped metallic disc. Who can say which is the obverse and which is the reverse? Nevertheless, *ahiṁsā* is the means and Truth is the end. Means to be means must always be within our reach, and so *ahiṁsā* becomes our supreme duty and Truth becomes God for us. If we take care of the means, we are bound to reach the end sooner or later. If we resolve to do this, we shall have won the battle. Whatever difficulties we encounter, whatever apparent reverses we sustain, we should not lose faith but should ever repeat one *mantra*: 'Truth exists, it alone exists. It is the only God and there is one way of realizing it; there is but one means and that is *ahiṁsā*. I will never give it up.'[18]

Perhaps in an ecstatic poetic mood Gandhi proclaims, "*Ahimsa* is my God, and Truth is my God. When I look for *ahiṁsā* Truth says: 'Find it through me.' When I look for Truth, *ahiṁsā* says: 'Find it through me'."[19] The Einsteinian discovery that even an infinitesimal particle of matter at the velocity of light acquires *infinite of energy*, seems rather similar to the energy released by the combination of *satya* and *ahiṁsā*: "With *satya* combined with *ahimsa* you can bring the world to your feet,"[20] and "When once it is set in motion its effect, if it is intensive enough, can overtake the whole universe."[21]

Realizing such a close interrelationship between *satya* and *ahiṁsā* in Gandhi's pattern of thinking and acting, it would, perhaps, be more authentic to name the Gandhian technique of non-violent resistance *ahiṁsātmaka satyāgraha* than just to call it, as Gandhi himself does, *satyāgraha*. The relentless pursuit of *satya* by means of *ahiṁsā*, is then, *ahiṁsātmaka satyāgraha* — the non-violent, self-suffering, other-regarding agape-love.[22]

18. *From Yeravda Mandir*, Chapter II. See Iyer 2: 230-31.

19. *Young India*, June 4, 1925.

20. *Ibid.*, March 10, 1920.

21. *Ibid.*, September 23, 1926.

22. For an excellent treatment of *agape*-love see Gene Outka, *Agape:*

AHIṀSĀTMAKA SATYĀGRAHA

Origin and Meaning

The seed of the idea of *satyāgraha*, received from a Gujarātī hymn started to germinate in the apt soil of the Sermon on the Mount and began to grow in the light and shade of the *Gītā*, until, finally, it took the definite shape of a full grown plant ready to blossom with the nourishment received from Tolstoy's *Kingdom of God is Within You*, and Ruskin's *Unto This Last*.[23] The compound Sanskrit word *satyāgraha* is formed of two words, *satya* and *āgraha*. *Satya* means truth. *Āgraha* means holding fast (adherence, insisting on) to something without becoming obstinate or uncompromising.[24] Hence *satyāgraha* stands for clinging to truth, holding fast to truth, insistence on truth. It is relentless pursuit of truthful ends by non-violent means. It is "the vindication of Truth, not by infliction of suffering on the opponent but on one's own self."[25] Gandhi himself describes it thus: "Satyāgraha is literally holding on

---

An Ethical Analysis (New Haven: Yale University Press, 1972). See also Soren Kierkegaard, *Works of Love*, tr. Howard and Edna Hong (New York: Harper and Brothers, 1962); Gerald Gilleman, S. J., *The Primacy of Charity in Moral Theology*, tr. William F. Ryan, S. J., and André Vachon, S. J., (Westminster, Maryland: The Newman Press, 1959).

23. The famous Gujarātī hymn which Gandhi often speaks about is given in his *Autobiography*.

> For a bowl of water give a goodly meal;
> For a kindly greeting bow thou down right with zeal;
> For a simple penny pay thou back with gold;
> If thy life be rescued, life do not withhold.
> Every little service ten-fold thy reward;
> But the truly noble know all men as one,
> And return with gladness good for evil done.
> — *Autobiography*, p. 31.

24. According to Bhikhu Parekh, Gandhi uses the word *āgraha* in the ordinary Gujarātī and not in the classical Sanskrit sense. See Parekh, *Gandhi's Political Philosophy: A Critical Examination*, p. 143.

25. Gandhi, *Speeches and Writings of Mahatma Gandhi*, p. 501.

to Truth and it means, therefore, Truth-force. Truth is soul or spirit. It is, therefore, known as soul-force."[26]

In 1906 Gandhi organized a new kind of resistance movement in South Africa and named it "Passive Resistance." Mangalal Gandhi, a nephew of Gandhi, coined the word *sadāgraha* to designate the passive resistance movement.[27] Gandhi was not satisfied with this term. Gandhi himself, then, coined the term *satyāgraha* in order to bring out the full significance of his movement.

Gandhi's passion for truth and consistent opposition to injustice, oppression, fraud and falsehood right from his childhood had prepared him into the spirit of *satyāgraha*. Discussing the origin of *satyāgraha* with Joseph J. Doke, Gandhi said:

> I remember how one verse of Gujarati poem, which as a child, I learned at school, clung to me. In substance it was this:

---

26. Gandhi, *Satyagraha*, p. 3.

27. Nirmal Kumar Minz, *Mahatma Gandhi and Hindu Christian Dialogue* (Madras: The Christian Literature Society, 1970), p. 2. See also Susane Hoeber Rudolph and Lloyd I. Rudolph *Gandhi: The Traditional Roots of Charisma* (Chicago: The University of Chicago Press, 1983). As the resistance movement in South Africa advanced, Gandhi felt the need for a term that would best articulate his aspiration of non-violence. He even announed in *The Indian Opinion* a prize to be awarded for the best term. The word *sadāgraha*, proposed by Maganlal Gandhi, though it implied firmness in a good cause, was not up to Gandhian expectation since this word did not really express the sentiments he wished to convey. So later on he adopted the word, *satyāgraha'*. "I liked the word (*sadagraha*), but it did not fully represent the whole idea I wished it to connote. I therefore corrected it to *satyāgraha*. Truth (*satya*) implies love, and firmness (*agraha*) engenders and therefore serves as a synonym for force. I thus began to call the Indian movement *satyagraha*, that is to say, the force which is born to Truth and Love or non-violence, and gave up the use of the phrase 'passive resistance.'" *Satyagraha in South Africa*, tr. V.G. Desai, 2nd edn. (Ahmedabad: Navajivan, 1950), p. 109; as quoted by Iyer, *The Moral and Political Thought of Mahatma Gandhi*, pp. 269-70.

"If a man gives you a drink of water and you give him a drink in return, that is nothing;
Real beauty consists in doing good against evil."

As a child, this verse had a powerful influence over me, and I tried to carry it into practice. Then came The Sermon on the Mount. . . . When I read the Sermon on the Mount, such passages as 'Resist not him that is evil but whosoever smiteth thee on thy right cheek turn to him the other also,' and 'Love your enemies and pray for them that persecute you, that ye may be sons of your Father which is in heaven,' I was simply overjoyed and found my own opinion confirmed where I least expected it. The Bhagavad Gita deepened the impression and Tolstoy's "The Kingdom of God is Within You" gave it permanent form.[28]

Satyāgraha vs Passive Resistance vs Pacifism

Satyāgraha is not the same as passive resistance; nor is it to be equated with Pacifism. Gandhi puts it very well:

Satyagraha differs from passive resistance as the North Pole from the South. The latter has been conceived as a weapon of the weak and does not exclude the use of physical force or violence; whereas the former has been conceived as a

---

28. See Joseph J. Doke, M.K. Gandhi, London: *The London Indian Chronicle*, India edition (Madras: G.A. Ganesan, 1919); as quoted by V.P. Verma, *Political Philosophy of Mahatma Gandhi, and Sarvodaya* (Agra: Educational Publishers, 1959), pp. 146-47.

Gandhi's decision to resort to the technique of *satyāgraha* was made while in South Africa. He recollects his Moritzburg experience in South Africa which gave him the impetus to shirk cowardice and embrace the non-violent fight thus: "I observed on the very first day that the Europeans meted out most insulting treatment to Indians. . . . I was pushed out of the train by a police constable at Moritzburg, and the train having left, I was sitting in the waiting room shivering in the bitter cold. I did not know where my luggage was, nor did I enquire of anybody lest I might be insulted and assaulted once again. Sleep was out of the question. Doubt took possession of my mind. Late at night, I came to the conclusion that to run back to India would be cowardly. I must accomplish what I had undertaken." As quoted in Hiren Mukerjee, *Gandhi: A Study* (Calcutta: National Book Agency Ltd., 1958).

weapon of the strongest and excludes the use of violence in any shape or form. . . . It is a movement intended to replace methods of violence and a movement based entirely on Truth.[29]

Pacifism is usually equated with total non-resistance, whereas non-violent, active search for truth not only permits but positively requires a great variety of positive actions aimed at preventing as well as eliminating evil.[30]

It is due to the incapacity or adverse circumstances that a passive resister shuns violence. A *satyāgrahī*, on the other hand, positively refrains from violence even if he or she is in a position to use violence effectively. Never to take advantage of the weakness of the opponent is absolutely fundamental to Gandhian *satyāgraha*. Even to harass or intimidate the opponent is foreign to it; whereas traces of such a temptation might linger in passive resistance. The latter could be undertaken as a "political weapon of expediency" whereas *satyāgraha* is an indispensable moral discipline and virtue. Any imposition of

---

29. *Young India*, January 14, 1940.

30. For a description of the notion of pacifism see Joseph T. Culliton, C.S.B., ed., *Non-violence — Central to Christian Spirituality: Perspectives from Scripture to the Present* (New York: The Edwin Mellen Press, 1982), Introduction, p. 1. This book challenges the attitude of a vast number of Christians considering non-violence as peripheral to mainline Christian spirituality. Culliton "sets out to show the centrality of non-violence to Christian spirituality." p. 38. See also W.R. Miller, *Nonviolence, A Christian interpretation* (New York: Schocken Books, 1966).

Tracing the history of passive resistance Miller writes: "Historically passive resistance has been used by oppressed people who desire immediate justice and immediate human rights. They are concerned with social and legal change rather than with truth as an eternal principle. The passive resister takes an ethical position which demands results — pragmatic results which correct a social or political injustice. He is concerned with the success or failure of his actions! The method he uses to obtain change is non-cooperaion such as the use of the walkout or the boycott. If non-resistance means "going the second mile," passive resistance means refusing to go the first mile." Miller, *Nonviolence, A Christian Interpretation*, p. 54.

physical force on a party (say *A*) to rectify an error perceived to be present by another party (say *B*) is simply a manifestation of a superior physical force and assumption of innocence by *B*. As far as Gandhi is concerned, it is never an indication of a better knowledge of truth in *B*. When physical brute force is used to settle conflicts this results in greater counter force. This, in turn, initiates a spiral of greater forces resulting in a chain of violence and counter-violence.

Contrasting his approach with passive resistance Gandhi says:

> If we continue to believe ourselves and let others believe, that we are weak and helpless and therefore offer passive resistance, our resistance would never make us strong, and at the earliest opportunity we would give up passive resistance as a weapon of the weak. . . . Again, while there is no scope for love in passive resistance, on the other hand, not only has hatred no place in *satyagraha* but is a positive breach of its ruling principle. While in passive resistance there is a scope for the use of arms when a suitable occasion arrives, in *satyagraha* physical force is forbidden even in the most favorable circumstances.[31]

---

31. *Satyagraha in South Africa,* p. 114. C.E.M. Joad writes about the power of Gandhian technique of *satyāgraha* to challenge any established order of untruth: "Inevitably it challenges vested interests in the thought of the present, upsetting man's minds, alarming their morals, and undermining the security of the powerful and the established. . . . He has announced a method for the settlement of disputes which may not only supersede the method of force, but, as men grow powerful in the art of destruction, must supersede it if civilization is to survive." S. Radhakrishnan (ed.), *Mahatma Gandhi, Essays and Reflections on his Life and Work,* pp. 159-60; as quoted in K.M. Prasad, *Sarvodaya of Gandhi,* ed. Ramjee Singh (New Delhi: Raj Hans Publications, 1984), p. 146. Drawing our attention to the law of "critical limit" in Physics K.M. Prasad argues that "the day mankind learnt to pit it (non-violence) against brute force, the atomic nightmare would disappear like the memory of an ugly dream." Prasad, *Sarvodaya of Gandhi,* p. 154. The "critical limit" theory shows that the normal laws governing the behaviour of matter is reversed when the critical limit is reached. Perhaps *ahiṁsā* would be Gandhian moral weapon to expedite

Thus we see that *satyāgraha* is not the same as passive resistance or pacifism.

Positive Meaning

Positively this notion implies on the one hand an unfailing *insistence on* and a relentless *search for* truth. Bhikhu Parekh, a recent interpreter of Gandhian political philosophy, correctly reads the mind of Gandhi when he too insists on this duality of meaning.[32] Any sincere and honest searcher of truth, recognizing human capacity to know the truth of the matter, insists *on* truth as one sees it; at the same time, knowing human contingency, acknowledges that one might be wrong or only partially right, and is willing to make the "opponent" a co-searcher *for* truth. Even when this invitation is declined, due to any reason (self-interest, self-righteousness, pride, arrogance, prejudice, ill-will, ambition, dogmatism, greed, moral inertia, limited sympathy, or sheer obstinacy), the one who is willing to search *for* truth starts his insistence *on* truth in a truthful manner. This, in short, is the quintessence of *ahiṁsātmaka satyāgraha.* The process is continued until the other side agrees to have a common search through dialogue and discussion. Hence rationality and rational discussion bring in objectivity in the process of the very search for truth itself. An honest and truthful appreciation of each other's arguments and counter-arguments helps both the parties to arrive at a

---

the "critical limit" of the atomic and nuclear weapons in order to reverse the process of destructive arms race. Just before Gandhi was assassinated, a U.S. journalist, Margaret Bourke-White, asked Gandhi how he would meet the atom bomb with non-violence. Gandhi's answer may not show prudential consideration; but his moral conviction on the effectiveness of *ahiṁsā* stands out very clearly as a deeper realism: "I will not go underground. I will not go into shelters. I will come out in the open and let the pilot see I have not a trace of evil against him. The pilot will not see our faces from his great height, I know. But that longing in our hearts - that he will not come to harm - would reach up to him and his eyes would be opened." as quoted by Prasad, *Sarvodaya of Gandhi*, p. 154.

32. See Parekh, *Gandhi's Political Philosophy*, p. 143.

point of view based on the *insights* of both and acceptable to both.[33]

Three basic assumptions of Gandhi for such a procedural pattern are correctly examined by Parekh:

1. The basic agreement that no human being is in possession of Absolute Truth. The concerned parties should enter into discussion in an openness and with a humble heart precisely because neither party is in possession of Absolute Truth.

2. The absolute necessity of rational discussion. Precisely because they see Reality differently, they should enter into the world of the other through rational discussion trying to see their point of view, at the same time sincerely seeking to find out why the other sees matters differently.

3. The necessity of an "open-heart" attitude. Rational discussion is of no avail if selfishness, hatred and ill-will blind either parties leading them to moral rigidity and emotional shortsightedness, thereby blocking ultimately the process of empathetic understanding and critical self-reflection. Good-will and sympathy, characteristic of an other-regarding love, is a prerequisite for total objectivity.[34]

In fine, Gandhi's convictions to resort to *satyāgraha* could be succinctly summarized as follows:

1. Truth alone will be victorious. Since truth alone is the ultimate reality, it is imperative for the votary of it to resist all encroachments on it.

2. Suffering can be creatively used for the emancipation of the suffering millions.

3. The soul remains unconquered and unconquerable even by the mightiest force, and every human being, however

33. See Parekh, *Gandhi's Political Philosophy*, pp. 143-44.
34. *Ibid.*, pp. 142-45.

degraded in social circumstances, however poor in economic terms, has the divine spark in her/him, and so there is a force within that is greater than any external physical force, however coercive and destructive it may be.

4. There is limitless potentiality for growth in every human being, and one is capable of responding to kind, generous, and empathetic treatment.

5. Faith in the inherent goodness of human nature which could be evoked by truth and love manifested through suffering.

6. Finally, *ahimsātmaka satyāgraha* is the *only* appropriate means to the attainment of *Rāmarājya* and *sarvodaya* which, in the last analysis, leads to *mokṣa* itself.

Virtue of the Strong

Satyāgraha, as the virtue of the strong, needs courage:

> A coward never risks his life. A man who would kill often risks it. A non-violent person's life is always at the disposal of him who would take it. For, he knows that the soul within never dies. The encasing body is ever perishing. The more a man gives his life, the more he saves it.[35]

Practice of *ahimsā* and cowardice cannot go together; it is not the way of the coward:

> A man cannot practice *ahimsā* and be a coward at the same time. The practice of *ahimsā* calls forth the greatest courage. It is the most soldierly of a soldier's virtues.[36]

Only a brave person can face suffering and death with joy and renunciation without bitterness. At the same time, non-violence is not a cover for cowardice, it is the virtue of the brave. Contrasting *ahimsā* and cowardice Gandhi says:

> Non-violence and cowardice are contradictory terms. Non-violence is the greatest virtue, cowardice the greatest vice.

35. *Young India*, December 18, 1924.
36. *Speeches and Writings of Mahatma Gandhi*, p. 346.

Non-violence springs from love, cowardice from hate. Non-violence always suffers, cowardice would always inflict sufferings. Perfect non-violence is the highest bravery. Non-violent conduct is never demoralizing, cowardice always is.[37]

And further,

Non-violence is not a cover for cowardice, but it is the supreme virtue of the brave. Exercise of non-violence requires far greater bravery than that of swordsmanship. Cowardice is wholly inconsistent with non-violence.[38]

Non-violence does not mean meek and humble submission to the will and malpractices of a tyrant. It is a conscious and deliberate check on one's desire for vengeance.

Given a choice between cowardice and violence, Gandhi would prefer violence:

I do believe that, where there is only a choice between cowardice and violence, I would advise violence. But I believe that non-violence is infinitely superior to violence.[39]

Though in its dynamic state non-violence demands conscious suffering, it does not imply "meek submission to the will of the evil-doer, but it means putting of one's whole soul against the will of the tyrant."[40]

---

37. *Young India*, October 31, 1929.

38. *Ibid.*, August 12, 1926.

39. Young India, August 11, 1920. Gandhi remarks: "My non-violence does not admit of running away from danger and leaving the dear ones unprotected. Between violence and cowardly flight, I can only prefer violence to cowardice. I can no more preach non-violence to a coward than I can tempt a blind man to enjoy healthy scenes. Non-violence is the summit of bravery. And in my own experience, I have had no dificulty in demonstrating to men trained in the school of violence the superiority of non-violence. As a coward, which I was for years, I harboured violence. I began to prize non-violence only when I began to shed cowardice." Gandhi, *All Men Are Brothers* (New York: Columbia Universiy Press, 1958), p. 102. See also *Young India*, May 29, 1924; and *Harijan*, November 17, 1946.

40. *Young India*, August 11, 1920.

Implications of Non-violence

Gandhi's success consisted in the transformation of *ahiṁsātmaka satyāgraha* into a social and political technique. He made it very clear that non-violence not only implies the negative concept of non-offending and non-injury to others, but that it stands for the positive virtue of self-suffering and self-sacrifice. In the September 5, 1936 issue of *Harijan*, Gandhi himself has summarized the implications and conditions of *ahiṁsā* as follows:

1. Non-violence is the law of the human race and is infinitely greater than and superior to brute force.
2. In the last resort it does not avail itself to those who do not possess a living faith in the God of love.
3. Non-violence affords the fullest protection to one's self-respect and sense of honour, but not always the possession of land or movable property, though its habitual practice does prove a better bulwark than armed men to defend such possessions.
4. Individuals or nations who would practice non-violence must be prepared to sacrifice everything except honour.
5. Non-violence is a power which can be wielded equally by all — children, young men and women or grown-up people, provided they have a loving faith in the God of love and have, therefore, equal love for all humankind.
6. It is a profound error to suppose that whilst this law is good enough for individuals it is not for masses of humankind. The law of love, if courageously practised, is bound to elevate the quality and character of politics and civilization. The acceptance of the norm of non-violence would amount to a moral transformation of values. Emphasis must be laid on the method of self-suffering and self-purification used in the technique of *ahiṁsātmaka satyāgraha*, which is the backbone of the Gandhian way of revolutionary transformation.

Ahiṁsātmaka satyāgraha is the Gandhian way of creating a "ferment" in society for radical changes in human conditions and socio-political and economic relationships and structures. Clinging to his conviction that human nature can be best set right by the method of love, Gandhi consistently advocated his technique of non-violent self-sacrificial love and denounced violence even in small doses.

Non-violent approach, then, is not just an attitude, a tactic, a strategy, a "weapon."[41] It is not even just a personal virtue; but a course of conduct, a way of life, ultimately a spirituality, both for the individual and for the community in all walks of life — spiritual, socio-political.[42]

For Gandhi *ahiṁsā* is a passionate, fundamental belief, a *creed*. The motive force of his creed is Truth and its relentless pursuit in mundane affairs. The intent is the revelation of that Truth.

---

41. Margaret Chatterjee calls this Gandhian approach of suffering as "the non-violent *weapon* of suffering." See the title of Chapter 5 of her book, *Gandhi's Religious Thought*, p. 75. In truly Gandhian sentiments the self-sacrificial agapeistic love involved in *ahiṁsātmaka satyāgraha* cannot just be categorized as a weapon. Very often in a conflict-filled and hate-dominated world of human affairs, we have a tendency to use terms (for instance target strategy, weapon, enemy) that are drawn from a war situation wherein individuals, tribes, ethnic entities, cultures, nation-states are pitted against one another, and are expressive of at least a milder form of Hobbesian state of nature. Look at the title of Mark Juergensmeyer's book, *Fighting with Gandhi: A Step-by-step Strategy for Resolving Everyday Conflicts* (San Francisco: Harper & Row, Publishers, 1984). Even in theological writings people, unconsciously perhaps, bring in such frame of mind as shown in the title of John A. Coleman's book *An American Strategic Theology* (New York: Paulist Press, 1982).

42. Gandhi observes, "For me *Ahiṁsā* comes before Swaraj (self-rule). *Ahiṁsā* must be placed before everything else while it is professed. Then alone it become irresistible." (*Harijan*, July 20, 1930). Only "unadulterated *ahiṁsā*" can bring individual freedom. Hence true democracy or *swaraj* can be attained only by *ahiṁsā*. Only when we can love our enemies can we attain the zenith of self-fulfilment.

Ahiṁsātmaka satyāgraha is, thus, Gandhian ethic of action aimed at, first and foremost, personal transformation and individual conversion to truth. This will in turn, as Gandhi hopes, effect structural changes that create a general climatic condition enabling personal transformative changes and conversion to truth and resulting in a better atmosphere that facilitate as the personal conversional process. Every human being needs to "wake up to the Spirit within." Gandhi believes that *ahiṁsā* has the capacity to awaken humans to the spirit within in order to help maintain non-violence in their behavior and social relations:

> Destruction (himsa) does not need to be taught. Man as animal is violent, but as Spirit is non-violent. The moment a person awakes to the Spirit within, s/he cannot remain violent. Either he progresses toward *ahiṁsā* or rushes to his doom.[43]

Acting non-violently is *ipso facto* demonstrating the Truth. Hence an advocate of *ahiṁsā* cannot make a cowardly retreat. Courageous manifestations of *ahiṁsā* would bring their reward of the conversion of the one who considers himself/herself an enemy:

> *Ahimsa* really means that you may not offend anybody; you may not harbor an uncharitable thought even in connection with one who may consider himself to be your enemy. If you express your love — *Ahimsa* — in such a manner that it impresses itself indelibly upon your so-called enemy, he must return that love.[44]

There is another very important element in the Gandhian approach to social transformation, which, perhaps, is not adequately emphasized, and which is, by and large, absent in the current approaches and mechanisms of social transformatory process. It is his respect for the institution of law. In the Kantian tradition Gandhi holds that the individual alone is a moral

---

43. Gandhi, *All men are Brothers*, p. 87.
44. Gandhi, *Speeches and Writings of Mahatma Gandhi*, p. 280.

personality. No other entities, whether the state or other institutions, can claim moral personality. Deeply attracted to the Socratic view with regard to the state, in contrast to Durkheim's notion of the state as an entity having the function of guiding the collective conduct of a people, Gandhi advocated on appeal to eternal unwritten laws (the Divine Law inscribed in the hearts of individuals). Such an appeal to Divine law could even challenge, as Antigone did, the laws advocated by a group of people, the state, or the commandments of particular religions, or religious authorities. Like Socrates, one must be willing to suffer the consequences of one's challenge of established laws, civil or others, even if such laws are not only perceived to be unjust, and, in fact, are absolutely unjust. One ought to endeavour to change unjust and iniquitous laws going to the extent of even breaking them. Nevertheless, as long as the law is in effect, in spite of its unjust character, one must be willing to suffer the consequences of its infringement, i.e., to bear the punishment gladly to show respect to the institutional character of law as such.

No legal system can exist and function without a sense of moral obligation to obey a set of laws. At the same time, while this moral obligation to obey the law as such is categorical, to obey a particular law need not be a categorical necessity; indeed, it is unwarranted if a particular law is known to be absolutely unjust, iniquitous, and is against the common good. Morality itself becomes meaningless if legality becomes a categorical imperative. Given human contingency, however, one can only *tend towards* the Absolute and to the perception of Absolute Divine Laws and a Divine order of reality.

Gandhi's attempt to articulate the human finiteness tending to the Infinite and the final "meeting" (merging) of the two (the *ātman* merging into *Brahman*) could be analogously explained in terms of two parallel lines tending to meet at infinity.[45]

---

45. Two parallel lines tending to meet at infinity would be a good analogy

Theory and Praxis of Ahiṁsātmaka Satyāgraha

Satyāgraha replaces brutal violence by love, forgiveness and self-suffering. Based on *satya* and *ahiṁsā*, the end is sought through a conversion of the heart of the opponent to truth; though, at times, the conversion is brought about by moral pressure as well. The conversion of the heart of the "opponent" is intended not to bring him/her around just to "my" opinions and to see things just the way "I" see things around; but to see that truth may prevail and reign in everyone's heart. Fearlessly one has to practice *ahiṁsā* and with courage one has to search for truth, even loving one's enemy in the process. In one of his letters published in the *Modern Review*, October 1916, Gandhi writes:

> In its positive form, *Ahimsa* means the largest love, the greatest charity. If I am a follower of Ahiṁsā, I must love my enemy. . . . This active *ahimsa* necessarily includes truth and fearlessness. As man cannot deceive the loved one, he does not fear or frighten him or her. The Gift of life is the greatest of all gifts; a man who gives it in reality, disarms all hostility. And none who is himself subject to fear can bestow that gift. He must himself, therefore, be fearless. A man cannot practice *ahimsa* and be a coward at the same time. The practice of *ahimsa* calls forth the greatest courage. . . . It may never barter away honour.[46]

---

to understand the Gandhian notion of the finite humans tending to the Infinite Absolute. (I am grateful to Prof. Lloyd I. Rudolph for calling my attention to this.) Many a times the underlying assumption of clear and distinct theories and propositions seems to be absurd! Look at calculus, for instance. This branch, perhaps the brain, of Mathematics, the most exact of all pure sciences, makes a fundamental assumption, without which there will not be a calculus; the claim is that two parallel lines *tend to meet* at infinity. If two lines are parallel, by the very definition of parallelness, they will never meet; we know this from our rationality. But this "rational certainty" is suspended, in order to make a claim which, in fact, is absolutely necessary to the most exact of all pure sciences. What I am trying to say is that what some consider "absurd" could be the most reliable "truth" for some others.

46. "On *Ahiṁsā*: Reply to Lala Rajpat Rai," *Modern Review*, October 1916. See Gandhi, *Speeches and Writings of Mahatma Gandhi*, p. 346.

The purpose of both individual as well as group *satyāgraha* is not negative. It is not as to crush, defeat or punish the tyrants or break their will. It is not to embarrass them either. Motivated by love, it is a positive endeavour to convert the wrong doers, to bring about a change in their heart first and foremost so that they would be in a position to see reality in a different manner: "The end of non-violent war is always an agreement, never dictation, much less humiliation of the opponent."[47]

In essence it is a principle that has its root in love; and as Easwaran, a Gandhian disciple, articulates it well,

> (I)ts object should not be to punish the opponent or to inflict injury upon him. Even while non-cooperating with him, we must make him feel that in us he has a friend and we should try to reach his heart by rendering him humanitarian service wherever possible. . . . Although noncooperation is one of the main weapons in the armory of satyagraha, it should not be forgotten that it is, after all, only a means to secure the cooperation of the opponent consistently with truth and justice. . . . Avoidance of all relationship with the opposing power, therefore, can never be a satyagrahi's object, but transformation or purification of that relationship.[48]

Positively, true followers of *satyāgraha* (*satyāgrahīs*) who know their own spiritual relationship with an opponent, will treat the latter as a member of their own family. For friend or foe, Gandhi has the same set of rules, "I must apply the same rules to the wrongdoer who is my enemy as I would do my wrong-doing father or son."[49]

So Gandhian *ahiṁsātmaka satyāgraha* is after all a means to a state and condition wherein truth and justice prevail, the friendship and love reign not the hatred and injury. Gandhi calls this condition/kingdom of perfect harmonious relationship the *Rāmarājya*.

---

47. *Harijan*, March 23, 1940,

48. Easwaran, *Gandhi the Man*, p. 158.

49. *Speeches and Writings of Mahatma Gandhi*, 4th edn., p. 284.

Satyāgraha as a Technique

The three techniques of *satyāgraha* are: civil disobedience, non-cooperation, and fast unto death. Concerning civil disobedience Gandhi says, "Civil disobedience is the inherent right of a citizen. He dare not give it up without ceasing to be a man. Civil disobedience is never followed by anarchy. . . . To put down civil disobedience is to attempt to imprison conscience."[50] Non-cooperation "is not a movement of brag, bluster or bluff, it is the test of our sincerity. It requires solid and silent self-sacrifice. It challenges our honesty and our capacity for nation work."[51] It is used as a means to obtain the cooperation of the opponent consistent with truth and justice. Essentially it is a cleansing process. Non-cooperation is the expression of anguished love.[52] Fasting is part and parcel of his philosophy of Truth and non-violence. It is the acme of self-suffering. Such fasting can be even unto death. Fasting should be used only as a last resort: "A satyagrahi should fast only as a last resort when all other avenues of redress have been explored and have failed."[53] A fast, undertaken by one with great inner strength for fuller self-expression, and for the attainment of the spirit's supremacy over the flesh, is the most powerful factor in one's evolution. It is a fiery weapon. It is the highest expression of the prayer of a pure and loving heart.[54] Unlike other methods fasting cannot be used effectively by the masses. It can be resorted to only by select and qualified individuals. Since Gandhi knows about the consequences of this method of *satyāgraha*, he insists that it should be used very sparingly. Still Gandhi's own conviction is that fasting unto death is an integral part of *satyāgraha*. Most importantly, one must have earned the right to fast by proving one's moral

50. Prabhu and Rao, *The Mind of Mahatma Gandhi*, p. 74.

51. *Young India*, April 20, 1921.

52. See *Young India*, p. 241

53. *Harijan*, April 21, 1946.

54. Dhawan, *The Political Philosophy of Mahatma Gandhi*, p. 138.

integrity, depth of character, capacity to discern the truth, and by the effective detachment from the very life one has lived and the service rendered.[55]

Ideal Satyāgrahī

Having explained the various aspects of *satyāgraha*, it needs to be asked: what does Gandhi expect of a *satyāgrahī*, a true follower of his philosophy? He answers, "To evade no punishment, to accept all suffering joyfully and to regard it as a possibility for further strengthening his soul force — is the duty of every single one of my followers."[56] Living faith in Truth and in soul-force is a *sine qua non* condition to resort to *satyāgraha* whole-heartedly and successfully. Without this faith in God a *satyāgrahī* will not have the courage to die without fear, without anger and without retaliation. Such courage comes from the firm belief that God (Truth) is in everyone's heart and that there need not be any fear in the presence and possession of Truth.[57] The sole of the *satyāgrahī* is Truth, and "without Him the satyagrahi is devoid of strength before an opponent armed with monstrous weapons. But he who accepts God as his only protector will remain unbent before the mightiest earthly power."[58] Indeed, victory lies in the ability and power to die in the attempt to make the opponent see the truth.[59] To Gandhi, therefore, the first and last shield and buckler of the non-violent person is the unwavering faith in God.

Some people may brand this as idealistic, having no practical application. The eye-witness account of Mr. Webb Miller, a special U.S. correspondent for the United Press, describing the scenes in the Salt Depot picketing led by Sarojani

---

55. See Stanley E. Jones, *Mahatma Gandhi: An Interpretation* (London: Hodder & Stoughton, 1948), p. 144.

56. Tendulkar, *Mahatma: Life of Mohandas Karamchand Gandhi*, 1: 17.

57. *Harijan*, June 18, 1938.

58. *Harijan*, October 19, 1940.

59. *Speeches and Writings of Mahatma Gandhi*, p. 504.

Naidu and Manilal Gandhi at Dharsana Camp, Surat, Bombay
Presidency, during the non-cooperation movement in 1930,
which was published in the New York *Telegram*, is enough to
show that real *satyāgrahī*s can be fully imbued with Gandhian
ideals. Miller wrote:

> In the eighteen years of reporting in twenty two countries,
> during which I have witnessed innumerable civil
> disturbances, riots, street fights, and rebellions, I have never
> witnessed such harrowing scenes as at Dharsana. The
> western mind can grasp violence returned by violence, can
> understand a fight, but is, I found, perplexed and baffled by
> the sight of men advancing coldly and deliberately and
> submitting to beating without attempting defense.
> Sometimes the scenes were so painful that I had to turn
> away momentarily. One surprising feature was the discipline
> of the volunteers. It seemed they were thoroughly imbued
> with Gandhi's non-violence creed, and the leaders
> constantly stood in front of the ranks imploring them to
> remember that Gandhi's soul was with them. During the
> morning I saw hundreds of blows inflicted by the police,
> but saw not a single blow returned by the volunteers. So far
> as I could observe the volunteers implicitly obeyed Gandhi's
> creed of non-violence. In no case did I see a volunteer even
> raise his arm to deflect the blows from lathis. There were no
> outcries from beaten swarajists, only groans after they had
> submitted to their beating.[60]

These words speak for themselves about the practical
applicability of Gandhi's non-violent resistance.

Having realized that the success of non-violent direct
action depends on adequate discipline, Gandhi drew up certain
rules and regulations to be followed by a *satyāgrahī* in order
to help that person realize her/his moral and spiritual unity
with all.[61] In 1921 Gandhi drew up a pledge laying down the
discipline required of every *satyāgrahī* volunteer. In 1930 he

---

60. Richard B. Gregg, *The Power of Non-violence* (New York: Fellowship
Publications, 1944), pp. 25-28.

61. *Harijan*, September 15, 1940.

laid down a set of nineteen rules. In 1939 Gandhi briefly stated the qualifications of a true *satyāgrahī* as follows:[62]

1. He must have a living faith in God.
2. He must believe in truth and non-violence as his creed and, therefore, have faith in the inherent goodness of human nature which he expects to evoke by his truth and love expressed through his suffering.
3. He must be leading a chaste life and be ready and willing for the sake of his cause to give up his life and his possessions.
4. He must be a habitual *khādī*-wearer and spinner.
5. He must be a teetotaller and be free from the use of other intoxicants.
6. He must carry out with a willing heart all the rules of discipline as may be laid down from time to time.
7. He should carry out the jail rules unless they are specifically devised to hurt his self-respect.

Bjorn Hettne has expressed the logic of *satyāgraha* far more succinctly, perhaps, than Gandhi ever did:

> In short, satyāgraha would imply a form of political struggle in which you try to convince your opponent of the justice of your cause and convert him in the process. In Gandhian (admittedly rather metaphysical) terms your *Relative Truth* is supposed to be closer than your enemy's to *Absolute Truth* and it is also your duty to support *his* search for Truth. Thus, your enemy is looked upon as a potential ally who could be convinced by your firmness and willingness to suffer for the cause in a nonviolent way. Violence is, however, preferred before (to) cowardice because cowardice means to be untrue to oneself as a human being. Compared to cowardice, even violence means a step towards Truth. The enemy is also supposed to search for the Truth (doing what he believes right) and if you fight him with violence means you prevent him from finding Truth (that is, to join the right cause). This is a loss not only to him but also to

---

62. *Harijan*, March 25, 1939.

yourself.[63]

A METHOD OF INDIVIDUAL AND SOCIAL TRANSFORMATION
AND CONFLICT RESOLUTION

As a method of social change, an attempt is made through
satyāgraha to

1. usher in the welfare of all (*sarvodaya samāja*), and
2. to initiate a radical transformative change in persons
   and systemic structures (e.g., government, economic
   structures).[64] Gandhi was very emphatic (and I think he
   is quite right in this) that short-cut and short-term social
   reforms would bring about changes which do not
   necessarily elevate the ethical climate and the moral tones
   of institutions and individuals. Hence they are bound
   to fail in the long run. So he was not looking for short-
   cut and short-term substitutes for the lasting process of
   individual and institutional purificatory transformations.
   His attempt was to establish a firm foundation for
   genuine and lasting structures in accord with the dignity
   of persons and in keeping with the ultimate goal of
   humanity individually and collectively. Even one
   authentic *satyāgrahī* can, singlehandedly, initiate needed
   subtle changes for far-reaching results better than
   massive demonstrations based on impetuous enthusiasm
   and latent violence.[65]

---

63. Bjorn Hettne, "The Vitality of Gadhian Tradition," in *Journal of Peace Research*, 13 (3/1976): 229.

64. Though Gandhian attempt was immediately applicable to the then context of South Africa and in the Indian subcontinent, Gandhi envisioned a day that the whole world would understand and choose to follow his path.

65. This attitude need not necessarily mean that Gandhi was much less concerned with the quantity of people involved in *satyāgraha* than with quality. For a general *satyāgraha* number was one of his main concerns. Of course, Gandhi was very much for quality and/or character. Nonetheless one concern need not negate the other. See Iyer 3: 2-3.

Over years of experiments and relentless meditative search Gandhi evolved a unique way of managing and resolving individual as well as socio-political conflicts. It did not take much time for Gandhi to realize that achieving *swarāj* necessarily entailed a conflict of interests. The British adherence to power for their political and economic interests, and the determination of the masses in India for self government and freedom were in conflict. The means evolved by Gandhi to manage and resolve the conflict was *ahimsātmaka satyāgraha*.

Conflicts arise with respect to the very perception of truth itself. The "truth of the matter" is perceived differently and often truth itself is the source of conflict. Relative truth is all that is available to humans in their contingent existence. Hence, it is in the light of the human understanding of such relative truths that humans should resolve their conflicts. Absolute Truth in and of itself cannot be the source of conflict. It is the relative truth or human perception and understanding that produces conflict. Gandhi was more concerned with relative truths and the means of achieving Absolute Truth than with the Absolute Truth itself: "As long as I have not realized this Absolute Truth, so long must I hold by the relative truth as I have conceived it. That relative truth meanwhile be my beacon, my shield and buckler."[66] In this sense *satyāgraha* was relative. Here Jesudasan's insight is enlightening: "Gandhi made the source of conflicts also the way to their solution when he applied the reality of the knowledge of God as truth to social and politico-economic conflict solution."[67]

Amenable at heart to moral persuasions, every human being, including a Nero, an Alexander, a Chenghis, a Hitler, a Mussolini, a Dyer, or, the latest violent and brute actors and

---

66. Gandhi, *Autobiography*, Introduction, p. ix.

67. Jesudasan, *A Gandhian Theology of Liberation*, p. 94. Indeed, even pure sciences seek such seemingly contradictory solutions! Do not Doctors inject into a healthy body in small doses hormones of the very disease they want to prevent ?

murderers in contemporary world scene, have at least a ray of the spark of God left in them, dormant though it may be. Here is where action should start as far as Gandhi is concerned. Consider what Gandhi has to say to those who would argue that *satyāgraha* is ineffective in dealing with powers and tyrants who are not susceptible to moral appeal and impervious to world opinion:

> (Even) the hardest metal yields to sufficient heat; even so must the hardest heart melt before the sufficiency of the heat of non-violence. And there is no limit to the capacity of non-violence to generate heat. . . . During my half a century of experience, I have not yet come across a situation when I had to say that I was helpless, that I had no remedy in terms of non-violence.[68]

Manifesting his optimism in the transformability of human nature Gandhi affirmed:

> My faith in human nature is progressively growing. I have concluded on the basis of my experiments, that human nature can be easily molded. We have come to assume, because of our inertia, that human nature is always the same and seldom amenable to progress. Churchill and Hitler are striving to change the nature of their respective countrymen by forcing and hammering violent methods on them. Man may be suppressed in this manner but he cannot be changed. Ahiṁsā, on the other hand, can change human nature and sooner than men like Churchill and Hitler can.[69]

His firm faith in the basic goodness of humanity and human nature would not permit him to leave out anyone from the possibility of a change of heart, the likelihood of growth and openness to something of higher values. One will not always remain in a permanent, unredeemable, and arcane condition that is "solitary, poor, nasty, brutish, and short." Gandhi emphasized the same idea on another occasion:

---

68. Quoted in S. Radhakrishnan, *Great Indians*, p. 42. See Prasad, *Sarvodaya of Gandhi*, p. 153.

69. Speech at prayer meeting, October 22, 1941, *Collected Works*, 75: 45.

It is tested by experience that the primary virtues of mankind are possible of cultivation by the meanest of the human species. It is this undoubted universal possibility that distinguishes the humans from the rest of God's creation. *If every one great nation were unconditionally to perform the supreme act of renunciation, many of us would see in our lifetime visible peace established on earth.*[70]

Human nature responds to the advances of love. A little spark of goodness left in the heart of even the worst and lowest of individuals, can be aroused and strengthened by the redemptive suffering of self-sacrificing love. K.M. Prasad reads Gandhi's mind correctly when he says,

satyāgraha touches human nature itself, not only its cultured areas; and human nature, no matter how much violent externally, is at bottom decent. Everybody has in his heart at least a little spark of goodness which can be aroused and strengthened. Nobody is absolutely beyond redemption.[71]

When a *satyāgrahī* suffers an assailant's violence patiently, cheerfully, fearlessly, and without ill-will, while at the same time boldly holding on and stating the truth of the matter without succumbing to pressure or pain, then, the courage of conviction and the unflinching endurance of pain startle the assailant who finally, losing self-confidence and acquiring moral balance, starts responding to the demands of the *satyāgrahī*s. Gandhi was convinced that a change in the inner attitude of an assailant was always a real possibility; in fact, a necessary outcome.

THE HEALING POWER OF AHIMSĀ

The world's attention was drawn by Gandhi to the healing power of the nonviolent approach to personal as well as institutional relationships. Gandhi discovered the power in every human to bring about to practice *ahiṁsā*, to bring healing to wounded and broken relationship and positive

---

70. "Answer to the Cosmopolitan," *Harijan*, June 18, 1938 (original emphasis). See Iyer 2: 29-30.

71. Prasad, *Sarvodaya of Gandhi*, p. 153.

reconciliation. With considerable success he translated this innate capacity into concrete historical praxis.

The essence of non-violence is suffering injury in one's own person as a substitute for doing violence to others.[72] As positive love that is other-regarding, *ahiṁsā* in its purest form is sacrificial love. One who positively inflicts injury on others is certainly incapable of finding his or her kinship with the other. Self-suffering, undertaken for the sake and on account of another, may awake the humane elements in the other.[73] One who is willing to accept voluntary suffering as a way of protest, shows that there is no grudge or ill-will against the misguided opponents and that their conversion to truth is what is desired. The quarrel is with the wrong situations and misguided attitudes, not with people. Self-suffering, undertaken for the conversion of the wrong-doer, and as a protest against his or her actions, has the positive capacity to rouse the "better nature" of the opponent. The good fight is against the *wrong actions* and *not* against the *wrong-doer*. An advocate of physical violence does not draw this person-deed distinction. The "intoxicating excitement of killing"[74] distorts judgements and embitters personal relations.

LAW OF SUFFERING AND THE WAY OF THE CROSS

Non-violence is nothing but the law of suffering. According to Gandhi "progress" in the practice of non-violence is to be measured by the extent of suffering undergone by the *satyāgrahī*. The purer the suffering, the greater is the progress.[75] This suffering should be undertaken joyfully. The more one can suffer for another, the better one shows one's love and concern for the other.[76] Gandhi was convinced that non-

72. M.K. Gandhi, *For Pacifists* (Ahmedabad: Navajivan Publishing House, 1960), Reprint, p. 16.

73. Gandhi, *For Pacifists* p. 25

74. *Collected Works*, XXV: 365.

75. *Young India*, June 1920.

76. Martin Luther King understood the meaning of Gandhian self-

violence "means conscious suffering. It does not mean meek submission to the will of the evil-doer, but it means putting one's whole soul against the will of the tyrant."[77]

Gandhi was convinced that personal suffering has both preventive and purificatory effect. All-embracing *ahiṁsā* "transforms everything it touches. There is no limit to its power."[78]

RESOLUTION OF CONFLICTS

The way of aggression both organized and unorganized, state and private, has failed in history to provide lasting, harmonious and dignified solution to political, economic, individual or social conflicts. Gandhi, seeks an alternative strategy for conflict resolution.

Resolution of conflict is seen as a cooperative endeavour of searching for the truth. With constant critical inquiry one has to be true in thought, word and deed to one's sincerely held beliefs, and at the same time dialogue to arrive at agreements with respect to the nature and character of the truth of common search. One needs to actively engage in the

suffering love when he told his congregation that by practicing *agape* they can tell their enemies, "We shall match your capacity to inflict suffering by our capacity to endure suffering. We will meet your physical force with soul force. Do to us what you will and we will still love you. . . . Bomb our homes and threaten our children, and, as difficult as it is, we will still love you. Send your hooded perpetrators of violence into our communities at the midnight hour and drag us out on some wayside road and leave us half-dead as you beat us, and we will still love you. Send your propaganda agents around the country, and make it clear that we are not fit, culturally and otherwise, for integration, and we'll still love you. But be assured that we'll wear you down by our capaciy to suffer, and one day we will win our freedom. We will not only win freedom for ourselves; we will so appeal to your heart and conscience that we will win you in the process, and our victory will be a double victory." Martin Luther King Jr., *The Trumpet of Conscience* (New York: Harper and Row, 1968), pp. 74-75.

77. *Young India*, August 11, 1920.

78. Gandhi, *Autobiography*, p. viii.

search for truth, and make progress in the art of being good and in the art of the possible.

It is an inevitable feature of human life that what appears to be true to one may appear as false to the other. To be moral, according to Gandhi, is to lead a life of truth; it is to lead an integrated life eliminating completely all traces of incoherence, illogicality and hypocrisy from one's way of life. This further implies positively fighting against the obvious untruths. A moral agent is inevitably called to "take a stand and fight when his opponent either refuses to talk or to do what they both agreed to be right or true thing to do in a given situation."[79] The means of achieving an objective is *integral* to the goal; not external to it. The goal does not exist at the *end* of a series of actions. Means create ends as Bhikhu Parekh puts it: "The so-called means were ends in an embryonic stage and represented the seeds of which the so-called ends were a natural flowering."[80] The fight for truth has to be conducted by truthful means.

Though often presented as a simple moral method of relying on the power and strength of the soul (soul-force) the Gandhian technique of conflict resolution (*ahiṁsātmaka satyāgraha*) involves an ingenious complex mix of various mechanisms. It aims at touching the heart, awakening the sense of humanity and rationality, and activating the innate moral sentiments. There is something Socratic about Gandhi in his call to the court of conscience. By the pricking of one's conscience one could be awakened "to be" in the world of inter-human relationships. Appealing to the truth of the oneness of humanity, the message of *satyāgraha* is that the "interest" of a fellow-human being has a moral claim on every actor on the world stage.

Gandhi evolved a complex three-fold method to resolve conflicts of various origin — individual or social.

79. Parekh, *Gandhi's Political Philosophy*, p. 142.

80. Parekh, *Gandhi's Political Philosophy*, pp. 142-43.

1. The patient use of a persuasive, practical power of right reason.
2. Appeal to the contritional, conversional capacity of the heart/soul, and to the innate sense of humanity present in everyone including the worst of criminals or tyrants.
3. Resorting to the technique of *satyāgraha* as a final means.

An explanation of these three mechanisms will be unfolded in analysing his reasons and arguments against the use of violent force for conflict resolution.

REASONS AGAINST THE USE OF VIOLENCE

Gandhi was absolutely averse to the use of violence as a method of change. Though he sympathized with those who advocated violence as a technique of socio-economic and political change, and tried to understand the spontaneous outbursts of violence in people under unbearable circumstances or severe provocations, he vehemently opposed the use of violence as a matter of deliberate policy. The chief reasons for his conviction are the following.

Since violence is based on untruth, it could never be a way of attaining truth. Since all, including the worst oppressors, are truth-seekers, the "pursuit of truth did not admit violence being inflicted on one's opponent but that he must be weaned from error by patience and sympathy."[81] Truth could be approached fully only through love.[82] Gandhi affirms that *satyāgraha* which excludes the use of violence is the only right approach to conflict resolution because "man is not capable of knowing the absolute truth and therefore not competent to punish."[83]

---

81. Jag Parvesh Chander, ed., *Teachings of Mahatma Gandhi* (Lahore: The Indian Printing Works, 1945), p. 494; as quoted by Joan V. Bondurant, *Conquest of Violence: Gandhi's Philosophy of Conflict*, rev. edn. (1965), fourth printing (Berkeley: University of California, 1971), pp. 16-17.

82. Tendulkar, *Mahatma*, 3: 176.

83. *Speeches and Writings of Mahatma Gandhi*, p. 506.

At its core, violence negates the fundamental notion that all people are ontologically one. It was Gandhi's fundamental belief that all persons were essentially one; and that goodwill and love, not hatred and violence, were the only valid bases for interpersonal relationship.

Eliminating the opponent through violence does not reduce the prevalent inhumanity; in fact, it would only compound it. Gandhi's vehement opposition to violence was because it not only attacks sin and evil but also the sinner and the evildoer. Attacking a person is like offending the greatest truth, the unity and sacredness of all Being. Truth demands a categorical rejection of violent means in conflict resolution.[84] Absolutely convinced that it was the only way to solve the numerous problems of humankind, Gandhi applied *ahiṁsā* in all walks of life including mass movements: "nonviolence is the universal law under all circumstances. Disregard of it is the surest way to destruction."[85] He was so strong on this point that once he declared categorically,

> I would like to repeat to the world times without numbers that I will not purchase my country's freedom at the cost of violence. My marriage with nonviolence is such an absolute thing that I would rather commit suicide than be deflected from my position.[86]

Assuming infallibility and negating corrigibility, violence presumes epistemological certainty. Such a presumption of "epistemological infallibility" is contrary to day-to-day human experience. One cannot be *totally* right and an opponent just may not be *absolutely* wrong in the perception of reality and the reading of the signs of the times. Allowing sufficient room for one's own fallible nature to reflect critically and act accordingly would totally eliminate violence as a moral option.

Besides, in Gandhi's view, the use of violence denies the

---

84. See *Harijan,* July 1939.

85. *Harijan,* July 15, 1939.

86. *Young India,* December 12, 1931.

basic epistemological fact that all knowledge is fallible and corrigible and that we could see truth only in fragments and from different angles of vision. When humans perceive truth differently, how can the perception of truth of some people be made a scale to evaluate and, in turn, "punish" violently the perception of truth and the subsequent actions of some others ? In order to morally justify the violent action of harming or even killing someone, one must assume that one is absolutely right, and that the opponent is totally wrong. It further assumes that the action taken is the appropriate means to achieve the desired result. These pretentious assumptions are absolutely inappropriate as far as Gandhi is concerned.

Violence works on the principle that one can impose one's opinions and beliefs on another and that one may do this with the use of physical might. But a violent act does not necessarily change the perception of truth of an opponent; it does not encourage the conversion process of the latter either. When ultimately conversion to truth is what is aimed, violence cannot achieve this goal. If everyone starts imposing their "truths" onto another there will be chaos in the world; only "might" will become the ultimate means of keeping order, if at all order can be preserved in this way. This approach violates the integrity of a person as a moral being and negates the moral order of reality.

Gandhi rejected violence further on pragmatic grounds. It does not take deep reflection to see that violence begets violence. And the spiralling cycle of violence will have the cumulative effect of relegating peaceful cooperative dialogue and reconciling forgiveness to the realm of illusions. It is certain that every act of violence leads to a vicious cycle of mutual fears, misunderstandings, and suspicions from which the parties concerned are not able to extricate themselves easily. If pride and the desire for power are added to the physical might it certainly leads to a proliferation of arms and ammunitions. Armed to the teeth, not with truth but with superior (military, atomic) force, either side might be the instant winner to the detriment of truth itself and even, perhaps, to the decimation of the human species.[87]

Another consideration is Gandhi's limited, but appropriate, reliance on reason and rationality. Perhaps, blind reliance on rationality and realism has led many to advocate violence as the only effective method of fighting injustice. Obviously such advocacy itself may be the result of an over-confidence about rationality's capacity for objective impartial judgement. Knowing that human rationality is limited (which we know by our rationality), to act as if it is not, by claiming that one has the absolute truth and that one is absolutely right in the perception of truth, is in itself a contradiction.

Besides, insistence that all disputes are amenable to rational resolution is fundamentally irrational too. Reason and rationality has its own limit: "I have come to the fundamental conclusion that if you want something really important to be done, you must not merely satisfy the reason, you must move the heart also. The appeal of reason is more to the head."[88] Having experienced that the very rationality is used to justify even violent responses Gandhi gave to rationality only a limited autonomy, much less than even Aquinas would permit, always leaving some space in human experience for not possessing the truth in its entirety. Using only rational discussion for resolution of conflict is often found to be ineffective in practice. Referring to the then South African situation, Gandhi wrote, "The human intellect delights in inventing specious arguments in order to support injustice itself."[89]

Advocates of the use of violence, using the principle of lesser evil, have insisted that the use of violence is justified when it is

---

87. For a detailed description of these Gandhian insights see Parekh, *Gandhi's Political Philosophy*, pp. 147-49. Also see Chatterjee, *Gandhi's Religious Thought*, pp. 76-77.

88. *Young India*, November 5, 1931.

89. *Satyagraha in South Africa*, p. 76.

to eliminate a greater evil. But Gandhi was opposed to the use of violence as a means of social change. Use of violence as a deliberate policy was not only not admissible to Gandhi, but it was absolutely repugnant to his reason and rationality as well. Something based on untruth could never be a means to attain truth. Violence is based on untruth. The assumption that some people have totally lost their moral impulse, and in that process lost their *ātman*, was not admissible to Gandhi. Even in the worst of criminals there will be a little bit of the human in them. The spark of the divine in one's heart cannot just be wiped out even by the meanest of human actions. Gandhi's faith in the goodness of the human being refused to believe that some people are so wicked that they had lost all traces of *ātman* and its moral impulses. Gandhi would argue for resonating to the little bit of the moral sensitivity and humanity left, in order to arrive at the goal of truth.

If persons, cultures and civilizations were reflective and self-critical, they can to some extent rise above hostility, and consider other's interest with a degree of impartiality. Looking at events as a judge, with an impartiality of a Daniel perhaps, distancing oneself from one's own people, prejudices, and self-interests and impartially analysing charges, events, persons, one can arrive at the objective truth. In any situation demanding conflict resolution both the head and the heart (rationality and affectivity/morality) should be allowed to play a reasonable role.

The distinction that Gandhi makes between the person doing the wrong thing, and the wrongdoing of the person, helps him to embrace suffering as a way of protest to fight against wrongful actions and pursue truth with the manifest intent of the conversion of the wrong-doer to truth. In such a pursuit of truth as affirmation of life, *ahiṁsā* is the only appropriate means. By introducing *ahiṁsā* as the operative principle of *satyāgraha* in interpersonal relations and conflict resolution in the process of building harmonious societal relationships, Gandhi's concept of truth, which is nonabsolute in human encounters, avoids the practical difficulty of ethical relativism.[90]

Further, if the philosophy of the use of force and violence is admitted to resolve conflicts, one always looks for the weak spot of the opponent. The aim of defeating the enemy makes one pursue and attack the shortcomings in an effort to take advantage of the weakness of the opponent. Such an approach is positively forbidden in the Gandhian program. In *satyāgraha* physical force is forbidden even in the most favourable circumstances.[91]

Truth is the source of, and the foundation for the resolution of conflicts. Relativity in the human perception of truth need not necessarily lead to absolute relativity and confusion. Ethical relativism is avoided through the interaction of *satya* and *ahiṁsā*. That which brings about a harmonious community is truth. Hence the pursuit of truth in and of itself increases harmony in societal life.

The oppressors too are in need of liberative transformation; indeed, they stand in greater need of liberation. Gandhi's basic assumption is that a dehumanized oppressor is as much a victim of his/her own oppressed condition as those who are ordinarily called the oppressed. Such an oppressor too needs to be liberated. This is relatively hard. It is hard precisely because the patient (oppressor) does not realize and will not admit that s/he is sick! All his life Gandhi sought to free the British as much as the people of India from the clutches of imperialism. True *swarāj* occurs only when both oppressor and oppressed are set free. As a nonviolent resister, the *satyagrahi* seeks liberation for the self styled opponent, or enemy, so that both can live in peace, harmony and friendship.[92]

90. See Bondurant, *Conquest of Violence*, pp. 20-21.

91. *Satyagraha in South Africa*, p. 114. See Prasad, *Sarvodaya of Gandhi*, p. 143.

92. In Gandhi's own life he came to a state of not hating or keeping

By denying the very notion of "adversary" from his spirituality (way of life) Gandhi could make everyone, including those who consider themselves to be enemy or foe, to be a co-searcher, a participant in the pursuit of truth and a truthful solution to conflicts. The one who considers himself or herself as an enemy needs to be weaned from his or her error. It could be said that Gandhi's way is a positive refusal to be treated as an enemy.[93]

MEANS-END NEXUS

Mention has been made earlier of Gandhi's insistence on the purity of means. The most salient characteristic of the Gandhian technique of *ahiṁsāmaka satyāgraha* is his insistence of the harmony of means and ends. There is an intrinsic relationship between means and end. Gandhi believed in the continuity of means and ends. Drawing inspiration from organic analogies, he likened the relation between means and end to the relation

---

grudge against anyone including those who some time or other have hurt or oppressed him:

"I hold myself to be incapable of hating any being on earth. By a long course of prayerful discipline, I have ceased for over forty years to hate anybody. I know this is a big claim. Nevertheless, I make it in all humility. . . . But I can and do hate evil wherever it exists. I hate the system of government that the British people have set up in India. I hate the ruthless exploitation of India even as I hate from the bottom of my heart the hideous system of untouchability for which millions of Hindus have made themselves responsible. But I do not hate the domineering British as I refuse to hate the domineering Hindus. I seek to reform them in all the loving ways that are open to me. My non-cooperation has its roots not in hatred, but in love." As quoted in Easwaran, *Gandhi the Man*, p. 56.

93. The radical love that he manifested to the so called "enemies," such as Jan Christian Smuts, the leader of South Africa in the early 1900s, shows Gandhi's's non-cooperation rooted in love. In 1914 when Gandhi left South Africa after many years of struggle for justice and truth, and in that process disturbing the "peace" of South Africa, he left a gift for General Smuts: a pair of sandals that Gandhi had made while in prison. Smuts wore them every summer for years afterward. See John Dear, *Our God is Nonviolent: Witnesses in the Struggle for Peace & Justice* (New York: The Pilgrim Press, 1990), pp. 12-13.

between seed and the tree. When asked once why one should not obtain a good by means whatsoever, including violence, Gandhi said:

> Your belief that there is no connection between the means and the end is a great mistake. Through that mistake even men who have been considered religious have committed grievous crimes. Your reasoning is the same as saying that we can get a rose through planting a noxious weed — the means may be likened to a seed, the end to tree; and there is just the same inviolable connection between the means and the end as there is between the seed and tree — We reap exactly as we sow — If I want to deprive you of your watch, I shall certainly have to fight for it, if I want to buy your watch, I shall have to pay for it; and if I want a gift I shall have to plead for it; and, according to the means I employ, the watch is stolen property, my own property, or a donation. Thus we see three different results from three different means. Will you still say that means do not matter?[94]

Gandhi sums up the issue in a statement given to the press on December 4, 1932, on the eve of his famous fast unto death:

> Those who have to bring about radical changes in human conditions and surroundings cannot do it except by raising a ferment in society. There are only two methods of doing this — violent and non-violent. Violent pressure is felt on the physical being, and it degrades him who uses it as it depresses the victim, but non-violent pressure exerted through self-suffering, as by fasting, works in an entirely different way. It touches not only the physical body, but it touches and strengthens the moral fiber of those against whom it is directed.[95]

Gandhi emphasized the purity of means because, while the end is beyond human control, the means are within human reach and that the means employed determine the nature of

---

94. *Hind Swaraj*, p. 105; as quoted by Prasad, *Social Philosophy of Mahatma Gandhi*, p. 145.

95. As quoted by Stanley Jones, *Mahatma Gandhi: An Interpretation*, p. 117.

the resulting ends. One cannot just diminish the importance of means, by saying that "means are after all means." For I would say "means are after all everything." As the means so the end. . . . There is no wall of separation between means and end. Indeed the Creator has given us control over means, none over the end. Realization of the goal is in exact proportion to that of the means. This is a proposition that admits of no exception.[96]

Even tyrants and dictators invariably claim to work for laudable ends while perpetrating the most atrocious crimes.[97] But Gandhi would say that even "(T)he attempt to win *Swarāj*, for instance, is *Swarāj* itself."[98] If one seeks the goal of the greatest good of all (*sarvodaya*), the means must be appropriate to that end. Gandhi's argument is disarmingly simple. If one uses violence to achieve a social order, the resulting social order will be a violent one. To achieve a peaceful social order, one has to use non-violent means. What Gandhi is trying to bring out is that the effects of violence and of violent means are far-reaching, beyond the dreams of the often well-intentioned people who resort to them. Violence has an inherent capacity of spiralling effect, leading to more and more violence.

With his added emphasis on means, especially in conflict-resolution, Gandhi has reversed the Machiavellian dictum that the "end justifies the means."[99] If Truth as God is the "highest

---

96. *Young India*, July 17, 1924; *Selected Works*, VI: 149.

97. History is full of examples showing that violent means only sow the seeds of further violence *ad infinitum*. Aldous Huxley in his *Ends and Means* cites a few incidents of the after-effects of some "iron dictatorships" in Europe. Just to cite one example, the dictatorship of the Jacobins resulted in military tyranny, twenty years of war and idolatrous natioalism. Even a cursor glance at some of the contemporary scenes of military dictatorships, the attempted coups, the resulting chaos and the subsequent military rule proves spell of what Gandhi is trying to articulate.

98. *Speeches and Writings of Mahatma Gandhi*, p. 685.

99. See Niccolo Machiavelli, *The Prince*, translation by Leo Paul S. de Alvarez (Texas: University of Dallas Press, 1980), Ch. XVIII, pp. 107-10.

end to be realized,"[100] then, the sovereign way to the goal and "the only inevitable means is Love, i.e., non-violence."[101]

Hence the end is inseparable from the means. One cannot attain the God or Truth, unless one tries to be truthful in thought, word and action.[102] Thus, Gandhi rejected the notion that the end justifies the means.[103]

THE NON-VIOLENT CREED

Mention has already been made that with Gandhi non-violence was a creed. Non-violence is not a prudentially expedient, pragmatically sound political policy. It is not just a strategy either. With Gandhi it is a passionate fundamental belief; it is a *credal policy*.[104] Of course, it is not Gandhian knowledge and experience of the ultimate failure and eventual frustration of the terrorists and violent revolutionaries that led to his search for an alternative technique. In his practice of non-violence,

---

100. Truth is the highest end to be realized for Gandhi; see *Selected Writings*, 4: 213.

101. Gandhi goes even to the extent of saying "I believe that ultimately the means and the end are convertible terms, I should not hesitate to say that God is Love." See *Young India*, December 31, 1931. Cf. *Hindu Dharma*, p. 68.

102. *Selected Writings*, 4: 213. If Gandhi's writings on the subject of *Ahiṁsā* is very rich and subtle, his practice of this reality is very complex and involved. His essay on *ahiṁsā* in *From Yeravda Mandir: Ashram Observances* is very informative with respect to his notion on the topic in question. In this essay Gandhi tries to weave the web of *satya-ahiṁsā* relationship. See *Selected Writings*, 4: 216-19.

103. See *Young India*, April 9, 1925; *Young India*, September 29, 1940. Also see *Niti Dharma*, p. 42.

104. See Pratibha Jain, *Gandhian Ideas, Social Movements, and Creativity* (Jaipur: Rawat Publications, 1985), p. 32. In his speech at Worker's School, Bogra, Gandhi explains his credal conviction of *ahiṁsā*: "ahimsa is not a policy with me, but a creed, a religion . . . Because I know that it is not *himsa* or destructive energy that sustains the world, it is *ahiṁsā*, it is creative energy. . . . *Ahiṁsā* inspires you with love than which you cannot think of a better excitment. . . . *Ahiṁsā* is my God, and Truth is my God." *Young India*, June 4, 1925.

like Socrates who reminded his friends that an unexamined life is not worth living, Gandhi appeals to all of humanity to examine the meaning of life in terms of ultimate concerns.

CONCLUSION

Ahiṁsātmaka satyāgraha is a way of life, a spirituality, embraced by Gandhi so that, in and through it whatever makes for fragmentation of life be overcome especially by eradicating violence from human hearts and from the face of the earth and paving the way for *Rāmarājya* wherein the eternal law of righteousness, the *sanātana dharma*, would prevail. Founded on the notion of the oneness of reality, the dignity of the human person, and the human obligation to strive to attain the purpose of life, and supported by self-sacrificial, suffering agape-love, it is intended to effect personal, socio-economic and political transformation, not by force but by conversion of the heart, so that the unity of humans may be achieved in the kingdom of mutual human enrichment and reconciling relationship and, above all, Truth may prevail in the ultimate analysis.[105]

---

105. There are many others who experienced and articulated the ontological unity of the human race. Thomas Merton, for instance, understood fully the ontological oneness of the human family: "No more nuclear war! No more injustice! The God of peace is never glorified by human violence. Let us live together as the brothers and sisters that we are." His trip to Asia, as Jim Douglass, an activist-theologian points out, was a quest to explore what Merton called "an ontology of nonviolence." Merton's question reveals his own search for that ontology in the cave of his own heart: "If we want to end war, hadn't we best begin by ending the wars in our own hearts?" [See John Dear, *Our God is Non-violent* (New York: Pilgrim Press, 1990), p. 93]. In his closing prayer, at the end of a conference in Calcutta in the fall of 1968, he invited participants to join hands and to be aware of "the love that unites us, the love that unites us in spite of real differences, real emotional friction. The things that are on the surface are nothing, what is deep is the Real. We are creatures of love." [*The Asia Journal of Thomas Merton* (New York: New Dimensions, 1975), p. 318. As quoted by John Dear, *op. cit.*, p. 93]. The prayer that gushed out of his heart proclaims his inner experience of the tension:

The way of organized or unorganized state or individual forms of violence aiming at providing lasting, harmonious and a dignified solution to political, economic or social conflicts has failed in history. And Gandhi seeks an alternative to conflict-resolution.

Born of agape-love, the Gandhian way of life treats friends and foes alike without making any preferential treatment of either. Denouncing coercion and physical force, Gandhi reiterates that a change of heart is what is called for.

The self-sacrificial, contritional-conversional, agape-love immanent in *ahiṁsātmaka satyāgraha* implies a willingness to lay down one's life in an unconditional manner for all, including the opponent, in a non-retaliatory fashion, for the entire human family, recognizing the ultimate unity and worth of every human being in a deep-seated appreciation of truth — the truth that all are equal and one, and that the spark of God is present in everyone. Respecting the opponent, while, nonetheless, steadfastly adhering vehemently to truth and justice, is

---

"Oh God, we are one with You . . . . You have taught us that if we are open to one another, You dwell in us. Help us to preserve this openness and to fight for it with all our hearts. Help us to realize that there can be no understanding where there is mutual rejection. Oh God, in accepting one another wholeheartedly, fully, completely, we accept You, and we thank You, and we adore You, and we love You with our whole being, because our being is in Your being, our spirit is rooted in Your Spirit. Fill us then with love, and let us be bound together with love as we go our diverse ways, united in this one spirit which makes You present in the world." (*The Asian Journal of Thomas Merton*, pp. 318-19).

In his famous essay, "The Root of War Is Fear," Merton points out the unity underlying the divisions of humanity: "What is imporant in nonviolence, is the contemplative truth that is not seen. The radical truth of reality is that we are all one." [Jim Forest, *Thomas Merton's Struggle with Peacemaking* (Erie, PA.: Benet Press, 1980), 29]. In one of his final talks in Calcutta, he concluded: "My brothers and sisters, we are already one. But we imagine that we are not. And what we have to recover is our original unity. What we have to be is what we are." William H. Shannon ed., *The Hidden Ground of Love: The Letters of Thomas Merton* (New York: Farrar, Straus & Giroux, 1985), p. x.

essential to such redemptive self-suffering love.

We have seen that in Gandhi's philosophy the emphasis is on the individual transformation as the starting point as well as the centre of social regeneration. To Gandhi the problems of the group are fundamentally the problem of the individual. The main reason for this emphasis is that change and progress in societal structures depend on the soul-force of the individual.

In response to "the inner voice," Gandhi sought how to manage a humanly unmanageable situation. He was convinced that "while perfection is above sorrow and suffering, the way to it lies through sorrow and suffering."[106] Gandhi knew very well that selfishness perverts our vision of the morally good; ignorance blinds our vision of the moral law. Independent of our feelings and opinions, the laws of the moral world are eternally valid, unlike human-made laws. We are bound to obey them even more strictly than the laws of the state: "Indeed, disobedience to the law of the state becomes a peremptory duty when it comes in conflict with the law of God," because, in God's world, Truth and righteousness should for ever remain the law.[107]

The power to do good "exists always within us, and we have only to develop it by appropriate means."[108] To work unremittingly "for the good of humankind" is the highest moral law and our paramount duty.

Believing firmly that a transformed relationship of loving concern where truth, justice and love prevail, cannot be brought about by any sort of brutal violence, Gandhi conceived of a non-violent social revolution, a revolution brought about by change of heart, by love, and not by force or violent upheavals. This he sought with the purpose of helping to reorganize society into a new social order (to a kingdom of

---

106. Pyarelal, *The Last Phase*, p. 324.

107. Gandhi, *Niti Dharma*, p. 47.

108. *Ibid.*, p. 39.

transformed relationship — *Rāmarājya*), wherein peace and prosperity reigns along with freedom and equality, with an equal distribution of power and opportunity.

Suffering injury in one's own person has an inherent capacity to rouse the "better nature" of the opponent.[109] Denouncing any imposition of compulsion or coercion of the opponent, Gandhi reiterates that a change of heart of persons considered to be oppressive is the goal. In the political realm, the technique of the mass *satyāgraha* attempting to paralyze an unjust Government through a self-suffering technique, was the means he resorted to. It was not the fulfilment of individual rights that Gandhi often referred to, but, in a Socratic way to the call of duty that every person ought to follow.

Toward a Spirituality of "Drinking From Our Own Wells" In Search of a New Spirituality by Gutiérrez

There definitely emerges a spirituality in the theological reflection of Gutiérrez. This spirituality "is not concerned simply with a particular area of Christian existence; it is a style of life that puts its seal to our way of accepting the gift of filiation (the basis of fellowship) to which the Father calls us."[110] Emphasizing the necessity of this new "style of life," he adds, "We need a vital attitude, all-embracing and synthesizing, informing the totality as well as every detail of our lives; we need a 'spirituality'."[111] The nature of such a spirituality needs to be explored. The mechanism of arriving at such a spirituality needs to be analysed. What that spirituality prescribes in terms of concrete action has to be articulated. My immediate concern here is to explore the nature

---

109. Gandhi, *For Pacifists*, p. 225; See Saxena, *Ever Unto God: Essays on Gandhi and Religion*, p. 146.

110. Gutiérrez, *We drink from our own wells*, p. 4.

111. Gutiérrez, *A Theology of Liberation*, p. 203. Gutiérrez mentions others like Arturo Gaete, Arturo Paoli, and Ernesto Cardenal who too have observed the necessity of a "spirituality of liberation." See his footnote no. 48, in *A Theology of Liberation*, p. 212.

of the way of life demanded of the followers of Jesus according to Gutiérrez and to see how that demand is expected to be met in the contextual, challenging, historical situation especially of Latin America. By this approach I hope to find the ways and means proposed by Gutiérrez in his liberation agenda to facilitate the process of liberative transformation expediting the coming of Kingdom of transformed relationship established by God in His *Verbum caro factum* (word made flesh) Jesus the Christ with the hope of eschatological fulfilment in the day of the Lord. In this way an attempt is made to arrive at the social ethical principles and prescriptions for action, in the liberation spirituality proposed by Gutiérrez.

Though diverse theological routes are taken to define such a spirituality by various liberation theologians, there is a clear consensus concerning the core of its nature.[112] Spirituality is a comprehensive term that signifies the entire pattern of life of the Christian, the manner in which the Christian lives. The condition of a specific society/culture at a particular historical context and the setting of the surrounding world are the point of view for this particular mode of life. Such a spirituality must involve all aspects of life. It embodies a synthesis of all actions in the ecclesial community of the Church and in the

---

112. A Christological approach to a liberation spirituality is most consistently developed by Jon Sobrino. Among his other writings see particularly *Christology at the Crossroads: A Latin American Approach* (Maryknoll, New York: Orbis, 1978), especially pages 388-95. Also see "Following Jesus as Discernment," *Discernment of the Spirit and of Spirits, Concilium,* 119, ed. Casiano Floristan and Christian Duquoc (New York: The Seabury Press, 1979), 14-24. Juan Luis Segundo's approach could be termed as a theology of the Spirit. The term "spirituality" does not play a major role in Segundo's writings. See Juan Luis Segundo, *Grace and Human condition* (Maryknoll, New York: Orbis, 1973), pp. 86-94; Alfred T. Hennlly, *Theologies in Conflict: The Challenge of Juan Luis Segundo* (Maryknoll, New York: Orbis Books, 1979), pp. 140-56. There is an ecclesiological approach developed in Gutiérrez's *Theology of Liberation.* It should be mentioned that these various approaches are not mutually exclusive. For instance, Christo-centrism is definitely one of the main criteria of this spirituality in *We Drink from Our Own Wells* by Gutiérrez.

world of human interaction. In the painful struggle of the poor of Latin America, in and through an intimate solidarity with them, Gutiérrez was able to identify the traits of this new spirituality of liberation.

His attempt is three-fold:

1. To consider the contextual experience that forms the matrix of the spirituality that he sees emerging.
2. To define the main aspects of a spirituality demanded in the following of Jesus; and
3. To bring out the relationship between the historical situation and the challenge of following Jesus in the ecclesial community.

Gutiérrez is convinced that the historical starting point for the following of Jesus and for reflection on this following is to be found in the experience that comes from the Spirit. . . . In our insertion into the process of liberation in which the peoples of Latin America are now engaged, we live out the gift of faith, hope, and charity that makes us disciples of the Lord. This experience is our well. The water that rises out of it continually purifies us and smooths away any wrinkles in our manner of being Christians, at the same time supplying the vital element needed for making new ground fruitful.[113]

This implies that one needs to go beyond theological categories to develop "vital attitude, all-embracing and synthesizing, informing the totality as well as every detail of our lives; we need a 'spirituality.' Spirituality, in the strict and profound sense of the word is the dominion of the Spirit."[114] That way Gutiérrez explains the prime necessity of a spirituality and acknowledges the requirement of an ethic in his theology of liberation.

In contrast to the polarities of the earlier "dominant" spirituality, Gutiérrez propose a unifying effort in four

113. Gutiérrez, *We Drink from Our Own Wells*, p. 5.
114. Gutiérrez, *A Theology of Liberation*, p. 203.

dimensions of Christian life — the dimensions of immanence and transcendence, material and spiritual, action and contemplation, and, finally, personal and social.[115] A description of the nature of liberation spirituality will unfold the unifying effort of Gutiérrez.

THE NATURE OF LIBERATION SPIRITUALITY

The full title of his book, *We Drink from Our Own Wells: The spiritual journey of a people,* indicates the matrix as well as the core idea of the spirituality that Gutiérrez proposes.[116] The insight of St. Bernard of Clairvaux, that "everyone has to drink from his own well,"[117] evokes in Gutiérrez a contextual question: "From what well can the poor of Latin America drink?" This question reveals that the contextual experience is the matrix of the spirituality now in the pangs of birth. One's spirituality ought to flow from an in-depth and comprehensive Christian insight able to meet the challenges

115. Roger Haight name these as polarities or tensions that govern the Christian life. These are manifested in the structure of liberation spirituality itself. "In the case of each of these polarities or tensions liberation spirituality may be seen as a reaction against a one-sided view of the Christian life and more positively as a spirituality that hold the two poles of the various tensions together." Haight, *A Alternate Vision: An Interpretation of Liberation Theology,* pp. 236-37. Since liberation theologians, especially Gutiérrez, are trying to put these "poles of tensions" together, there definitely exists a unifying effort to arrive at a holistic spirituality. Hence the use of the phrase "unifying effort."

116. In his earlier works Gutiérrez had not gone specifically into elaborating the nature and characteristic of his liberation spirituality. Of course, he was keenly experiencing the necessity and, accordingly, had given overall directional tendencies that such a spirituality should take place (see his *Theology of Liberation,* pp. 203-08). In this work (*We Drink from Our Own Wells*), he delves deep into the nature and demands of such a "spiritual journey" of the people, especially the poor, of Latin America. Hence most of my references would be from this latter work.

117. *De consideratione libri quinque ad Eugenium tertium,* II,I,2; P.L. Migne, CLXXXII, 745D; cited in E. Gilson *Theologie et histoire de las spiritualite* (Paris: Vri, 1943), p. 20. See Gutierrez, *We Drink from Our Own Wells,* p. 138, notes 4.

raised by the relationship between faith and the political order, by the defence of human rights, or by the struggle for justice. The spirituality that Gutiérrez visualizes "is like living water that springs up in the very depths of the experience of faith,"— one that reveals the full significance of "liberation."

What it is Not

Liberative spirituality is not based on a "perfect-imperfect" dichotomy, nor is it "geared to minorities," nor is it oriented to an "individualistic bend."[118] Individualistic virtues as personal perfections have been extolled in the spiritual journey of the past. Such privatization of spirituality turned it into a purely individual venture, one person's journey to God. Such a "spiritualist" following of Jesus is challenged by Gutiérrez as not being authentic in the Biblical perspective of Christo-centricity. Such individualism and spiritualism "combine to impoverish and even distort the following of Jesus. An individualistic spirituality is incapable of offering guidance in this following to those who have embarked on a collective enterprise of liberation. Nor does it do justice to the different dimensions of the human person, including the so-called material aspects."[119] Further, in the past "Christian spirituality has long been presented as *geared to minorities.*"[120] Understanding religious life as a state of perfection, the way proper to religious life assumed some kind of "flight" from the world. Such individualism and limitation to a minority have led to a distortion of valid spiritual intuitions and experiences, considering that religious life, in the narrow sense of this term, encompassed a "state of perfection;" it implicitly supposed, therefore, that there were other, imperfect states of Christian life. Religious life was marked by a full and structured quest for holiness; in the other states there were found, at best, only the less demanding elements of this

118. See Gutiérrez, *We Drink from Our Own Wells*, pp. 13-14.

119. *Ibid.*, pp. 15-16.

120. *Ibid.*, p. 13.

spirituality. The way proper to religious life supposed some kind of separation from the world and its everyday activities (one form of the well-known *fuga mundi*, "flight from the world").[121]

So liberation spirituality is not reductionist. It challenges all Christians to break out of their individualism, elitism, and/or romantic spiritualism or mere inner search for personal piety. Gutiérrez points to a spirituality that pays close attention to the Biblical traditions with a new outlook.[122]

A Life-Affirming Spirituality

Gutiérrez treats various aspects of his liberation spirituality quite extensively. First and foremost, this spirituality of *We Drink from Our Own Wells* touches every aspect and dimension of human life, affirming life in its totality. With its source in a God who positively wants human liberation from all forms and forces of death, and who offers unconditional life to humans in all its dimensions, total transformation, this liberation spirituality, as envisioned by Gutiérrez, affirms the whole life and all of life. In line with the authentically biblical, Gutiérrez takes pains to let God's saving action in history penetrate all the dimensions of human existence. The saving act is directed to all forms and forces of death — physical, mental, cultural, religious, economic, political or social. All destruction and death-dealing mechanisms aimed at individual persons, cultures, or traditions are rejected. Hence his theology of liberation is a theology of life confronting the reality of death; not only physical and cultural death, but also death in the Pauline sense, since sin is also a death.[123]

---

121. See Gutiérrez, *We Drink from Our Own Wells*, p. 13.

122. This new outlook and viewpoint derive precisely from the phenomenon of what Gutiérrez calls the "irruption of the poor" in history.

123. In fact, sin is "the ultimate root of all social injustice." See Gutiérrez, *The Truth Shall Make You Free*, p. 35. Also see *ibid.*, p. 31; *A Theology of Liberation*, pp. 35, 109-10

The spirituality that Gutiérrez speaks of "is walking in freedom according to the spirit of love and life."[124] This life which is affirmed is "not blind; implicit in any Christian life is a view of the meaning of such a life and an understanding of human existence itself in Christian terms."[125] The life affirmed is authentic Christian existence.

Witness to *life* "takes on a special meaning in Latin America where the forces of death have created a social system that marginalizes the very poor who have a privileged place in the kingdom of life."[126] Jesus finds his dwelling in his messianic work. Similarly, a follower of Jesus is called to life-affirming activities: "To give witness to life implies passage through death."[127] Though the situation in Latin America remains, by and large, one of suffering, poverty, disappearance and death, people have discovered a new faith in God who liberates and gives life. They are also experiencing a time of martyrdom, a time of prayer, a time of hope, and a time of solidarity:

> The struggles of the poor for liberation represent an assertion of their right to life. The poverty that the poor suffer means death: a premature and unjust death. It is on the basis of this affirmation of life that the poor of Latin America are trying to live their faith, recognize the love of God, and proclaim their hope. Within these struggles, with their many forms and phases, an oppressed and believing people is increasingly creating a way of Christian life, a spirituality.[128]

In his explanation of Mark 8: 27-35, Gutiérrez explains the nature of real disciples. The answer to the question "Who do you say that I am?" in the final analysis "is our life, our personal history, our manner of living the gospel."[129]

---

124. Gutiérrez, *We Drink from Our Own Wells*, p. 35.
125. Haight, *An Alternative Vision*, p. 241.
126. Gutiérrez, *We Drink from Our Own Wells*, p. 45.
127. *Ibid.*
128. Gutiérrez, *We Drink from Our Own Wells*, p. 28.
129. *Ibid.*, p. 51.

A Dynamic Spirituality

Constant and careful listening to the people of God, especially the poor, makes this spirituality dynamic; attentive listening to the movement of the Spirit in the community of the faithful, makes it seminal. Gutiérrez's insistence on Christian "praxis" explains the nature of such dynamism seen in the manner of life that he advocates. The very definition of liberation theology as "critical reflection on Christian praxis in the light of the Word," puts emphasis on praxis.[130] Praxis encompasses "a transforming activity marked and illuminated by Christian love."[131] It is not just a Marxian praxis that Gutiérrez implies by "historical praxis," a notion very often overlooked by his numerous critics: "Gutiérrez most often uses praxis to connote a Christian living out of the faith."[132] Praxis implies *transforming activity*; it does not simply mean mere activism. The motive force behind the praxis is Christian *charity*. A Marxian type of social analysis and its reading of history and its diverse manifestations in the light of such social analytic interpretation are *not* the motivating force of the praxis that Gutiérrez speaks

---

130. Gutiérrez, *A Theology of Liberation*, p. 13. See also Gutiérrez, *The Truth Shall Make You Free*, p. 35.

131. Gutiérrez, *La verdad los hara libres, confrontaciones* (Lima: Centro de Estudios y Publicaciones, 1986), p. 138; as quoted by Arthur F. McGovern, *Liberation Theology and Its Critics: Toward an Assessment* (New York: Orbis Books, 1989), p. 32.

McGovern correctly mentions that Gutiérrez gives eight reasons for his emphasis on "praxis" in the pages preceding the given definition of liberation theology: "The centrality of charity in Christian life expresses a commitment to praxis by emphasizing living out one's faith through actions. But other developments have also pointed to the importance of relating faith to action: developments in spirituality ("the contemplative in action"), new attention in theology to revelation as illuminating the human situation, the life and activity of the church as a focus of theology, the Vatican II method of reading "the signs of the times," Maurice Blondel's philosophy of human action, the influence of Marx's idea of praxis, and finally the place of "historical praxis," of Christians seeking to 'do' the truth." McGovern, *Liberation Theology and Its Critics*, p. 32.

132. McGovern, *Liberation Theology and Its Critics*, p. 33.

of. Of course, social analysis plays a constitutive part in his liberative theological agenda. He does not imply a mere social activism devoid of transforming activity and conversion, and aims at a transformation wrought by the Spirit and a conversion to Christo-centrism.

At the same time, some of his critics are right in saying that Gutiérrez does not delve deep into various dimensions of "means and methods" questions.[133] What is the direction that a liberating praxis should take ? What are the means of liberation agenda necessary to usher in the Kingdom? What are the means and methods to be avoided? These questions await answers from Gutiérrez. It is true that Gutiérrez describes a wide array of movements and groups that fall under the general heads of "the process of liberation in Latin America" and "the church in the process of liberation" (in Chapter 6 and 7 of *A Theology of Liberation*) but, as Arthur F. McGovern points out, "in determining concretely the direction that liberating praxis should take, this same broad base seems hardly adequate."[134]

A Christo-centric Spirituality

Liberation spirituality is the "particular way of being a Christian" who is defined as a follower of Jesus.[135] The following of Jesus takes place within a person's particular historical context and cultural situation. For Christians Jesus Christ is the point of mediation of their faith in and contact with God; He is the prototype and paradigm of the Christian life. Further, a Christian discerns the will of God in accordance with the structures through which Jesus followed the will of his Father.[136]

---

133. An overview of some of the critics (Latin American, European, North American) is given by Arthur F. McGovern. See Chapter 3 of his *Liberation Theology and Its Critics*, pp. 47-61.

134. McGovern, *Liberation Theology and Its Critics*, p. 33. A critique of the position of Gutiérrez will be taken up in my final chapter.

135. Gutiérrez, *We Drink from Our Own Wells*, p. 1.

136. Though this Christological approach to spirituality is very consistently given by Jon Sobrino (*Christology at the Cross roads*, pp. 388-

Christ-centeredness is crucial to this spirituality of liberation.[137] It is important to note that Gutiérrez starts his book on the spiritual journey of a people (*We Drink from Our Own Wells*) with the clause, "A Christian is defined as a follower of Jesus". Jesus is the *centre* of the spirituality of "We drink from our own wells." This Jesus-centrality gives the struggle for human freedom, which is the core of liberation theology as such, its unique dimension. Paying close attention to the intimate encounters with Jesus that are handed down to us in the *New Testament*, Gutiérrez takes pains to articulate this centrality making its exposition the core of his book.[138]

The following of Jesus implies commitment to a mission. The mission that requires the followers, like their master, "to pitch camp in the midst of human history and there give witness to the Father's love."[139] Further, it is a witness to life. One's witness to "life" implies a passage through death.[140] In his understanding of Mark 8: 27-35, where Christ is asking about his disciples' understanding of his identity, Gutiérrez explains the nature of the real following. This question, "Who do you say that I am ?," is directed to every Christian. Our answer cannot just be theoretical or theological. Addressed to the various events of our daily life, and the life of the entire church, "(I)t (this question) permanently tests the Christian faith, leading it to its ultimate consequences."[141] The following of Jesus means, "paying the price of rejection, of calumny, or even of the surrender of their own lives," and is ultimately,

95), Gutiérrez too gives an added emphasis to Christ-centredness of the spirituality of liberation that he proposes.

137. See Henri J.M. Nouwen's "Foreward" to the book *We Drink from Our Own Wells*, p. xvii.

138. Ch. 3 ("Encounter with the Lord"), Ch. 4 ("Walking according to the Spirit"), and a good portion of Ch. 5 ("People in search of a God"), specifically deals with this question of Jesus-centrality.

139. Gutiérrez, *We Drink from Our Own Wells*, p. 41.

140. *Ibid.*, p. 45.

141. *Ibid.*, p. 51.

"oriented to the horizon of resurrection, definitive life."[142]

Following of Jesus is also opting for the cross. The only way to receive the gift of filiation, the status of the children of God is

> an option for Christ's cross, in the hope of his resurrection. This is what we celebrate in the Eucharist: we express our wish and intent to make our own the meaning Jesus Christ gave to his life, and to receive the Spirit, the gift of loving as he loved.[143]

Ultimately the person of Christ is the way: "To follow the way is to live in Christ the Lord (Col. 2: 6). For the Christian way is not directed by an external law; it is identified with a person, with Jesus, the free man."[144] The person of Christ is the Law. Dealing in detail with the conversion experience of Paul, Gutiérrez argues for this identification. Drawing on Acts 9: 1-5, Gutiérrez sees the connection between the "the way" and the spiritual conversion experience of Paul. Thus an encounter with the Person of Christ in the poor constitutes an authentic spiritual experience. It is a life in the Spirit, the bond of love between Father and Son, between God and human being, and between human being and human being. It is in this profound community that Christians involved in a concrete historical liberation praxis strive to live — in love for Christ in solidarity with the poor, in faith in our status as children of the Father as we forge a society of sisters and brothers, and in the hope of Christ's salvation in a commitment to the liberation of the oppressed.[145]

In short, once we understand the depth of love that is manifested in accepting Christ as the way, the norm for all other actions, the Law guiding as well as directing human endeavors, "even faith and hope will cease to be necessary,

---

142. Gutiérrez, *We Drink from Our Own Wells*, p. 51.

143. Gutiérrez, *The Power of the Poor in History*, p. 52.

144. Gutiérrez, *We Drink from Our Own Wells*, p. 82.

145. Gutiérrez, *The Power of the Poor in History*, p. 53.

because we shall see God 'face to face.' Only love will remain, the love that, as we already know, is the supreme fruit of the Spirit." In this way, one is not performing an action with the hope of a reward; ultimately, one recognizes that the fruit and reward of good actions, are good actions themselves; the reward of virtue is virtue itself. Here one cannot but love, knowing that the reward of love is love itself.

The way in question, the way that seals the witness given by the Christian community, is the way of the Spirit — which is to say, the way of love that expresses itself in deeds. It is the way of salvation, the way of the Lord, the way of God. Paul calls this way "the law of the Spirit of life in Christ Jesus," which has set us free "from the law of sin and death" (Rom. 8: 2), because "if you are led by the Spirit you are not under the law" (Gal. 5: 18). We live in the regime of grace: "you are not under the law but under grace" (Rom. 6: 14), and of freedom: "for freedom Christ has set us free; stand fast therefore, and do not submit again to a yoke of slavery (*douleias*)" (Gal. 5: 1).

A Way of "Walking According to the Spirit"[146]

Christo-centrism, thus, takes us to walking in accordance with the Spirit: "Spirituality, in the strict and profound sense of the word is the dominion of the Spirit," says Gutiérrez.[147] This Spirit, which "will guide you into all the truth" (John 16: 13), the truth that "will set you free" (John 8: 32), "will lead us to complete freedom, the freedom from everything that hinders us from fulfilling ourselves as men and sons of God and the freedom to love and to enter into communion with God and with others. It will lead us along the path of liberation."[148] Inaugurated at the initial encounter with the Lord, this *following* (discipleship), makes its journey "walking according to the Spirit" (Rom. 8: 4).

146. In his book *We Drink from Our Own Wells,* Gutiérrez devotes a whole chapter (Chapter 4) to this theme of "Walking according to the Spirit"

147. Gutiérrez, *A Theology of Liberation*, p. 203.

148. *Ibid.*, pp. 203-04.

Explaining the deep meaning of Paul, Gutiérrez affirms:

> By this he means a life proper to the follower of Jesus and
> opposed to ways of life inspired by other perspectives. The
> disciple of the Lord lives in and according to the Spirit who
> is freedom and love because the Spirit is *life,* and not
> according to the "flesh," which is law and sin because it is
> *death.* Jesus himself promises us the gift of the Spirit, which
> is to accompany us on the road that leads us to "all the
> truth" (John 16: 13). The presence of the Spirit sets the
> "messianic people" (*Lumen Gentium,* no. 9) in motion for its
> quest of God.[149]

A life according to the Spirit is "a life that is in accordance
with God's will — that is, a life in accordance with the gift of
divine filiation that finds expression in human fellowship."[150]
Hence filiation and fellowship are the two dimensions of a
life centered in the Spirit.

In this life-journey process we have not yet fully attained
the goal. And it is possible to retrogress on the journey. There
is a dynamism (this dynamism stands in contrast to the
passivity and even weakness of the human person that are
conveyed by the word "flesh") as well as vitality — "The
Spirit is life" (Rom 8: 10) — that are expressed in this 'way of
life in accord with the Spirit.'

A Grass-root intimacy Spirituality

Careful listening to the people of God, *a fortiori* the poor, and
to their daily experiences and encounters makes this
spirituality something very special.[151] The daily concrete
experiences of the Christian community in Latin America form
the general context from which this spirituality is drawn.

149. Gutiérrez, *We Drink from Our Own Wells,* p. 55.

150. *Ibid.,* p. 62.

151. Henri Nouwen calls this the "inductive character" of the spirituality
as developed by Gutiérrez in *We Drink from Our Own Wells.* By this he
means that "this spirituality is drawn from the concrete daily experiences
of the Christian communities in Latin America." (See his "Foreword" to
Gutiérrez's work, *We Drink from Our Own Wells,* p. xix.)

Gutiérrez affirms, "The fact is that daily contact with the experiences of some, a reading of the writings of many, and the testimony of still others have convinced me of the profound spiritual experiences that persons among us are living today."[152]

The faith-elicited question evoking hope is "What is God doing in the midst of suffering ?" Gutiérrez gives moving texts written by various Christians who, in spite of their intense suffering and persecution, are witnesses of the hope-giving God. Out of the intimacy he experiences with the lowly and the abandoned erupted this seminal spirituality — a new way of walking in the journey of life, in solidarity with the poor.

An Historically-involved Community Enterprise

As a community enterprise, this spirituality "is the passage of a people through the solitude and dangers of the desert, as it carves out its own way in the following of Jesus Christ."[153] "The "walking" is that of an entire people," The biblical paradigms "bring home to us the fact that the journey is a community journey and that it is also all-embracing."[154]

This journey is undertaken in concrete history involving oneself in tangible historical realities. God reveals the mystery of God's personhood in concrete history, and God's word comes to us in proportion to our involvement in historical becoming. But this history is a conflictual one, a history of conflicts of interest, of struggles for greater justice, a history of the marginalization and exploitation of human beings, of aspirations for liberation. To make an option for the poor, for the exploited classes, to identify with their lot and share their fate, is to seek to make this history that of an authentic community of brothers and sisters.[155]

---

152. As quoted by Henri J.M. Nouwenn, in his "Foreword" to *We Drink from Our Own Wells*, p. xxi.

153. Gutiérrez, *We Drink from Our Own Wells*, p. 41. p. 137.

154. *Ibid.*, p. 4.

155. Gutiérrez, *The Power of the Poor in History*, p. 52.

A Preferentially-opted spirituality

A reflection on Jesus-centrality and the Biblical God as experienced and mediated in the scriptures leads Gutiérrez to claim that the Christian spirituality he proposes is a preferentially opted spirituality; an option made in favour of the poor: "The spirituality of liberation will have its point of departure in the spirituality of the *anawim*."[156] Christian commitment ought to be manifested in time spent working

156. Gutiérrez, *The Power of the Poor in History*, p. 53.

The study of George M. Soares-Prabhu, a biblical scholar, concerning the biblical poor and God's special concern for the poor is worth noting. His findings confirm what Santa Ana and other liberation theologians have written on this topic. The Hebrew word, *anawim* is very often used to designate the poor in the Bible. It derives from the root meaning "to be bent, bowed down, afflicted," and it implies persons who have been dehumanized and reduced by oppression to a condition of *diminished worth*. In a secondary sense it also takes a religious meaning; those who are powerless and in poverty "bend before God" and put their faith and trust in God. There are other words also used to designate the poor: *ebyon*, connoting a person in material need; *dal*, its root means low, weak, and powerless; *rash*, that has an unambiguous sense of economic poverty. Of these, Soares-Prabhu notes, *anawim* offers the most significant meaning, embracing the various aspects contained in the other terms. In the Bible *anawim* (the poor of Yahweh) is connoted as victims of oppression; they are also those through whom history is redeemed. Soares-Prabhu spells out the role of the poor in three propositions:

1. The poor in the *Old Testament* are primarily the sociological poor. They comprise several groups: impoverished and indebted peasants who live in distress without being utterly destitute; the destitute, including unemployed and landless workers, bonded laborers, and beggars; all those who are afflicted or oppressed (they are not just the economically needy; and the spiritually poor (in postexilic times). In the *New Testament* the Greek word *ptochos* is often used to refer to the poor; it connotes persons who are destitute and must beg for a living. Though many exegetes in the past are given to spiritualize the meaning of poor, nowadays they are coming to recognize the poor as a sociological category.

2. Though wisdom literature sometimes attributes poverty to internal factors (laziness, drunkenness), the rest of the Bible ascertain poverty in external factors: the exploitation of the poor by elite, dominant groups. In

directly with the poor in the struggle for liberation. In his time spent with the poor Gutiérrez discovered three things:

> I discovered that poverty was a destructive thing, something to be fought against and destroyed, not merely something which was the object of our charity. Secondly, I discovered that poverty was not accidental. The fact that these people are poor and not rich is not just a matter of chance, but the result of a structure. It was a structural question. Thirdly, I discovered that poor people were a social class. When I discovered that poverty was something to be fought against . . . it became crystal clear that in order to serve the poor, one had to move into political action.[157]

---

the *Old Testament* the poor are opposed not so much to the rich, but to the powerful, the wicked who exploit them. In the *New Testament* the emphasis is not on conflict and exploitation. Here the contrast is between the poor and the rich who are indifferent to the poor.

3. The poor have a significant role in biblical history. They are not presented as a group of passive victims. The poor continue to be the bearers of salvation and hope in the *New Testament*. Clearly the early church thought of itself as a church of the poor (1 Cor 1: 26-28). George M. Soares-Prabhu, S.J., "Class in the Bible: The Biblical Poor a Social Class?," in *Vidyajyoti* 49 (1985): 325-46. Also see John R. Donahue, "Biblical Perspectives on Justice," in *The Faith That Does Justice: Examining the Christian Sources for Social Change,* edited by John C. Haughey (New York: Paulist Press, 1977), pp. 68-112.

157. José Miguez Bonino recounts the experiences of Gutiérrez in a statement that is quoted in the *Theology of the Americas,* ed. Sergio Torres and John Eagleson (Maryknoll, New York: Orbis, 1976), p. 278; as quoted by McGovern, *Liberation Theology and Its Critics,* p. 28. They are cited also by Robert McAfee Brown, *Gustavo Gutiérrez: An Introduction to Liberation Theology* (Maryknoll, New York: Orbis, 1990), p. 32. In his end-notes McAfee Brown mentions that the autobiographical dimension is not retained in the published version of the talk given by Gutiérrez at a meeting of liberation theologians in Spain in 1972. Bonino also was present at the meeting. The reference we have from Bonino is his reconstruction of the notes he took at the meeting. See Brown, *op. cit.,* Note No. 4, p. 206.

In his recapturing the personal thrust of Gustavo's comments from the published text as well as from Bonino's brief reconstruction, Brown observes concerning the third aspect of Gutiérrez's discovery, "Consequently, to opt for the poor is to opt *for* one social class and *against* other social classes, to

This movement to political action in no way manifests a reductionist approach to liberation. For Gutiérrez insists, "Christ's liberation is not reduced to political liberation, but Christ's liberation occurs in liberating historical events . . . in the concrete historical and political circumstances of today."[158] Commitment to the process of liberation forces Christians to make a "qualitative leap" (the radical challenging of a social order and of its ideology, and the breaking with old ways of knowing), and to experience the budding of a new type of understanding of faith that helps us to link knowing and transforming, theory and practice.[159] Faith becomes a "liberating praxis" battling with sin which now has the wider structural connotation of "oppressive structures created for the benefit of the few and for the exploitation of people, races, and social classes," rather than the ordinary understanding of sin as

---

become aware of the reality of "class struggle," and to side with the dispossessed, identifying with their concerns and their struggles." (emphasis mine; Brown, op.cit., p. 32) I just wonder whether the real mind of Gutiérrez is captured here. Is an opting *for* one social class *against* another social class for Gutiérrez? Either Gustavo's mind is read incorrectly in Brown's recapture; or Gutiérrez has changed his position; (a third possibility would be a printing error). See what Gutiérrez has to say: "The option for the poor . . . is preferential and not exclusive."(Gutiérrez, *The Power of the Poor in History*, p. 127). The alleged exclusivity is part of the "distorted interpretations abroad," and it "would be an evident mutilation of the gospel message. That message is directed to every human being, as someone loved by God and redeemed by His Son. The gospel is not anyone's private property, to do with as one might wish. *Preference* for the poor is written into the gospel message itself. But this alleged exclusivity, if it gained the upper hand, would — paradoxically — deprive that very preference of its historical "bite."" Gutiérrez, *The Power of the Poor in History*, p. 128. A clarification of this is crucial for comparison of Gandhi and Gutiérrez.

158. *Mission Trends*, No. 3, p. 65; as quoted by Brown, *Gustavo Gutiérrez*, p. 33. Brown mentions that portions of the talk given by Gutiérrez at El Escorial is published in English in "Praxis of Liberation and Christian Faith," Mexican-American Cultural Center, San Antonio, 1976, and as "The Hope of Liberation," in Aderson and Stransky, eds., *Mission Trends*, no. 3, Paulist/ Eerdmans, New York and Grand Rapids, 1976, pp. 64-69.

159. See Brown, *Gustavo Gutiérrez*, p. 33.

individual inadequacies.[160] Brown singles out the two important reminders that Gutiérrez offered in his concluding remark:

1. Our praxis involves an *identification with persons,* especially the interests and conflicts of those social classes that suffer "misery and exploitation," and Christ's liberating praxis must be announced "from within that process."

2. The crucial factor, however, will not be "our" identification with "them." It will be the liberation of previously subjected groups who can "freely and creatively express themselves in society and among the people of God." so that they can become "the artisans of their own liberation."[161]

The first point illustrates the matter under discussion of the preferential option and the second leads to an important notion of liberation spirituality, namely, the notion of the empowerment of the powerless to become architects of their own liberation, the gratuitous gift of God given in Jesus Christ.

This preferential attention is given to the poor irrespective of the moral or personal situation in which they find themselves. Gutiérrez reasserts what was already emphasized at Pueblo,

> The preference for the poor is based on the fact that God, as Christ shows us, loves them for their concrete, real condition of poverty, "whatever may be" their moral or spiritual disposition. . . . The preferential option is for the poor as such, the poor as poor. The value of their attitude of openness toward God is not neglected. . . . But this does not constitute the primary motive of the privilege of the poor.[162]

This preference is written into the gospel message itself and the privilege of the poor has its theological basis in God.[163]

---

160. *Gustavo Gutiérrez,* p. 33.

161. *Mission Trends,* p. 69; as quoted by Brown, *Gustavo Gutiérrez,* pp. 33-34.

162. Gutiérrez, *The Power of the Poor in History,* p. 138.

163. Gutiérrez, *The Power of the Poor in History,* Gutiérrez makes a

To believe and to love such a God who loved us first, is "to be in solidarity with the poor and the exploited of this world in the midst of social confrontations and popular struggle for liberation. To believe is to proclaim the kingdom as Christ does — from the midst of the struggle for justice that led him to his death."[164]

Also the prophets have categorically proclaimed the truth of the gratuitous character of God's love for the poor:

> Prophetic language makes it possible to draw near to a God who has a predilection for the poor precisely because divine love refuses to be confined by the categories of human justice. God has a preferential love for the poor not because they are necessarily better than others, morally or religiously, but simply because they are poor and living in an inhuman situation that is contrary to God's will. The ultimate basis for the privileged position of the poor is not in the poor themselves but in God, in the gratuitousness and universality of God's *agapeic love*.[165]

A Spirituality of Empowerment

Emphasizing the newness of this newly erupted spirituality Gutiérrez says,

> Our increasingly clear awareness of the harsh situation in Latin America and the sufferings of the poor must not make us overlook the fact that the harshness and suffering are not what is truly new in the present age. What is new is not wretchedness and repression and premature death, for these, unfortunately, are ancient realities in these countries. *What is new is that the people are beginning to grasp the causes of*

---

further observation: "The exploited strata of society are the concrete, historical agents of a new understanding of the faith. The God of the Bible reveals himself through those despoiled of their dignity as a people and as human beings. He manifests himself in those the gospel calls "the poor" and "the least"." See Gutiérrez, *The Power of the Poor in History*, p. 213.

164. Gutiérrez, *The Power of the Poor in History*, p. 20.

165. Gutiérrez, *On Job: God-Talk and the Suffering of the Innocent* (Maryknoll, New York: Orbis Boks, 1987), p. 94.

*their situation of injustice and are seeking to release themselves
from it.* Likewise new and important is the role which faith
in the God who liberates is playing in the process.[166]

Gutiérrez considers the present moment of history as an
exceptional and favourable time in the history and life of the
Latin American Church. Gathering courage from the very
source of their life — a living faith in the God of Jesus Christ;
and God's preferential, committed love — they "see the truth
and speak out when others remain silent," in the sure
knowledge of the preferential love that God has for them.[167]

Gutiérrez advocates empowerment of the people especially
the poor to become agents of their own history: "The future
of history lies with the poor and the exploited. Authentic
liberation will be the deed of the oppressed themselves; in
them the Lord will save history."[168] Emphasis should be put
on the "action" of the poor in confronting their life-situation.
In his approach to the *new way* of doing theology, "a theology
of liberating transformation of the history of mankind and
also therefore that part of mankind — gathered into *ecclesia*
— which openly confesses Christ,"[169] Gutiérrez would have
the poor become active agents of the process of liberative
transformation. The oppressed need to "break with their
present situation and take control of their own destiny."[170]

Methodology is the Spirituality

When Gutiérrez speaks of the commitment to the struggles of
the poor, he is not just raising a simple question of theological
methodology. He is talking "about a specific way of
understanding what it means to be a Christian. We are framing
method (Greek *hodos*, 'way' or 'path') within the broader
context of the Christian life. And in the Acts of the Apostles

---

166. Gutiérrez, *We Drink from Our Own Wells*, p. 20. My emphasis.
167. Gutiérrez, *We Drink from Our Own Wells*, p. 23.
168. Gutiérrez, *The Power of the Poor in History*, p. 53.
169. Gutiérrez, *A Theology of Liberation*, p. 15.
170. *Ibid.*, p. 35.

we find that the Christian life is actually described as "the way" initiated by Jesus. — (Acts 9: 2, 18: 25, 19: 9)."[171] Therefore a real and committed theological methodology

> reflects a way of living the faith; it has to be with the following of Jesus. As a matter of fact, *our methodology is our spirituality.* There is nothing surprising about this. After all, the word "method" comes from *hodos,* "way." Reflection on the mystery of God (for that is what a theology is) is possible only in the context of the following of Jesus. Only when one is walking according to the Spirit one can think and proclaim the gratuitous love of the Father for every human being.[172]

There is a call here to follow a "way" (*derek* in Hebrew) characterized by certain behaviour, in the manner of life one ought to lead. Witnessing at once reflects a manner of thinking and a mode of acting. In short, this "way of life," laying emphasis on an ethical approach, "extends to the whole of life."[173] Interpreting St. Paul (1 Cor. 4: 17) Gutiérrez argues "to follow the *way* is to practice certain *conduct* . . . conduct in the service of God. It is a manner of life that is taught through witness and that can in turn be followed by others."[174] What we see here is that the "walking" is the road itself.[175] The particular style of life is the particular way of living one's faith in the Lord, of living according to the Spirit. This is the methodology. This is, at the same time, the spirituality.[176]

---

171. Gutiérrez, "Reflections from a Latin American Perspective: Finding Our Way to Talk about God," in Fabella and Torres, Editors, *Irruption of the Third World,* p. 225.

172. Gutiérrez, *We Drink from Our Own Wells,* p. 136. My emphasis.

173. *Ibid.,* p. 81.

174. *Ibid.*

175. Does the "walking" create it own particular "path", its own "road" specific and peculiar to itself? Gutiérrez often speaks of "walking" according to the Spirit; and in that process one proclaims the gratuitous love of the Father for every human being. Is the "path" already laid out in advance and now it is only a question of "walking"? This is a question Gandhi would ask Gutiérrez. I shall return to this in my concluding chapter.

176. Here it is question of understanding spirituality in the strict sense

A Contemplative in Action

Any serious approach to spirituality has to grapple with the question of presence to the world and presence to the Lord. The problem is how to reconcile both "presences" without a *split* in spiritual experience. Living in a one-dimensional fashion seems to be the easy way out. Running away from the world — to the desert, to the forests, to the caves of mountains, or to the banks of rivers — or an absolute immersion in the world of mundane affairs without an experience of the Lord or the spiritual are common in history. The lack of vital unity that is

---

of the word. According to Gutiérrez, there is an epistemological break in the work and understanding of theologizing. This implies a break in the way we live as Christians. See Gutiérrez, "Reflections from a Latin American Perspective: Finding Our Way to Talk about God," in Fabella and Torres, editors, *Irruption of the Third World*, p. 226.

The intimate and inseparable connection between theology and spirituality, and between liberationist theology and an integral spirituality might be captured, according to Roger Haight, in the notion of contemplation. As his reflection is very informative, I quote him at length: "Theology, as an interpretation of reality in terms of the symbols of Christian revelation, provides a vision of reality, a way of seeing the world and history in relation to God. For Christians this faith vision evokes the contemplative attitude out of which they fashion the whole of their lives in the world. This contemplation does not escape from the world and history in an ascending vertical direction. Rather it is a contemplation rooted in hope, faith and love that experiences God within the world and, as transcendent as God is, nowhere else. This contemplative attitude of this spirituality hopes that God will forge the Kingdom of God in the end time out of what we actually see and experience in history. This spirituality has a faith that sees the Kingdom of God in the little bits and pieces of history where people are being served and cared for by other people. This faith sees God's hand working through human agency in this; these little victories in the struggle for the emancipation and liberation of other human beings are the ultimate experiential ground of faith that justifies hope. And, finally, the faith and hope of this spirituality is informed by love, because only through participating in this movement of history can faith and hope continue to survive. One thus contemplates God within history; and one is a contemplative in and by one's action in history." Haight, *An Alternative Vision: An Interpretation of Liberation Theology*, p. 256.

found in such approaches "is the separation that takes place . . . between prayer and action. Both are accepted as necessary, and in fact they are. The problem is to establish a connection between them. Good-will solutions ("everything is prayer"; "I pray with the people") do not eliminate the problem."[177]

In fact, they compound it. Gutiérrez offers an authentic unity "based on a synthesis of elements that are seemingly disparate but that in fact enrich one another."[178] The clue is to be found in various spiritualities offered in course of the history of the Church especially in that of an Ignatian spirituality. Ignatius of Loyola's emphasis on effective action and on a prudent charity represents a convincing contribution to Christian spirituality at the threshold of the modern age. In the Ignatian insight of "finding God in all things" one can find the unity of action-contemplation, which a first-generation jesuits summed up in the phrase "contemplative in action."[179] The recovery of the vital unity between prayer and action must be, asserts Gutiérrez, the result of an effort to be faithful, in both prayer and concrete commitments, to the will of the Lord in the midst of the poor.

A Spirituality of Conversion

There is an unmistakable call to conversion in Gutiérrez. The process of evangelical conversion takes place in concrete conditions of history and in historical becoming. As central

---

177. Gutiérrez, *We Drink from Our Own Wells*, p. 17.

178. *Ibid.*, p. 18.

179. See Gutiérrez, *The Truth Shall Make You Free: Confrontations*, p. 44. This "Contemplation in Action" of Ignatian spirituality is, according to Gutiérrez, "one of the most notable and fruitful of the successful efforts for a synthesis." See *We Drink from Our Own Wells*, p. 143. Gutiérrez emphasizes the same in another place: "The poor person, the other, becomes the revealer of the Utterly Other. Life in this involvement is a life in the presence of the Lord at the heart of political activity, with all its conflict and with all its demand for scientific reasoning. It is the life of — to paraphrase a well-known expression — contemplatives in political action." Gutiérrez, *The Power of the Poor in History*, p. 52.

element of all spirituality, this conversion is an abandonment of oneself and an opening up to God and others. It implies breach, but most of all it implies new departure. And this is precisely why it is not a purely "interior," private attitude, but a process occurring in the socio-economic, political, and cultural milieu in which we live, and which we ought to transform.[180]

As the "starting point of every spiritual journey," conversion requires a cleavage with the life lived up to the juncture of this new starting point. It further implies the decision to embark upon a new journey on a new path. The option for this innovative enterprise is not something static, done once and for all; but "it entails a development, even a painful one, that is not without uncertainties, doubts, and temptations to turn back on the road that has been travelled."[181] The ongoing continuity of the development of the new journey undertaken is a sign of "growth in maturity," a deepening of the faith with the passage of time, an entering into a deeper communion with God.[182]

Conversion, further, implies the very recognition of the possibility of vitiating our relationship with God and of infringing our solidarity with one another. In other words, the perception of personal as well as social sin in our lives and in our world is a step into the journey to solidarity with the poor and oppressed.[183] When it exists, such infringement hinders the creation of a just and human society. This simply shows that conversion process is an absolute necessity and a positive requirement for solidarity with the poor — a solidarity "not with 'the poor' in the abstract but with human beings of flesh and bone."[184] Thus Gutiérrez makes it very clear that

180. Gutiérrez, *The Power of the Poor in History*, pp. 53-54.
181. Gutiérrez, *We Drink from Our Own Wells*, p. 95.
182. *Ibid.*, pp. 95-96.
183. *Ibid.*, p. 97.
184. *Ibid.*, p. 104.

"the solidarity required by the preferential option for the poor forces us back to a fundamental Christian attitude: a grasp of the need for continual conversion. We are then able to find in the break with former ways and in our chosen new way deeper dimensions of a personal and social, material and spiritual, kind."[185] A determined decision, a steadfast "stubbornness," is necessary to overcome difficulties and obstacles on the road that is undertaken.

Magnificat: An Admirable Expression

Finally, it is a spirituality that perceives the Magnificat as its prime paradigm. The spirituality of liberation expressed in the Magnificat is revealing in its comprehensiveness. A thanksgiving song for the gifts of the Lord, it is the expression of the humble joy of being loved "for the Almighty has done great things for me" (Lk 1: 49). At the same time, in this "most liberating and political passage in the *New Testament*," thanksgiving and joy "are intimately bound up with the liberating activity of God in favour of the oppressed and God's bringing low the mighty: "He has pulled down princes from their thrones and exalted the lowly. The hungry he has filled with good things, the rich sent empty away. (Luke 1: 52-53)."[186]

While exploring effective means to bring about changes needed to expedite the Kingdom, this new spirituality fully recognizes the gratuitousness of God's unconditional love. While experiencing joy, the people, suffering though they may be, give evidence "of a profound sense of prayer and of a conviction that in the final analysis love and peace are unexpected gift of God."[187]

Conclusion

Thus in fact, when understood it in its totality, spirituality includes, what is meant by the notion of liberation. It

185. Gutiérrez, *We Drink from Our Own Wells*, p. 106.

186. Gutiérrez, *The Power of the Poor in History*, p. 53.

187. Gutiérrez, *We Drink from Our Own Wells*, p. 111.

comprehends *all of life,* including the way in which Christians, *followers* and not just *imitators* of Christ, live every facet of their existence — personal, social, economic, political, cultural, business, as well as prayer, meditation, contemplation, and action. The fullness of reality would be the point of reference for such a spirituality. There is no province of human existence outside the sphere of influence of such a spirituality. In such a "contemplative action" a personal and communal encounter with Christ and a commitment to God are inseparable from an encounter and commitment to the neighbour — one who is in need, especially the poor. In this simultaneous commitment to God and the other, the realization of the kingdom of God is expedited. Caves in mountains, the arid deserts, or the serene cathedrals, decorated temples and mosques are too limited to contain the wholesome presence of the God of such a spirituality. At the same time, the heart of an individual is big enough to reveal Him through loving actions. Thus we see that spirituality is a way of living one's faith. It has to do with the following of Jesus in every concrete encounter of a person, in sleep or in wakeful hours.

As a community enterprise, spirituality is, concludes Gutiérrez in his book on the spiritual journey of a people, "the passage of a people through the solitude and dangers of the desert, as it carves out its own way in the following of Jesus Christ. This spiritual experience is the well from which we must drink. From it we draw the promise of resurrection."[188]

Conclusion

Thus we see that both Gandhi and Gutiérrez have proposed spiritualities of action specific to their pattern of "doing" theology and "searching" for truth. The Gandhian method of *ahiṁsātmaka satyāgraha* for socio-political transformation insists very much on means consonant with the goal of human search

---

188. Gutiérrez, *We Drink from Our Own Wells,* p. 137.

for truth. Gutiérrez's proposal of "Drinking from our own wells" points to a spirituality of contemplative-action. Those who have embraced such spiritualities of liberation could easily make Tagore's supplication their own:

This is my prayer to thee, my lord —
strike, strike at the root of penury in my heart.
Give me the strength lightly to bear my joys and sorrows.
Give me the strength to make my love fruitful in service.
Give me the strength never to disown the poor
or bend my knees before insolent might.
Give me the strength to raise my mind high above daily trifles.
And give me the strength to surrender my strength
to thy will with love.[189]

And,

It shall be my endeavour to reveal thee in my actions,
knowing it is thy power gives me strength to act.[190]

---

189. Tagore, *Gītāñjalī*, p. 21.
190. *Ibid.*, p. 3.

5

The Goal of Liberative Transformation

Introduction

EVEN though their notions of liberation sprung from their respective foundations, and corresponding means were advocated by them, both Gandhi and Gutiérrez envisioned an utopian "order" where love, peace, justice, communion, freedom, and harmony would reign. That order is not independent of their vision of the final destiny of humankind as a whole. This is the goal of their respective liberation agenda. Gutiérrez calls it as the symbol of the Kingdom of God. The final goal of the Gandhian *swarāj* is his utopian notion of *Rāmarājya* — the reign of Rāmacandra, the great hero of the *Rāmāyaṇa* epic.[1] In their effort to outline the elements of personal and social transformatory processes both Gandhi and Gutiérrez envisioned an ideal community which they firmly believed could fashion human living into a pattern of mutual enrichment and expedite the coming of the reign of God.

1. The Gandhian utopia of a democratic polity is suggested by the symbol of *Rāmarājya*, the reign of Rāma, the kingdom of Rāma. It is a religious symbol equivalent to the kingdom of God, understood mainly as a temporal reign. As a popular leader of the Indian masses, Gandhi knew that the presentation of his utopian vision in a religious-emotional symbol would bring home to the masses the ideal to be reached. Gandhi was rather vague in his description of such a reign of Ram. His vision was only roughly sketched and not worked out in detail.

Gandhian Rāmarājya

The option for an ascetical, mystical, or purely spiritual life un-involved in the mundane activities of everyday life had no relevance to the pursuit of the good life and ideal society that Gandhi envisaged. He, visualized an ideal community, a society of mutuality, love and concern, which he named *Rāmarājya* (Kingdom of Rāma). This "kingdom" could shape the social living in a new manner worthy of the human. Gandhi's vision emerged only slowly, as he gave clearer attention to the interweaving of the mundane and the divine dimensions in human life.

Though the immediate context of Gandhi's *swarāj* was Indian society, he had a global vision of a liberated society, of a new and unique social order. Centred around real human happiness, it aimed at the development of the human spirit — the soul within. His starting premise is that the social reconstruction is impossible unless we try to remake individuals as well.

Gandhi envisioned a society of mutual regard and common human concern. The translation of his notion of the essential unity of all life into concrete terms in social, political, and economic realms lay at the foundations, as it were, of his envisioned *Rāmarājya*. This *Rāmarājya* in its mundane form stands on the foundation of ethics and morality. In the social arena Gandhi advocated a *sarvodaya samāj* — a society where the welfare of one and all is actively sought after.[2] In the political sphere he championed decentralization and a stateless democracy. In the realm of economics he proposed his famous trusteeship theory. The universal character of Gandhian *swarāj*, combined with self-determination in polity, enabled Gandhi to enlarge his objective beyond the periphery of a particular nation state to the concept of a society wherein his essential

---

2. *Sarvodaya samāj* is made up of three Sanskrit words, *sarva* = all, *udaya* = rise, and *samāj* = society. Hence it implies a society in which the greatest good of all is the end sought after.

unity of all life could be translated into concrete social, political, and economic terms.

Sarvodaya stresses the immense significance of the village community. Gandhi always advocated a village economy. By means of reorganizing village communities he wanted to deepen the bonds of love and mutual accountability. From both the psychological and ethical standpoints there is great value in small communities. From the psychological standpoint they intensify the bonds of mutuality. From the ethical angle they are centres which impose a system of social norms that integrate the individual to the community. This will help in putting a healthy restraint upon the excessive individualism which grows uninhibited in cities.

Gandhi was not trying to found a celestial city on earth. Nor was he willing to separate the various dimensions of human life, political, religious, spiritual, temporal, demarcating what is Caesar's from what is God's, "the city of God and the city of man." His "vision splendid," in the phrase of Margaret Chatterjee, is grounded "in a metaphysic of existence which embraces the inorganic, the organic, the individual and society — all environed in the divine dimension in which they have their being."[3] Thus, envisioned in the horizon of the divine, this society is woven into a united whole. Humans stand in a relational dimension with the organic and the inorganic, and with one another, in the divine horizon in which they have their being and existence. In a strange mix of natural law argument, Gandhi held that ordinary humans are endowed with a natural capacity to employ a non-violent strength in the cause of transforming human society and human relationship. Living in harmonious relationship can create and release powerful energy to bring about changes to achieve a new equilibrium. No human encounter is neutral. Every human encounter releases some sort of energy. A conflictual one leads to the release of destructive force that disharmonizes and

3. Chatterjee, *Gandhi's Religious Thought*, p. 137.

destroys concord. An encounter in a common search (for truth, for instance), a living together in harmony and in serenity, helps the community to achieve a new and higher equilibrium of concord and peacefulness. In order to achieve this equilibrium Gandhi stressed the value of *tapasyā*.[4] His proposal of *tapasyā* was to release a new life-affirming energy to neutralize, as it were, the disharmonizing energy that is usually let loose by conflictual, *a fortiori*, military encounters and by "this mad rush to kill." He thought, that hatred and enmity could be neutralized by the positive actions of self-suffering love.

One has to strive positively for the establishment of such a society. Precisely because conflictual processes release disharmonizing forces, disturbing and even destroying the equilibrium of peaceful coexistence, that a new, positive, harmonizing force, especially through *tapasyā* (self-suffering), ought to be discharged. This is aimed at, not on individual ascetical perfection, but to achieve a transformation of society and social relations. Such a *tapasyā* has the inherent capacity to build bridges of harmonious relational existence. The establishment of such a society of mutuality and love is the whole aim of Gandhian liberation.

Gandhi denounced the acquisitive, competitive, consumeristic society produced by the modern industrial and techno-centric civilization which breeds impersonality, the denial of the individual and of personal creativity in the work place. Gandhi was not attracted to a Marxist ideal of a classless society either; centralization of production and loss of

---

4. *Tapasyā* could be described as moral fervor, self-sacrifice, austerity. The deeper meaning of *ahiṁsā* is *tapasyā* (self-suffering), the quality of accepting pain within oneself instead of inflicting it on another. Such an acceptance is of the very nature of love that is *ahiṁsā*. "The test of love is *tapasyā* and *tapasyā* means self-suffering." *Young India*, June 12, 1922. See also *Young India*, July 1931; *Young India*, April 18, 1929. In a *satyāgraha* struggle, *tapasyā* would imply a stage of emotional persuasion of the other (an opponent) through self-suffering so that *satya* (truth) may prevail. See Jesudasan, *A Gandhian Theology of Liberation*, p. 97.

individual freedom could find no place in his scheme. He urged for an alternative social order where freedom and individual creative experience could be fulfilled.

This new society of the Gandhian imagination cannot come about without intense suffering, a suffering not just imposed by external forces but voluntarily undergone for a selfless cause, undergone not in the pursuit of individual ecstatic experiences of the Himālayan caves and personal emancipation from the physical bondage, but for the common good, with the objective of transforming the self and others and for the very affirmation of the physical world which stands in the horizon of the divine.

Though he started his liberation process in the context of a struggle for political freedom, Gandhi did not consider political power as an end in itself, but a means to enable people to better their condition in all aspect of life.[5] In the Gandhian vision of a liberated society, political entities and powers are not ends in themselves.

Gandhi's model of the liberated society is intrinsically moral. His unitive and non-dichotomized vision of belief and action, in the context of *mukti, swarāj,* and the presence of moral human beings, was a source of optimism for Gandhi. He wanted an economics that is ethical, a politics that is preoccupied with moral concerns, and a society where the humans are sincerely concerned about one another. He opposed the separating of economics and ethics. Responding to a remark made by Rabindranath Tagore, Gandhi emphasized,

> I must confess that I do not draw a sharp or any distinction between economics and ethics. Economics that hurt the moral well-being of an individual or a nation are immoral and, therefore, sinful. Thus the economics that permit one country to prey upon another are immoral.[6]

---

5. See *Young India*, July 2, 1931.
6. *Young India*, October 13, 1921.

As far as Gandhi is concerned, true economics stands for social justice promoting the good of all, including the weakest.[7] The *Rāmarājya* that he envisaged includes an economy that is liberated, rather than liberal, a polity that has attained *swarāj*, and a people who acts in a mutually responsible *dhārmik* manner. In this liberated economy, the "political" in its root meaning of the communitarian, moral, and religious, affect the economic praxis. In such an economy, the prime issue, then, is not just how wealth is allocated but rather on how wealth is created and acquired.

Envisioning a future world order made up of "ever-widening," "never-ascending circles" of communities, he wrote in a famous passage:

> It (the world human society) will be an oceanic circle whose centre will be the individual, always ready to perish for the village, the latter ready to perish for the circle of villages, till at last the whole becomes one life composed of individuals never aggressive in their arrogance, but ever humble, sharing the majesty of the oceanic circle of which they are integral units.[8]

Suspicious of the state and its violent character, Gandhi told Nirmal Kumar Bose in an interview which was published in *The Hindustan Times*, a prominent daily news paper published from Delhi:

> The State represents violence in a concentrated and organized form. The individual has a soul, but the State is a soulless machine, it can never be weaned from violence to which it owes its very existence. . . . I look upon an increase of the power of the State with the greatest fear, because although while apparently doing good by minimizing exploitation, it does the greatest harm to mankind by destroying individuality, which lies at the root of all progress.[9]

---

7. See *Harijan*, October 9, 1937.

8. *Harijan*, July 28, 1946.

9. *The Hindustan Times*, October 17, 1935; Iyer III: 599.

Hence Gandhi aims at a social order in which "everyone is his own ruler. He rules himself in such a manner that he is never a hindrance to his neighbour. In the ideal state, therefore, there is no political power because there is no state."[10] Gandhi was aware that his "vision splendid" might be branded as utopian and brushed aside. So he added: "I may be taunted that . . . this is all utopian and therefore not worth a single thought. If Euclid's point, though incapable of being drawn by any human agency, has an imperishable value, my picture has its own for mankind."[11]

Thus, the entire superstructure of his social order is based on non-violence. The social order he envisioned was free from moral degradation, economic exploitation, and political subjugation. Based on Truth, non-violence, non-centralization, and *tapasyā*, Gandhi projected a classless, casteless and stateless society in which everyone would find freedom, justice, equality of opportunity, and fulfilment of economic needs. Thus he aimed at a unique social order seeking over-all human happiness and development.

The Kingdom of God According to Gutiérrez

The goal of liberation is expressed by Gutiérrez through the symbol of the Kingdom of God.[12] The symbol of the Kingdom is central to Jesus' teaching. Christ came to proclaim the Kingdom of God to us. His whole life is a revelation of God and of God's Kingdom. The "Kingdom of God" means that God reigns, that "his love, his fatherhood, and a community of brothers and sisters, is going to reign among all human beings."[13] With its coming, the domination of satan, of sin, and of death over human beings is at an end. Gutiérrez's emphasis is that the category of the Kingdom of God, God's

---

10. *Young India*, July 2, 1931.

11. *Harijan*, July 28, 1946.

12. In Part 2 of his *El Dios de la vida* (1988) Gutiérrez deals at length with the subject of the Kingdom of God.

13. Gutiérrez, *The Power of the Poor*, p. 14.

eschatological saving action, has a bearing upon our history here and now. In its objective form, the Kingdom of God is the Kingdom of human fulfilment, the utopic Kingdom of peace and harmony, of justice and joy.[14] Quoting Luke 4: 16-21, Gutiérrez asserts that Christ "is proclaiming a kingdom of justice and liberation, to be established in favor of the poor, the oppressed, and the maginalized of history."[15] In Christ we are faced with the mystery of God's revelation and the gift of his Kingdom of love and justice.[16] In his messianic practice, Christ has revealed the Kingdom to us. Indeed, His messianic practice is the proclamation of the Kingdom of God and the transformation of the historical conditions, especially of the marginalized and the poor.

Human freedom plays a part in the fashioning of this Kingdom. It is God who provides a goal or a direction for that freedom indicating what that freedom is for. It is for the building up of the Kingdom of a transformed relationship of love in history, and beyond the historical process to a life eternal that God offers us as an invitation from love to love — an invitation to a life in Him that one ought to strive.

History is transformed into the Kingdom, and events in history receive their value in the light of the Kingdom transforming history. The kingdom is not the simple *telos* (goal) the progress of history, neither is it a total replacement of human history.

Ultimately the salvific meaning released by Jesus into history and historical praxis by Jesus is *not* some notion of a just comprehensive social order that the humans expect to bring about. The Kingdom of God will not be fully realized in history. Its complete fulfilment is not within the power of mere human freedom either. And yet, the proclamation of the Kingdom by Christ challenges and thus offers a means of

14. See Haight, *An Alternative Vision*, p. 93.
15. Gutiérrez, *The Power of the Poor*, p. 14.
16. *Ibid.*, p. 95.

discernment to human consciousness to see this Kingdom in the bits and pieces of history where mutual love is experienced and justice is established.

The most complete symbol of God's will for history is the Kingdom. God is revealed in history in the process of realizing the Kingdom. The Kingdom means the transformation and fulfilment of history according to the will and nature of God who liberates, establishes justice and right, and gives life. When we do not receive the Kingdom, God himself is denied. In a history of sin and death, the demands of the Kingdom are not met, and God is absent. God is *not*, whenever and wherever the Kingdom is *negated*.[17]

There is an intrinsic relation between God and His Kingdom; and so it is impossible to speak of separating God from the Kingdom:

> God's will is precisely that the kingdom be brought to reality. If we separate God from the divine intent and design, we surely must not believe in God. We are rejecting God's reign. . . . Indeed, the God of the Bible is inseparable from God's will, from the kingdom. Hence any attempt to encounter or comprehend God in isolation from the kingdom is the fabrication of an idol — is the adoration of a different god from the God of Jesus Christ. A god without a kingdom is a fetish, the work of our hands, the negation of the Lord, for a god without a kingdom is contrary to the Lord's designs.[18]

Explaining the growth of the Kingdom as a process that happens historically in liberation, Gutiérrez points out that

17. Gutiérrez, *Dios*, 46; See Araya, *God of the Poor*, p. 75.

18. Gutiérrez, *Dios*, 45-46; as quoted by Araya, *God of the Poor*, p. 76. Miguez Bonino explains a relationship of unity-in-difference: "Thus the kingdom of God is not the negation of history but rather the elimination of its frailty, corruptibility, and ambiguity. Going a bit more deeply, we can say it is the elimination of history's sinfulness so that the authentic import of communitarian life may be realized. In the same way, then, historical 'works' take on permanence in so far as they anticipate this full realization." Bonino, "Historical Praxis and Christian Identity," in *Frontiers of Theology in Latin America*, ed. Gibellini, p. 273.

"Liberation is a precondition for the new society" and "without liberating historical events, there would be no growth of the Kingdom. But the process of liberation will not have conquered the very roots of oppression and the exploitation of man by man without the coming of the Kingdom, which is above all a gift."[19]

Both the growth of the Kingdom and the human liberation are directed toward the complete communion of persons with God and among themselves. The ultimate design of God for human history is that the Kingdom come to realization. The coming of the Kingdom as God's final design for His creation is experienced in the historical process of human liberation. This is very clearly emphasized by Gutiérrez when he says:

> The growth of the Kingdom is a process which occurs historically *in* liberation, insofar as liberation means a greater human fulfilment. Liberation is a precondition for the new society, but this is not all it is. While liberation is implemented in liberating historical events, it also denounces their limitations and ambiguities, proclaims their fulfilment, and impels them effectively towards total communion. This is not an identification. Without liberating historical events, there would be no growth of the Kingdom. But the process of liberation will not have conquered the very roots of human oppression and exploitation without the coming of the Kingdom, which is above all a gift. Moreover, we can say that the historical, political liberating event *is* the growth of the Kingdom and *is* a salvific event;

19. Gutiérrez, *A Theology of Liberation*, p. 177. Leonardo Boff expresses the same sentiment when he says that "The Kingdom of God is the realization of a fundamental utopia of the human heart, the total transfiguration of this world, free from all that alienates human beings, free from pain, sin, divisions, and death. . . . He (Christ) not only promised this new reality but already began to realize it, showing that it is possible in the world. He therefore did not come to alienate human beings and carry them off to another world. He came to confirm the good news: this sinister world has a final destiny that is good, human, and divine." Leonardo Boff, *Jesus Christ Liberator: A Critical Christology for Our Time* (Maryknoll, New York: Orbis Books, 1978), pp. 44-47.

but it is not *the* coming of the Kingdom, not *all* of salvation. It is the historical realization of the Kingdom and, therefore, it also proclaims its fullness. This is where the difference lies. It is a distinction made from a dynamic viewpoint, which has nothing to do with the one which holds for the existence of two juxtaposed "orders," closely connected or convergent, but deep down different from each other.[20]

---

20. Gutiérrez, *A Theology of Liberation*, 15th anniversary edn., p. 104. The "Final Document" of The International Ecumenical Congress of theology (Sao Paulo, 1980) provides us with an explanation of the profound and complex relationship between human history and the Kingdom:

The coming of the Kingdom as God's final design for . . . creation is experienced in the historical processes of human liberation.

On the one hand the Kingdom has a utopian character, for it can never be completely achieved in history; on the other hand, it is foreshadowed and given concrete expression in historical liberations. The Kingdom pervades human liberations; it manifests itself *in* them, but it is not identical *with* them. Historical liberations, by the very fact that they are historical, are limited, but are open to something greater. The Kingdom transcends them. Therefore it is the object of our hope and thus we can pray to the Father: "Thy Kingdom come." Historical liberations incarnate the kingdom to the degree that they humanize life and generate social relationships of greater fraternity, participation, and justice.

To help understand the relationship between the Kingdom and historical liberations we might use the analogy of the mystery of the Incarnation. Just as in one and the same Jesus Christ the divine and the human presence each maintain their identities, without being absorbed or confused, so too is the eschatological reality of the Kingdom and historical liberations.

The liberation and life offered by God surpass everything that we can achieve in history. But these are not offered outside history nor by the passing history. It is all too clear, however, that there are other forces in the world, those of oppression and death. These are the forces of sin, personal and social, that reject the Kingdom and, in practice, deny God. . . .

The Kingdom is grace and must be received as such, but it is also a challenge to new life, to commitment, to liberation and solidarity with the oppressed in the building of a just society. Thus we say that the Kingdom is *of God*; it is grace and God's work. But at the same time it is a demand and a task for human beings" (nos. 33-36, pp. 236-37; as quoted by Araya, *God Of The Poor*, p. 107).

This radicalness and totality of the salvific process gives human history its profound unity, its hope, and its full eschatological communion in the fullness of time. In existential life humans give their response in faith and hope that the Kingdom come. Though in its utopian aspect this Kingdom is not fully attainable through human struggles in history, "faith in God is basically nothing else but continually giving historical, imperfect form (*topos*, "topia") to the trans-historical utopia of the kingdom."[21] Thus there is a tension in the "already" and "not yet" character of the Kingdom; it is already present and active in history; but, at the same time, it is awaiting for its full eschatological fulfilment in the day of the Lord. In its quality of "eschatological plenitude" the Kingdom is not the work of humans but of God. Though "it is a gift of God . . . (it) requires certain behaviours from those who receive it. It is *already* present in history, *but* it does not reach its complete fulfilment therein. Its presence already produces effects, but these are "not *the* coming of the Kingdom, not *all* of salvation"; they are anticipations of a completion that will be realized only beyond history."[22]

Though the growth of the Kingdom is not reduced to temporal progress, any effort to build a just society is liberating indeed, and thus an experience into the growth of the Kingdom.[23] Further, "we see that the very meaning of the growth of the Kingdom is also the ultimate precondition for a just society and a new humanity."[24] The fundamental obstacle to the realization of the Kingdom is sin, the root of all misery and injustice, the negation of love. One reaches this "root" and this "ultimate precondition" only through accepting the

---

21. Araya, *God of the Poor*, p. 106; see also Sobrino, "Dios," p. 109; *Christology*, p. 230; L. Boff, *Jesucristo*, 257-58.

22. Gutiérrez, *A Theology of Liberation*, 15th anniversary edn., Footnote 103, p. 227.

23. *Ibid.*, pp. 103-04.

24. *Ibid.*, p. 103.

liberating gift of Christ. At the same time, any historical struggle against alienation and exploitation is an attempt to eliminate negations of love.

Thus the very theological notion of the Kingdom is a call to new life, to commitment, to liberation, and to communion and solidarity especially with the oppressed and the dehumanized in the building of a just and harmonious society. It is a gift as well as a task. It is a gift by the very fact of the announcement of the Kingdom of God in Christ; it is a task precisely because humans are free to respond to the given announcement.

Conclusion

Both Gandhi and Gutiérrez envision to bring about fundamental changes in political, social and economic affairs. Breaking with alienating and life-denying structures, they attempt to shape a genuine human history. Moral and political energy is to be channelled in order to create and maintain a societal system responsive to human needs and challenges.

In this chapter as well as in the earlier ones one may clearly see that there are points at which Gandhi and Gutiérrez meet. Yet there are very significant differences in their respective approaches to the process of liberative transformation. A conversation between our two figures will definitely help us to draw conclusions in our contemporary search to articulate a more adequate paradigm for a process of liberative transformation and socio-political and economic action. To this I turn in my concluding chapter

6

Evaluation and Conclusion

It is evident that aspiration for liberation is a human phenomenon. The manifold forms it takes are conditioned by cultures and historical circumstances but it is not the prerogative of one particular religion. A close look at the reflection and attempted struggle for liberative transformation as proposed and undertaken by our two figures, Gandhi and Gutiérrez, indicates that there are points at which they meet. Yet there are areas where they differ. A conversation between them will help us to draw insights and to identify elements in our attempt to direct socio-political and economic process in the framework of working toward a more adequate paradigm of liberative transformation especially in the context of India. This would, in turn, enable us to identify some features of a socio-political and economic ethics.

Option for the Poor vs Option for Truth

Right at the outset it should be pointed out that the "central organizing perspective," is different for Gandhi and Gutiérrez. For Gutiérrez I take it to be the preferential option for the poor. For Gandhi it is the option for Truth. The socio-economic and political analysis, the theological reflections and the spirituality proposed in the light of such analysis and reflections are undertaken by Gutiérrez from the central view point of the preferential option for the poor. This is *the perspective* around which the foundational bases of Gutiérrez cohere and in the light of which he has chosen both to employ his sources (scripture, Christian mysticism, social sciences) and to propose the spirituality of "drinking from our own wells." From the focus-point of Truth in Gandhi's belief-system there emerges his continued search, reflections, experiments, and proposals for socio-political and economic actions in the larger framework of his liberation agenda. Gandhi's embrace (search, experiments and option) of Truth is the perspective from which his *ahiṁsātmaka satyāgraha* emanates and around which the foundational bases of his belief-system cohere.

There are similarities in their very starting points. Personal and historical experiences give them an impetus to consider that things need not be as they are; in fact, they should not and ought not be as they are. In an "experience-reflection-action-more experience-reflection-action" continuum Gandhi developed a conceptual framework and outlined a comprehensive programme of action to re-affirm the dignity and the sacredness of the human person. He attempted thus to reconstruct society in its socio-economic, political, moral, and religious dimensions wherein individual sacredness, personal dignity and the common good are never sacrificed. In a similar fashion, in the context of a doctrinal religious history, the experience of intense and unwanted human suffering, and with the intention of discerning the meaning of "the signs of the times" in the light of God's action in history through a Biblical hermeneutics, Gutiérrez starts his spiritual journey of "drinking from our own wells." "What is God saying to us in the midst of suffering?" or "How to speak of a God of love and life to the suffering poor of Latin America in the midst of poverty and death?" are basic questions of Gutiérrez.

Their differences in the theological bases and social analysis are significant enough to affect their prescriptions for action. The Biblical theology of Gutiérrez, the preferential option for the poor as the central organizing perspective of his liberation theology, and his perception of realities and historical praxis from such a perspective affect his specific theology, his interpretation of the nature of God. A hermeneutic of the signs of the times under the light of the Gospel brought Gutiérrez to the God of the poor. Gandhi's emphasis upon the existential and his consideration of the life-journey as a search for truth made him affirm God as Truth and consider life as a continuous series of experiments with Truth.

Both Gandhi and Gutiérrez show that religious traditions provide a milieu which creates our moral vision, nurtures our moral loyalties, informs our moral outlook and sustains our moral character. Beyond the deontological and utilitarian ethical framework, there is the sphere of religious ethics which creates, informs, and sustains our moral outlook and character. This implies that religious dimensions do make a difference in one's total outlook on life. So any serious attempt toward a new paradigm for liberative transformation of the human should consider seriously the religious sphere that undergirds· our ethical/moral thinking.

The form and content of the Gandhian ethics of action, *ahiṃsātmaka satyāgraha*, follow systematically and logically from his concept of God as Truth and from his notion of the human qua moral agent who always stands in relation to Truth (God), to other human beings and to the universe. The inter-human relationships, the notion of the unity of the humans, together with his insightful understanding of the mechanism for realization of Truth, especially in a process of conflict resolution, make him reject violence even in small doses. One of Gandhi's primary concerns was an explication of how religious life, faith and belief-systems form a responsible self. The actions of human agents in all realms of life (socio-economic, political) have ethical and religious significance. The consequence is that economics, politics, or any other science, for that matter, are not outside the realm of ethics and morality. This indicates that responsible action in mundane realms, and at every stage and sphere of human life, is a moral ought.[1] Gandhi's views are firmly based upon his assumptions and concepts regarding human nature, human perfectibility, human fulfilment, and person-to person and person-to-God relationships. In the background of very clear convictions regarding what the essential nature of the human is, what one should be and can become, and what one's place in the universe is, Gandhi realized the tragedy of the human acting with a false understanding of oneself and by a fundamentally flawed organization of society. Going up the steep slope of truth is more difficult than slipping down into the abyss of brutality. To be involved in the public realm working for *swarāj* and *Rāmarājya* is to be involved in the sacred *dharma* (duty). Hence a committed involvement in the uplift of all, especially the *Harijans* (the untouchable outcastes — people of God) and in the attainment of freedom, were simply a journey undertaken in search of Truth.

Gutiérrez proposes a spirituality of "contemplative action" embracing every facet of Christian existence. The spirituality he proposes is Biblical, Christo-centric, dynamic, life-affirming, and agapeic. It is a "walking according to the Spirit," affirming life in its manifold manifestations and advocating the empowerment of especially the poor "to take control of their own destiny." This spirituality is seen as a demand in the following of Jesus. A conversion to Christo-centrism is seen as essential to the liberation-transformation process. Gutiérrez is convinced that an authentic conversion to God in and through Christ can bring one to "an abandonment of oneself" for the sake of one's neighbour, going beyond a purely "interior" and "privatized" spirituality. He is confident that "contemplative action," wherein a personal and communal encounter with Christ and a commitment to God are inseparable from an encounter and commitment to the

---

1. So one need not await the primordial *tabula rasa* of Rawlsian "original position" to commence change in a socio-political or economic structure. See John Rawls, *A Theory of Justice.* Cambridge, Massachusetts: Harvard University Press, 1971, pp. 17-22; 118-92.

224 Gandhi and Gutiérrez

neighbour, especially the neighbour in need (the poor), opens the door for the coming of the Kingdom of God.

One can make a reasonable claim that the journey of Gutiérrez is primarily a theological journey; or more accurately a "spiritual journey" in the company of theology under the guidance of the person of Christ as the Law. Spelling out and giving emphasis to concrete norms in the realm of action, the journey of Gandhi is an ethical undertaking, or more specially, an "action journey" under the umbrella of Truth and supervised by *dharma* (duty). There is a moral wisdom in Gandhi's search for a rational understanding. Such moral wisdom captured in moments of intuitive glow in the cave of his heart had a compelling force for Gandhi, urging him to action. With action as his domain, Gandhi earnestly endeavoured to translate his metaphysical and religious beliefs and assumptions into ethical principles to guide his concrete options in the *swarāj* agenda.

As seen above, conversion to Christo-centrism is essential to the liberation-transformation process of Gutiérrez. On the other hand, for Gandhi, the conversion, if I may use such a term, is to Truth, and not to any person as such (to Rāma or Kṛṣṇa or, for that matter, to any of the *avatārs*). This has ethical implications too. In the Christo-centric spirituality of Gutiérrez, Christ becomes the norm, the law, to judge the adequacy of *walking* in the life-journey. Here the "height" and the "depth" of the norm depend on the pattern and adequacy of "Christ" interpretation. In the Gandhian paradigm the journey itself is an indication of its own adequacy since the scale of evaluation is the concrete realization of Truth in day to day affairs. The adequacy of one's journey is not tested against the imitation and/or following of a person. Gandhi considered the *search* for Truth more important than the attainment of Truth itself. The end-creating mechanism of means becomes clear under this light: the means themselves are the scale of evaluation of one's ethical/moral integrity. This is why Gandhi insisted so much on the means. Ethical/moral questions arise in the very mechanism of the *journey itself* in the Gandhian paradigm. So in the Gandhian paradigm the main question will be the adequacy of the ethical, whereas for Gutiérrez the basic question is concerning the adequacy of the theological. In short, Gutiérrez's agenda is a theological one, whereas Gandhi's is ethical. The "theological journey" of Gutiérrez has ethical implications; whereas the "ethical journey" of Gandhi has theological ramifications. While there is a theological simplicity underlying the moral clarity in Gandhi, acute theological clarity but ethical/moral thinness mark the journey of Gutiérrez. What is, perhaps, needed is a harmonious combination of both, namely, a theocentric ethic.[2]

Both Gandhi and Gutiérrez see the modern world as dehumanizing in its present form of existence and operation. They call for a prophetic denunciation of it in an active effort for socio-economic and political structural changes in order to usher in freedom and to accelerate the process of the liberative transformation of the human. Both see very clearly that the world of humans is not yet a home for humanity. The immediately experienced world of Gutiérrez is marked by violence, poverty, and death — a world of life denial and of exploitation. For Gandhi it is experienced as a world of negation and ignorance — a world of denial of self-rule and equal status, a rejection of mutuality and acceptance, lack of self respect and absence of mutual respect. Both propose radical changes. It is clear that it is Gandhi's religiosity that led him to politics. His religious convictions gave him the motive force for his theo-political theory of action, namely *ahiṁsātmaka satyāgraha*. His relentless search for truth made him embrace a way of life (spirituality) whereby insertion into various fields of human interaction (economics, politics, sociology, spirituality/mysticism and/or religion) would usher in a

---

2. Herein lies, I think, the importance of pioneering works of persons like James M. Gustafson. See Gustafson's seminal work in two volumes, *Ethics from a Theocentric Perspective*.

harmonious united whole, without dichotomizing different dimensions of human life, especially of religion and politics. In a similar fashion it is the religious vision, through a biblical hermeneutics and a specific understanding of God's action in history, that led Gutiérrez to propose an immanent insertion into the world of the poor to work toward an economic and political transformation of the existing social structures. Though history becomes the primary reference point of Gutiérrez, there is the important transcendent aspect of human liberation that is fundamental to his calling for structural transformation in his paradigm of liberation.

Both would agree on the importance of a conversion of the individual and the transformation of various socio-political and economic structures that oppress and dehumanize. Their direction of movement of the process of transformation seems to be different. Their various emphases on the starting point of transformatory processes are very obvious.

Their major differences are to be found in their primordial understandings about what is required to transform this imperfect world into a better one where harmony and concord prevails. Since it is the systemic social oppression that oppresses and dehumanizes the world of human affairs, according to Gutiérrez, such oppressive social structures ought to be transformed first and foremost. On the other hand, Gandhi has argued forcefully that any real and lasting transformation of this world order to the better has to begin with an individual's realization of inherent dignity and of willingness to search for Truth. Individual persons are not considered as enemies or adversaries by Gandhi. The adversary is the social order that dehumanizes the human. The opponent is an oppressive systemic structure. The enemy is the wrong action. Thus what is to be combatted/opposed is the wrong actions of peoples, and not the individuals who are instruments for such wrong actions. It is possible in the Gandhian paradigm to hate the wrong actions, to denounce the oppressive systemic structures without considering those who are instrumental to it as enemies. What is to be attempted is the transformation of the sinner, the offender, the victims as well as victimizers of oppression. Both the oppressor as well as the oppressed are victims in the Gandhian analysis. Hence both stand in need of liberation. And both should work *together* to attain *swarāj*. Though most of the time Gutiérrez speaks of the liberation of the oppressed, there are instances where he talks of the liberation of the oppressor as well. But Gutiérrez's primary agenda is to be with the oppressed poor and their liberation. Gandhi would ask Gutiérrez whether Gutierrez's oppressor group are oppressed in some manner; and if they are, then, what concrete mechanism he would use to expedite their liberation. Gutiérrez would ask Gandhi as to where he (Gandhi) would primarily locate responsibility for wrong actions; in the individual, and/or in the systemic structures? It should be emphasized that a personal realization of the inadequacy of one's grasp of truth and a humble attitude of search for fuller comprehension of truth leading to a change of heart, is what is needed first and foremost in the Gandhian approach. Gutiérrez also would insist on personal conversion and change of heart; but his main emphasis is on changes in the structures.

Further, Gutiérrez's approach is specifically Christian. The symbols, paradigms, the language, all these suggest a particular religious affiliation. To that extent it is parochial. Though Gandhi, a Hindu, draws inspiration mainly from his religious traditions and uses language and symbols accordingly, he is still open to other religious affiliations and personalities of various religious faiths, and even to persons of no particular faith at all to elicit various elements in building his belief-system. This gives him a broader platform to speak from and to be spoken to. Given India's diversities (religious, cultural, ethnic, tribal), a broader platform is more appropriate in one's search for an adequate paradigm for liberative transformation.[3]

3. It is interesting to note here that, when once I asked Gutiérrez whether his Liberation Theology as such would be applicable to India, without any hesitation he said, "No." This strengthens my case for

Swarāj vs Liberation

Concern for freedom is the meeting point. The concept of *swarāj* captures the quintessence of the Gandhian notion of freedom and the essence of liberative transformation. The inner freedom of being in control of the self that one ought to experience even before the experience of freedom of national independence, and the subsequent result of being able to rule oneself in politics, is inherent in the Gandhian *swarāj*. The external freedom that we attain will only be in direct proportion to the inner freedom in which we have grown. In other words, the social and institutional dimension of freedom depends upon and springs from the individual personal dimension — an experience of the intrinsic worth and dignity of an individual *per se*. This implies that, as far as Gandhi is concerned, the development of a polity and the organization of a people ruling themselves should be a reflection as well as an index of the degree of maturity of the individual moral agents in their experience of inner freedom.

Both Gandhi and Gutiérrez would agree that freedom is essential to the human being. Gandhi would consider it an inherent virtue, while Gutiérrez would regard it as an inalienable right. Both would clearly endorse the freedom "from" and the freedom "for" aspects. Gutiérrez has presented liberation as a *freedom from* domination inherent in certain unjust social structures to a *freedom for* a social order that is more attentive to the needs of the poor, and which is more appropriate and attuned to expedite the Kingdom. By equating freedom with *swarāj*, Gandhi built into his concept of freedom the notion of obligation, to oneself and to others, while keeping

---

proposing a broader platform for an appropriate paradigm for liberative transformation in the Indian context. This "no" could be stretched, if I might, to interpret that, when, in the context of South America, they "drink from their own wells," in the Indian context, the people could "swim in their own ponds." The process of "Inculturation" that is very much alive and active in Christian circles in India today might well be an attempt to "swim in their own ponds".

the aspect of voluntariness as the basis. Thus freedom from all that dehumanizes and oppresses, and freedom for self-determination are affirmed by both. The virtue of *swarāj* has moral priority for Gandhi. This moral priority is preserved by basing *swarāj* on *satya*. Gandhi's extension of the analogical relationship of *satya* and *ahiṁsā* to *swarāj* and *swadeśī*, is an oversimplification. His emphasis on *swadeśī* as the only legitimate means for the achievement of *swarāj* might be challenged in today's global context and the politico-economic interrelatedness that is increasingly characteristic of our shrinking world.[4]

Beyond the notion of freedom to be, there is the aspect of freedom as the capacity "to become." The empowerment of the masses to have "bread with dignity," to be aware of their capacity to regulate and control authority, and to grasp the causes of their situation of injustice in order to find release, is emphasized by both. Both of them advocate the empowerment of people to be agents of their own history. Both of them would see the need of breaking with situations of injustice so that those who suffer because of such unjust situations could take control of their own destiny.

Kingdom and *Rāmarājya*

The liberation agenda of our paradigm figures is oriented to their respective goals. Both aim at egalitarian, harmonious societies structured in accord with freedom and love. The *Rāmarājya* of Gandhi and the Kingdom of Gutiérrez have similarities. Most of us live by our visions, beliefs, and utopias, explicit or implicit. Gandhi's religious goals of perfection, though fervently focused on the perfection of the self (self-

---

4. Of course Gandhi's objective should be respected. His aim is to opt for a technology at a particular socio-cultural and historical context in such a way that a specific technological option would bring in maximum employment which in itself would enhance self dignity. Would Gandhi consider the Service Sector as a meaningful and self-fulfilling area of employment?

realization), exists in the context of the quest for a perfect society (*Rāmarājya*) — reflecting a cluster of hopes and values. Both of them envisage a restructuring of society itself. Gandhi was concerned about constructing a morally and ethically coherent life. Gandhi finds a very high correlation between the moral character of a people and the nature of their political organization. The world of the humans is seen as a unity.

Ahimsātmaka Satyāgraha and "Drinking From Our Own Wells"

Like Plato, Gandhi considered the search for Truth to be more important than Truth as such. With Gandhi the *ahimsā* is a creed that sprung forth from his basic foundational belief system. He succeeded in converting the virtue of *ahimsā* into a collective moral force against a structural evil present in society. In recent times Gutiérrez has been insisting on a spirituality of liberation. I think a reasonable claim could be made that Gandhi's insistence on the means and methods of attaining Truth is more rigorous than that of Gutiérrez. This is not to suggest that Gutiérrez is not serious about the means in the effort to work for the Kingdom. The question is one of degree. One can ask: what are the moral principles that Gandhi and Gutiérrez would employ to judge or to recommend an action? What kind of action guides do they propose for involvement in the transformation of societal structures? Do they differ? If so, how? and why?

The nature of the spirituality of action proposed by Gutiérrez and Gandhi, as we have seen above, help us to conclude that the interpretations of how one ought to make moral decisions, namely the ethical concerns for practical moral reasoning, are different for our paradigmatic figures. In the Gandhian paradigm there is an organic understanding of society. This understanding presumes a cosmic order (*ṛta*) that needs to be maintained for a harmonious human existence.

The observance of principles for the preservation of harmony is essential in this approach to situation of conflict. The moral imperative is grounded in being; and his argument is from "being" to "ought." Human's being is the basis of becoming. Hence the emphasis is on duty (*dharma*). Thus there is a deductive approach in the Gandhian paradigm. Though Gandhi lays much emphasis on experience and is clearly concerned about sinful oppressive social structures, there is a movement from first principles to clearly prescribed actions. His approach, then, is based on an application of principles. These principles could provide a high degree of moral certitude. When Gandhi says that *ahiṁsā* is the law of our species, and that *ahiṁsā* should be embraced as a creed' in one's search for Truth, what he is saying in effect is that being is the basis of our becoming.

As a biblical theologian Gutiérrez looks into God's revelation in history rather than searching for God's purposes revealed through nature.[5] Starting with the experience of the poor, and given an opportunity to encounter God through an insertion into their experience, Gutiérrez follows an inductive approach. His is not a movement from principles to prescribed actions, or an adherence to principles and procedures deduced from some sort of a Natural Law. In the tensions of the dialectics of history, he searches for norms of action in the light of a Biblical hermeneutic, which is a call of the poor to claim their privileged position and the power to act, to recover, as it were, their moral agency itself. So in the practical moral

---

5. The approach of finding God's purposes revealed in nature is the traditional Natural Law approach. The Roman Catholic tradition particularly relied on the philosophical basis of natural law to elicit moral principles and procedures in making moral decisions on a wide range of issues. This tradition has been extensively criticised in the last four decades. See Josef Fuchs, *Natural Law: A Theological Investigation* (New York: Sheed and Ward, 1965); John Mahoney, *The Making of Moral Theology: A Study of the Roman Catholic Tradition* (Oxford: Clarendon Press, 1987), pp. 72-115; James M. Gustafson, *Protestant and Roman Catholic Ethics*, pp. 80-85; Charles Curren, *Directions in Fundamentals in Moral Theology* (Notre Dame: Notre Dame University Press, 1985), pp. 119-67.

reasoning, the moral imperative is not grounded on being *per se*; nor is the movement of the argument from "being" to "ought." It is not duty that is stressed but the right and the privilege, especially of the poor, is asserted.[6]

In concrete historical situations, there is a possibility that Gutiérrez might, depending upon a particular context, as for example a nation's specific socio-political organization (such as military rule, dictatorship) and/or cultural differences, permit means and methods not agreeable to Gandhi — for instance, allowing moments of violence or armed insurgency which would imply physical violence in the Gandhian sense.[7] Gandhi would not allow any form of physical violence to be adopted as means in his *satyāgraha* struggle. He would understand and painfully sympathize with violence irrupted as a result of the *satyāgraha* movement. But he would not permit his *satyāgrahīs* to resort to physical violence in any form whatsoever because non-violence for him is the necessary and indispensable means of discovering truth. Violence in any form will further increase the wrong and the evil, taking humans far away from attaining the highest truth of spiritual unity.

Gandhi has developed an ethically coherent means in his liberation praxis. Gutiérrez speaks of spirituality of liberation and a wide range of activities that fall under the generic term of "the process of liberation."[8] In the Christian living out of faith, continually reflected in the light of the word of God, such a "process" needs to be concretely articulated. It is true

---

6. Other liberation writers too agree on this point. For instance, according to Ruben Alves moral action is that which enables the poor to determine their own destiny, the action which allows and encourages them to become true actors on the stage of history. See Ruben Alves, "Some thoughts on a Program For Ethics," *Union Seminary Quarterly Review* 26 (Winter 1971): 169-70.

7. In a conversation with Gutiérrez a few years ago, If I understood Gutiérrez correctly, this is what he told me at that time. I am not sure of his position today.

8. See Chapters 6 and 7 of *A Theology of Liberation*.

that Gutiérrez would argue that Christians should give priority to orthopraxis, namely, how one lives out one's faith. Gutiérrez is convinced that the point of the Gospel is not just orthodoxy, or "getting things right," but orthopraxy, or "making things right." There is a moral agency and moral colouring to everything one does or does not do; there is no moral neutrality. He would, further, propose that opting for the poor should take precedence over working for the non-poor. In developing categories for a new theology of liberation such a general notion of praxis might suffice. But in directing liberation praxis in a historical context such a broad notion is rather inadequate. In historical praxis, conflicting means are involved. Herein lies the real problem of choosing between means. Here Gandhi could well ask a question to Gutiérrez with regard to his selection of means in the liberation struggle. Gandhi would insist that Gutiérrez make a clear choice between the use of violence and nonviolence, between armed struggle and *ahiṁsātmaka satyāgraha*. Gandhi would say that Gutiérrez needs to move in the direction of developing explicit ethical criteria to help people make the right decisions especially in situations of conflict. Thus, Gutiérrez has to concretely spell out action guides involving normative principles and procedures. The Gandhian *satyāgraha* is search for truth through a dialogical process. It is possible that conflicts will arise in this process, especially when one side is not ready to honestly and sincerely search for truth. It may not be ready for dialogue; it may even break away from the very process of truth-search. This is especially the moment when emphasis on appropriate means (non-violence for Gandhi) and insistence on openness and the rejection of secrecy become all the more necessary. Gutiérrez has to address concretely such crucial problems in the historical praxis.

Gutiérrez too would have some questions for Gandhi concerning the role he (Gandhi) would give to institutional and structural changes in his liberation praxis. Gutiérrez would agree with Gandhi that individual conversion is a *sine qua non* in the process of liberative transformation. But this need not necessarily mean that a structure would change when individual conversion takes place; nor does "eschatological impatience" permit the awaiting for the conversion of every individual. This may not be realistically possible. Gandhi has to face this challenge.

Gandhi was concerned about constructing a morally and ethically coherent life. He found a very high correlation between the moral character of a people and the nature of their political organization. The world of the humans is seen as a unity. For Gandhi the religious relation is by and large an ethical/moral relation. Ethics and morality are the religiosity of the religious. Gandhi's stress is on character and not on religions, or even on a particular theology. Dogmatic credal assertions or theological speculations are of little importance. In Gutiérrez there is a shift in emphasis from the problem of belief to the problem of poverty. This shift in emphasis need not necessarily imply lack of emphasis on articulations of belief. Gutiérrez's aim is to capture and forcefully articulate the true and original Christian experience as given especially in the Gospel.

Both of them look at reality from the perspective of the victims of the established social order. Refusing to think in terms of Marxist antagonistic class interests, Gandhi developed his own basic principles and overall action guides. Considering social analysis as integral to his approach, Gutiérrez finds Marxist analysis useful as a tool to explain the root cause of poverty in Latin America especially in his dependency theory.[9] As far as Gandhi is concerned, emphasis on class conflict to

9. The use of Marxist analysis by liberation theologians including Gutiérrez is the issue most frequently raised in liberation theology. Even when the concerns of the Church authorities are focused on broader questions of the mission of the Church, fidelity to Church teachings, use of scripture, the question of Marxist influence looms large in their minds. In my view, paying too much attention to this one issue dilutes the larger concerns of Gutiérrez.

explain socio-political and economic realities does not necessarily solve the problem of oppression. In case of a value conflict between individual right and social responsibility, in continuity with the Kantian sense of moral duty, Gandhi would subordinate the former to the latter.

Reconciling Communion

A mechanism for reconciliation and communion is the strength of Gandhian *ahiṁsātmaka satyāgraha*. Gandhi's search for truth through *ahiṁsa* is to manifest to the "oppressors" (say *A* in plural) that even in motive and intent the *satyāgrahīs* (say *B* in plural) are well-wishers of *A*. The insistence on changing the oppressive and sinful social structures and conditions through *satyāgraha* is an attempt to make *A* examine their opinions and attitudes, and if needed (and in most cases it is needed) to change their deeply held values. It is not meant to inflict a defeat on *A*; but, rather, that truth may prevail in the last analysis. The whole process of the *satyāgraha* struggle is undertaken to kindle the little spark of God present even in the worst *A* so that this challenge makes *A* reflect and perceive the truth. Thus, a condition is created in such a way that *A* can realize the folly of their position and initiate their own process of change and transformation. It should be stressed that *A* make the decision to change. Structural changes become a possibility once individual truth-realization becomes a reality. Thus there is an open-ended dialogical process at work here. *B* want to make it very clear to *A* that

1. *B* do not entertain any hostility to *A*, and

2. *B* do not want to make *A* act against their will.

Also *B* do not want to create even the slightest fear in *A* of any intended physical harm or violence inflicted on *A*. Wishing *A*'s well-being is the manifest motive of *B*. This is made known to *A*. Secrecy has no place in *B*'s approach. The intended goal as well as the employed means are out in the open for anyone to see and to scrutinize. Every positive effort will be made to keep all avenues of communication with *A* open. At the same time, *B* will constantly pray for strength to carry on the process of continued insistence on truth, irrespective of the intensity of suffering that may be inflicted on *B* in the process of the search for truth. The nonviolent approach of *B* makes it possible for *A* to act according to the latters' will. If violence is used, *B* would be forcing *A;* and in that process, *B* would be making *A* act against their will, which *B* do not want. And, finally, believing in the redemptive power of self-suffering love, *B* is ready to accept any extent of suffering, including death, that comes as a result of their insistence of truth. Thus, in such a search for communion and reconciliation, *B* even refuse to be characterized as "enemy" of *A*. In this process of active search for truth there is an inherent mechanism of reconciled communion in the Gandhian paradigm. Accepting Pantañjali's dictum that "violence ceases in the presence of non-violence," Gandhi aims at the spiritual unity of all humans.

In Gutiérrez's paradigm such a mechanism is not so obvious. This is not to say that there is no channel at all open in Gutiérrez for communion and reconciliation. Again, as mentioned earlier, the difference is one of degree and of clarity. There are people who would not hesitate to point a finger at Gutiérrez saying that he uses combative language without seeing all its implications. Perhaps, "reading into" Gutiérrez creates more confusion.[10] One can see clearly instances of advocacy of communion in Gutiérrez.[11]

---

10. Arthur F. McGovern cites Cardinal Alfonso Lopez Trujillo, the past president of CELAM (the Conference of Latin American Bishops), as "the most prominent Latin American critic of Liberation theology." According to McGovern, "He (the Cardinal) blames Gutiérrez for texts that created the "atmosphere" leading to conflict in the church. . . . Quite possibly, says Lopez Trujillo, Gutiérrez felt obligated to use combative language and did not see all its implications." See McGovern, *Liberation Theology and Its Critics,* p. 48.

11. See Gutiérrez, *We Drink from Our Own Wells,* pp. 129, 137.

When short-term solution are prudently judged to be the
appropriate answer to a particular situation, the Gandhian
non violence may not be the most effective answer but works
in the long-run. The question is how long is the Gandhian
"long-run"? Does Gutiérrez's "eschatological impatience"
permit too long a "long-run"?

Towards a New Agenda of Liberative Transformation

Theories of liberation do not liberate. At best, they can inform,
reform and reshape our social consciousness. Perhaps, many
still live under the illusion that once theories are made rational,
they will automatically affect life-patterns. But that is not
necessarily so. Rational logicality need not necessarily in and
by itself result in change or initiate the process commended
by its own rational findings. What is needed is a constructive
translation of theoretical and theological reflections into
concrete life patterns proposing norms and guidance for
concrete action. Gutiérrez's notion of "doing" theology is a
step in the right direction. His work with the Basic Christian
Communities is an attempt at translation of his theological
findings into concrete action plans. Gandhi's *satyāgraha*
undertakings are positive attempts in action. Gandhi's
adamant clinging to *ahiṁsā* points to the right direction that
one should take. Positive emphasis should be given to the
spiritual unity of human beings that we *are* brothers and sisters,
sons and daughters of God (the Absolute Truth) that has a
special interest in seeing that a kingdom of transformed
relationship be brought into existence through human
interactions in history so that in continuum this kingdom could
be brought to its eschatological fulfilment.

The above conversation between the two paradigm figures
explores the role of the individual as a responsible agent in
the liberative transformation process, and the role of
institutions and structures in the liberation praxis. The two
figures given in Chapter 1 illustrate the movements with
respect to the respective paradigms of both Gandhi and

Gutiérrez in their liberation agenda. As mentioned earlier, Gandhi's insistence on individual persons and their pursuit of Truth, makes it clear that his movement seems to be from person to personal acts (realization process) and then to the systemic structures — a clockwise movement. On the other hand, in Gutierrez the process seems to be from person to systemic structures first, and then only to personal acts and convertion — a counter-clockwise movement.

I presume that the stage is now set to give a synthetic conclusion and proposal for a new agenda of liberation in the Indian context. Before going into the specifics of this proposal it should be emphasized that the basis of continued healthy existence of any society is ethics and morality. Theology and religious convictions can (and should) inform the ethics and morality. The conceptual foundations of ethics should enable one to find flexibility amid constancy in tackling the varied problems arising in situations where there are ample occasions of conflicts and strifes. Conflicts seem to be a constant companion of life's journey. How to tackle them constructively; how to build bridges of human relationships, reconciling and correcting wrongs done in the historical process of life, with a final goal of harmonious relationship, should seriously concern any serious person trying to offer hope in midst of apparent hopelessness.

Gandhi sought to achieve a balance of reason and intuition without succumbing to the temptation of the illusion of infallibility or the delusion of indispensability. Many a time he depended on intuition (inner voice) seeking understanding, warning against blind emotionalism or rationalization of selfishness. One could find here ample flexibility amid consistency.

The influence of structuring on the human condition is correctly highlighted by Gutiérrez. In any serious proposal for a new social order, adequate attention should be given to systemic structural influences. The liberation paradigm proposed by Gutiérrez could point the direction with respect to the systemic structures and their influence on the liberation praxis.

In the light of the insights drawn above from a comparison of our two paradigm figures from diverse cultural milieus, one could draw from both Gutiérrez and Gandhi various elements to propose a more adequate paradigm for India. A process of systemic and structural change simultaneous with a process of individual conversion (conversion to Truth) may result in a more adequate interpretation of economic and socio-political action which would lead to a better social order. This could be a richer paradigm than the ones represented by either of the figures under scrutiny.

First of all, the liberation agenda should move to a stage of liberative transformation. This paradigm insists on the aspects of both *liberation* and *transformation*. Here equal emphasis is given to the structural change and to the individual conversion process. They are not mutually exclusive. They share elements and conditions. A combination of the moral wisdom of Gandhi and the theological insights of Gutiérrez could provide a paradigm of liberative transformation. When One Combines,

(a) the added importance given by Gutiérrez to the analysis of "the moment of truth" (the *kairos*) and of the particular cultural, contextual situation through a right reading of the "signs of the times" in the light of God's action in history, through a critical reflection on historical praxis and through a biblical hermeneutics, especially of the Gospel, and

(b) the inviolable *sacredness* attributed to individual persons by Gandhi and the relentless search for Truth that forms the *antaryāmin* of his socio-economic and political transformation process and the basis of his *ahiṁsātmaka satyāgraha*, together with the self-sacrificial and reconciling power of self-suffering (*tapasyā*) love and the contritional-conversional model of *ahiṁsā* for conflict resolution, one would tend to arrive at the centre of the base of the figures. The two movements would together, then, proceed to the dimension of change and transformation. Therein both persons and systemic structures stand, not in opposition to one another as an either or, but in mutual enrichment giving rise to a better and more adequate paradigm of liberative transformation. The proposed movement could be captured in the following figure.

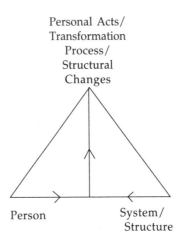

fig. 6.1: The New Paradigm of Liberative Transformation

The approach of Gutiérrez would give the needed emphasis on structural changes. The sacred dignity accorded to every human and the importance given to the search for Truth and the practice of *ahiṁsā* would render the Gandhian paradigm amenable to concrete means and mechanisms necessary for any ethical model for action oriented to a harmonious community of mutual enrichment. Such bringing together of salient elements from both Gandhi and Gutiérrez would enable one to be responsible to oneself, to others and to the socio-economic and political structures of our creation. Universal human good would then become the measure of all our historical endeavours. In such a framework, structural transformation would be comparatively easier. Through his critical social analysis and the importance given to history, Gutiérrez scrutinizes the value-laden presuppositions embodied in social structures and political practices. This is necessary to understand and adequately address the socio-economic, political, cultural, and religious problems that confront the world, *a fortiori*, India in this hour of history. The enlightened understanding of human responsibility and responsible freedom, together with the affirmation of mutual rights and duties in the conflictual world of human affairs, as proposed by Gandhi, is a *sine qua non* for the establishment of a meaningful and sustainable community of human beings in authentic communion and real stewardship.

Glossary

advaita	:	non-dualism of God and the universe.
ahiṁsā	:	non-violence, non-injury, non-coercion, self-suffering love, non-violent love, abstention from any hostile and harmful thought, word and deed.
anāsakti	:	non-attachment, spiritual detachment.
antaryāmin	:	the inner force which gives life to a being; in Hindu philosophy it is one of the qualities attributed to *Brahman*.
aparigraha	:	non-possession.
artha	:	material goods, possessions, political economy, material welfare.
ārtta prapatti	:	resignation to the will of God.
āśram	:	an institution on monastic lines, but necessarily of religious candidates; a commune of spiritual fellowship.
asteya	:	non-stealing.
ātman	:	soul, self, the spirit of *Brahman* (God) in human beings.
avarṇas	:	those without colour, hence the casteless.
avatāra	:	a descent of God, hence incarnation of God.

bansī	:	lute.
bhajans	:	religious hymns, popular religious chants.
bhakti	:	devotion, faith.
Brahman	:	the impersonal, absolute God.
buddhi	:	intuitive understanding, discriminative discernment, moral wisdom.
carkhā	:	spinning wheel.
daridra	:	the poor.
Daridranārāyaṇa	:	The Lord of the poor.
dharma	:	duty, righteousness, moral law, morality.
duragraha	:	holding onto untruth and what is evil, persistence in wrong-doing.
harijans	:	the people of God.
hiṁsā	:	violence.
jivan-mukta	:	one who has attained liberation while yet alive.
kama	:	human affection, desire, pleasure, happiness, love.
karma	:	the ethical consequences of a person's actions which determine one's life hereafter.
kevalajñāna	:	perfect knowledge.
līlā	:	plaything, the sport of God, divine play.
mahātmā	:	great soul.
māyā	:	appearance, non-reality, relatively real.
mokṣa	:	liberation, salvation, eventual emancipation, freedom from bondage.
nara	:	the human being.
Nārāyaṇa	:	the Lord, literally the Lord of humans.

neti, neti	:	Not this, not that.
nirguṇa Brahman	:	The God without qualities.
niṣkāmakarma	:	acting without looking for a reward, unattached action.
parama satya	:	the highest of truths, the Ultimate Truth.
*pañcāyat*s	:	a council of five elected officials especially in village government.
pūrṇa swarāj	:	total independence.
*puruṣārtha*s	:	the four basic ends of human life (*dharma* =duty; *artha* = wealth; *kāma* = love; *mokṣa* = heaven).
Rāmarājya	:	the reign of Rāmacandra, the great hero of *Rāmāyaṇa* Epic, the kingdom of Rāma; symbolically the reign of God, the kingdom of God.
ṛta	:	the cosmic order.
sadagraha	:	firmness in a good cause, the first coinage for the concept of *satyāgraha*.
saguṇa Brahman	:	the impersonal Supreme God with qualities.
sahasranāma	:	thousand names, a thousand names that are attributed to God.
saṁnyāsī	:	an ascetic.
śakti	:	force, power.
śaraṇāgati	:	self-surrender.
sarvodaya	:	the welfare of all.
sarvodaya samāj	:	a society where the welfare of one and all is actively sought after.
sat	:	to be (esse), being; also means abiding, actual, right, wise, self-existent essence, as anything really is, as anything ought to be;

in its highest sense it (*SAT*) stands for the absolute, archetypal Reality and for the absolute, archetypal Truth.

satya : truth, reality, valid, sincere.

satyāgraha : a relentless search for truth, holding onto to truth, soul-force, truth-force, suffering undergone for the cause of justice.

satyāgrahī : one who practices satyāgraha.

Satyanārāyaṇa : The God of Truth.

savarṇas : the coloured, i.e., the people of caste.

swadeśī : indigenous, of the soil, pertaining to one's country, belonging to or made in one's own country, name of a patriotic movement to promote products made in India during the independence struggle.

swarāj : literally a rule over oneself, hence self-rule, mastery over the self, self-determination, self-government, independence.

Toa-Te-King : the basic scripture of Taoism; *Tao* — the way of harmony, *Te* — the power.

tapasyā : self-suffering, penance, mortification, austerity.

tat vam asi : Thou are That.

varṇāśrama dharma : duties relevant to the four stages of life.

Viśvanātha : Lord of the Universe.

Viśvakarmā : The supreme creator of the universe; this is an aspect of *saguṇa Brahman*.

vyāvahārika : pertaining to the mundane.

vyāvahārika dṛṣṭi : practical point of view.

Bibliography

Agarwala, N.N., *India's Saviour Crucified: A Challenge for Us to Think and Act*. Agra: Agarwal, 1948.

Aggarwal, Suman Khanna, *Gandhian Vision*. Delhi: B.R. Publishing Corporation. 1999.

Alves, Ruben, "Some Thoughts on a Program for Ethics." *Union Seminary Quarterly Review* 26 (Winter 1971): 158-71.

Amaladoss, Michael, T.K. John, and G. Gispert-Sauch, *Theologizing in India*. Bangalore: Theological Publications in India, 1981.

Amin, Samir, *Unequal Development: An Essay on the Social Formations of Peripheral Capitalism*. Translated by Brian Pearce. Sussex, England: The Harvester Press Limited. 1976.

———, *Accumulation on a world Scale: A Critique of the Theory of Underdevelopment*. 2 vols. trans. Brian Pearce. New York: Monthly Review Press. 1974.

Amin, Shahid, "Gandhi as Mahatma," in *Selected Subaltern Studies*, ed., Ranajit Guha and Gayatri Chakravorty Spivak, pp. 288-348. New York: Oxford University Press, 1988.

Andrews, C.F., ed., *Mahatma Gandhi: His Own Story*. London: George Allen & Unwin. 1930.

———, *Mahatma Gandhi's ideas*. London: George Allen & Unwin, 1949.

Aquinas, Thomas, *The Basic Writings of Saint Thomas Aquinas*. ed., Anton C. Pegis. Volumes I & II. New York: Random House, 1945.

Araya, Victorio, *God of the Poor: The Mystery of God in Latin American Liberation Theology*. Maryknoll, New York: Orbis Books, 1987.

Arendt, Hannah, *On Revolution*. New York: Viking Press, 1965.

————, *The Human Condition.* Chicago: The University of Chicago Press. 1958.

————, *Crises of The Republic.* New York: Harcourt Brace Jovanovich, Publishers, 1972.

Arokiasamy, Soosai, *Dharma, Hindu and Christian According to Roberto de Nobili: Analysis of its meaning and its use in Hinduism and Christianity.* Roma: Pontificia Universita Gregoriana, 1986.

Arokiasamy, S., S. J., and G. Gispert-Sauch, S.J., *Liberation in Asia: Theological Perspectives.* Jesuit Theological Forum, Reflections series. Anand, India: Gujarat Sahitya Prakash, 1987.

Ashe, Geoffrey, *Gandhiji, A Study in Revolution.* London: Heinemann, 1968.

Augustine, Saint, *Confessions.* Translated with an Introduction by R.S. Pine-Coffin, Reprint. New York: Penguin Books, 1983.

Ballou, Robert O., ed., *World Bible.* New York: Viking Press, 1944.

Barth, Karl., *Church Dogmatics.* 2 volumes. Edinburgh: T.T. Clark, 1957.

Baum, Gregory, "Gandhian Socialism and Christian Church." *Concilium* 105. (1977): 13-22.

Becker, Ernest, *The Structure of Evil.* New York: George Brazilleer, 1968.

Benne, Robert, *The Ethic of Democratic Capitalism: A Moral Reassessment.* Philadelphia: Fortress Press, 1981.

Bernstein, Henry, *Underdevelopment and Development: The Third World Today.* Middlesex, England: 1973.

Bernstein, Richard J., *Praxis and Action: Contemporary Philosophies of Human Activity.* Philadelphia: University of Pennsylvania Press, 1971.

Berryman, Phillip, *The Religious Roots of Rebellion: Christians in Central American Revolutions.* Maryknoll, New York: Orbis Books, 1984.

————, *Liberation Theology.* New York: Pantheon Books, 1987.

Bhagwati, Jagdish, *The Economics of Underdeveloped Countries.* London Weidenfelf & Nicalson, 1971.

Biswas, S.C., ed., *Gandhi, Theory and Practice, Special Impact and Contemporary Relevance.* Simla: Indian Institute of Advanced Study, 1969.

Black, Jan Knippers, "Development and Modernisation Theory." *Cross Currents* XXVII (Spring 1977): 4Iff.

Bodenheimer, Susanne J., "The Ideology of Developmentalism: American Political Science's Paradigm-surrogate for Latin American Studies." *Berkeley Journal of Sociology* 17 (1972-73): 517-34.

Boff, Leonardo, *Jesus Christ Liberator: A Critical Christology for Our Time.* Maryknoll, New York: Orbis Books, 1978.

Boff, Leonardo, *Liberating Grace.* Translated by John Drury. Maryknoll New York: Orbis Books, 1979; second printing 1981.

Boff, Leonardo and Clodovis Boff, *Liberation Theology. From Confrontation to Dialogue.* San Francisco: Harper & Row Publishers, 1986.

————, *Salvation and Liberation: in Search of a Balance between Faith and Politics.* Maryknoll, New York: Orbis Books; Melbourne, Australia: Dove Communications, 1984.

Bondurant, Joan V., *The Conquest of Violence: Gandhi's Philosophy of Conflict.* Revised edition (1965); fourth printing. Berkeley: University of California, I971.

Bonino, Jose Miguez, *Doing theology in a revolutionary situation.* Philadelphia: Fortress Press, 1975.

————, *Toward a Christian Political Ethics.* Philadelphia: Fortress Press, 1983.

Bose, Nirmal Kumar, *Studies in Gandhism.* Second edition. Calcutta: India Associated Publishing Co., 1947.

————, *My Days with Gandhi.* Calcutta: Nishana, 1953.

————, *Lectures on Gandhism.* Ahmedabad: Navajivan Publishing House, 1971.

Bose, Nirmal Kumar and P.H. Patwardhan, *Gandhi in Indian Politics.* Bombay: Lalvani Publishing House, 1967.

Brown, Judith M., *Gandhi: Prisoner of Hope.* New Haven: Yale University Press, 1989.

Brown, Robert McAfee, "Spirituality and Liberation: The Case for Gustavo Gutiérrez." *Worship* 58 (Spring 1984): 395-404.

————, *Spirituality and Liberation: Overcoming the Great Fallacy.* Philadelphia: The Westminster Press, 1988.

———, *Gustavo Gutiérrez: An Introduction to Liberation Theology.* Maryknoll, New York: Orbis Books, 1990.

Buber, Martin, *I and Thou.* New York. Charles Scribner's Sons, 1970.

Bussmann, Claus, *Who Do You Say? Jesus Christ in Latin American Theology.* Translated from the German by Robert R. Barr. Maryknoll, New York: Orbis Books, 1985.

Cabestrero, Teofilo, ed., *Faith: Conversations with contemporary Theologians.* Maryknoll, New York: Orbis Books, 1980; second printing 1981.

Cahill, Lisa Sowle, *Between the Sexes: Foundations for a Christian Ethics of Sexuality.* Philadelphia: Fortress Press and New York: Paulist Press. 1985.

Calvez, Jean-Yves and Jacques Pen-in, *The Church and Social Justice.* Chicago: Henry Regnery Company, 1961.

———, *The Social Thought of John XXIII.* London: Burns & Gates, 1964.

Cardoso, Fernando Henrique and Enzo Faletto, *Dependency and Development in Latin America.* Translated by Marjory Mattingly Urquidi. Berkeley: University of California Press, 1979.

Cenkner, William, "Gandhi and Creative Conflict." *Thought* XLV (Autumn 1970): 422-32.

Chatterjee, Margaret, *Gandhi's Religious Thought.* Notre Dame, Indiana: University of Notre Dame Press, 1983.

Chatterjee, Partha, *Arms, Alliances, and Stability: The Development of the Structure of International Politics.* Delhi: Macmillan Co., 1975.

———, *Nationalist Thought and the Colonial World: A Derivative Discourse?* London: Zed Books for the U.N. University, 1986.

Chopp, Rebecca S., *The Praxis of Suffering: An Interpretation of Liberation and Political Theologies.* Maryknoll, New York: Orbis Books, 1986.

Cockroft, James D., Andre Gunder Frank, and Dale L. Johnson, *Dependence and Underdevelopment.* New York: Doubleday, Anchor, 1972.

Coleman, John A., *An American Strategic Theology.* New York: Paulist Press, 1982.

Comblin, Jose, *The Church and the National Security State.* Maryknoll, New York: Orbis Books, 1979.

Congregation for the Doctrine of the Faith. "Instruction on Certain Aspects of the 'Theology of Liberation'." *Origins* 14 (September 13, 1984): 193-204.

———, "Instruction on Christian Freedom and Liberation." *Origins* 15 (April 17, 1986): 714-28.

Cormie, Lee, "The Hermeneutical Privilege of the Oppressed." *Proceedings of the Catholic Theological Society of America* 33 (1978): 155-81.

———, "The Sociology of National Development and Salvation History." in *Sociology and Human Destiny*, ed., Gregory Baum, New York: Seabury Press, 1980.

Cosmao, Vincent, *Changing the World: An Agenda for the Churches.* New York: Orbis. 1984.

Culliton, Joseph T., C.S.B., ed., *Non-violence — Central to Christian Spirituality: Perspectives from Scripture to the Present.* Toronto Studies in Theology, vol. 8. New York: The Edwin Mellen Press, 1982.

Curran, Charles, *Directions in Fundamental Moral Theology.* Notre Dame: University of Notre Dame Press, 1985.

Damico, Linda H., *The Anarchist dimension of Liberation Theology.* American University Studies series. New York: Peter Lang, 1987.

Danto, Arthur C., *Mysticism and Morality: Oriental Thought and Moral Philosophy.* New York: Harper & Row, Publishers, 1973.

Dasgupta, Subhayu, *Hindu Ethos and the Challenge to Change.* Calcutta: The Minerva Associates, 1972.

Datta, Amian, *The Gandhian Way.* Shillong: North-eastern Hill University Publications, 1986.

Datta, Dhirendra Mahon, *The Philosophy of Mahatma Gandhi.* Madison: University of Wisconsin Press, 1953.

Dear, John, *Our God is Nonviolent: Witnesses in the Struggle for Peace & Justice.* New York: The Pilgrim Press, 1990.

Dalton, Dennis, *Mahatma Gandhi: Nonviolent Power in Action.* New York: Columbia University Press, 1993.

Desai, Mahadev, *Epic of Travancore.* Ahmedabad: Navajivan Publishing House, 1937.

Desrochers, John, *Christ The Liberator.* Bangalore: Centre for Social Action, 1977.

Dhawan, G.N., *The Political Philosophy of Mahatma Gandhi*. Bombay: The Popular Book Depot, 1946.

Diwakar, R.R., "Gandhi and Evolution of Man as a Social Being." *Gandhi Marg* 2 (May 1980): 105-13.

————, "Gandhi: From 'God is Truth' to 'Truth is God'." *Gandhi Marg* (February 1981): 617-26.

Doke, Joseph J., *An Indian Patriot in South Africa*. Reprint. Delhi: Government of India, 1967.

Dorr, Donal., *Option for the Poor: A Hundred Years of Vatican Social Teaching*. Maryknoll, New York: Orbis Books, 1983.

Dos Santos, Theotonio, "The Crisis of Development Theory and the Problem of Dependence in Latin America." in *Underdevelopment and Development*, ed., H. Bernstein, 57-80. Harmondsworth, England: Penguin Books 1973.

Douglass, Bruce, ed., *The Deeper Meaning of Economic Life: Critical Essays on the U.S. Catholic Bishops' Pastoral Letter on the economy*. Washington, D.C., Georgetown University Press, 1986.

Douglass, James W., *The Non-violent Cross: A Theology of Revolution and Peace*. Third Printing. New York: Macmillan Publishing Co., Inc., 1973.

Dussel, Enrique, "An Ethic of Liberation: Fundamental Hypotheses." *Concilium* 172 (April 1984): 54-63.

————, *Ethics and the Theology of Liberation*. Maryknoll, New York: Orbis Books, 1978.

Easwaran, Eknath, *Gandhi: The Man*. San Francisco, Glide Publications, 1972.

Edwards, Paul, ed., *The Encyclopedia of Philosophy*, 8 volumes. New York: Macmillan Publishing Co., Inc. & The Free Press, 1967.

Ellacuria, Ignacio, *Freedom Made Flesh: The Mission of Christ and His Church*. Maryknoll, New York: Orbis Books, 1976.

Ellis, Marc H., and Otto Maduro, *The Future of Liberation Theology: Essays in Honor of Gustavo Gutiérrez*. Maryknoll, New York: Orbis Books, 1989.

Engineer, Asghar Ali, ed., *Gandhi and Communal Harmony*. New Delhi: Gandhi Peace Foundation, 1997.

Erikson, Erik H., *Gandhi's Truth: On the Origins of Militant Nonviolence*. New York: W.W. Norton & Company, 1969.

Estey, George F., and Doris A. Hunter, *Nonviolence: A Reader in the Ethics of Action.* Waltham, Massachusetts: Xerox College Publishing, 1971.

Fabella, Virginia, ed., *Asia's Struggle for Full Humanity.* Maryknoll, New York: Orbis Books, 1980.

Fabella, Virginia M.M., and Sergio Torres, eds., *Irruption of the Third World: Challenge to Theology.* New York: Orbis Books, 1983.

Ferm, Deane William, *Third World Liberation Theologies: A Reader.* Maryknoll, New York: Orbis Books, 1986.

————, *Third World Liberation Theologies: An Introductory Survey.* Maryknoll, New York: Orbis Books, 1986.

Fisher, Louis, *The Life of Mahatma Gandhi.* London: Jonathan Cape, 1952.

Forest, Jim, *Thomas Merton's Struggle with Peacemaking.* Erie: Benet Press, 1980.

Fox, Richard, *Gandhian Utopia: Experiments with Culture.* Boston: Beacon Press, 1989.

Frank, Andre Gunder, "Sociology of Development and Underdevelopment of Sociology." in *Dependence and Underdevelopment,* ed., Cockroft, James D., André Gunder Frank, and Dale L. Johnson, 321-98. New York: Doubleday, Anchor, 1972.

Frankena, William K., *Ethics.* Second edition. Englewood Cliffs, New Jersey: Prentice-Hall, Inc., 1973.

Fuchs, Josef, *Natural Law: A Theological Investigation.* New York: Sheed and Ward, 1965.

————, *Personal Responsibility and Christian Morality.* Washington: Georgetown University Press, 1983.

Furtado, Celso, *Underdevelopment and Dependence: The Fundamental Connections.* Cambridge: Centre of Latin American Studies, University of Cambridge, 1974.

Gaede, Erwin A., *Politics and Ethics: Machiavelli to Niebuhr.* New York: University Press of America, 1983.

Galtung, John, *The Way is the Goal: Gandhi Today.* Ahmedabad: Gujarat Vidyapith Peace Research Centre, 1992.

Gandhi, M.K., *Ethical Religion (Nithi Dharma).* Translated from the Hindi by A. Ram Iyer, Second edition. Madras: S. Ganesan, 1922.

——, *Sermon on the Sea.* Edited by Haridas T. Mazurndar with an Introduction by John Haynes Holmes. Chicago: Universal Publishing Co. 1924.

——, *Hind Swaraj (Indian Home Rule).* Sixth edition. Madras: G.A. Natesan & Co., 1932.

——, *Speeches and Writings of Mahatma Gandhi,* 4th ed. Madras: G.A. Natesan & Co., 1933.

——, *Christian Missions.* Ahmedabad: Navajivan Publishing House, 1941.

——, *Non-Violence in Peace and War.* 2 volumes. Ahmedabad: Navajivan Publishing House, 1948, 1949.

——, *India of My Dreams.* Ahmedabad: Navajivan Publishing House. 1947.

——, *Hindu Dharma.* Edited by Bharatan Kumarappa. Ahmedabad: Navajivan Publishing House, 1950.

——, *Towards Lasting Peace.* Edited by Anand T. Hingorani. Bombay: Bharatiya Vidya Bhavan, 1956.

——, *From Yerawda Mandir: Ashram Observances.* Translated from Gujarati by V.G. Desai, Third edition. Ahmedabad: Navajivan Publishing House, 1957.

——, *Gandhi's Correspondence with the Government, 1942-44.* Ahmedabad: Navajivan Publishing House, 1957.

——, *All Men Are Brothers.* New York: Columbia University Press, 1958.

——, *Collected Works of Mahatma Gandhi.* 100 volumes to date. New Delhi: Publications Division of the Ministry of Information and Broadcasting, Government of India, 1958.

——, *For Pacifists.* Reprint. Ahmedabad: Navajivan Publishing House, 1960.

——, *In Search of the Supreme.* 3 volumes. Ahmedabad: Navajivan Publishing House, 1962.

——, *Ashram Observances in Action.* Ahmedabad: Navajivan Publishing House, 1965.

——, *Constructive Programme.* Ahmedabad: Navajivan Publishing House, 1968.

————, *Sarvodaya (The Welfare of All). Gandhi's paraphrase in Gujarati of John Ruskin's Unto This Last.* Ahmedabad: Navajivan Publishing House, 1968.

————, *Satyagraha in South Africa.* Translated from Gujarati *(Dakshin Afrika-na Satyagraha-na Itihas)* by V.G. Desai. Madras: S. Ganesan, 1928. Reprint of the rev. second edition. Ahmedabad: Navajivan Press, 1972.

————, *Autobiography: The Story of My Experiments with Truth (Satyana Prayogo athava Atmakatha).* Translated by Mahadev Desai. Ahmedabad: Navajivan Publishing House, 1945. Reprint. New York: Dover publications, Inc., 1983.

Gandhi, Rajmohan, *The Good Boatman: A Portrait of Gandhi.* New Delhi: Viking, 1995.

Gangrade, K.D., *Gandhian Perspective on Human Rights and Social Work Practice.* Lucknow: Lucknow University (Lecture), 2002.

Ganguli, B.N., *Gandhi's Social Philosophy: Perspective and Relevance.* Delhi: Vikas Publishing House Pvt. Ltd., 1973.

————, *Non-violent Resistance (Satyagraha).* Eighth printing. New York: Schocken Books, 1974.

Garcia, Ismael, *Justice in Latin American Theology of Liberation.* Atlanta: John Knox Press, 1987.

Gaur, V.P., *Mahatma Gandhi: A Study of His Message of Non-violence.* New Delhi: Sterling Publishers Private Limited, 1977.

Gibellini, Rosino, ed., *Frontiers of Theology in Latin America.* Second Printing. Maryknoll, New York: Orbis Books, 1979.

————, *The Liberation Theology Debate.* Translated from the Italian by John Bowden. London: SCM Press Ltd., 1987.

Giddens, Anthony, *The Nation-State and Violence.* Berkeley: University of California Press, 1987.

Gilkey, Langdon, *Naming the Whirlwind: The Renewal of God-Language.* Third Printing. New York: The Bobbs-Merrill Company, inc., 1969.

Gilleman, Gerard, S. J., *The Primacy of Charity in Moral Theology.* Translated from the second French edition by William F. Ryan, S. J., and Andre Vachon, S. J., Westminster, Maryland: The Newman Press, 1959.

Gilpin, Robert, *The Political Economy of International Relations.* Princeton, New Jersey: Princeton University Press, 1987.

Goizueta, Roberto S., *Liberation, Method and dialogue: Enrique Dussel and North American theological Discourse.* Atlanta, Georgia: Scholar Press, 1988.

Gottwald, Norman K., ed., *The Bible and Liberation: Political and Social Hermeneutics.* Maryknoll, New York: Orbis Books, 1983.

Goulet, Denis, *A New Moral Order.* Maryknoll, New York: Orbis Books, 1974.

————, *The Cruel Choice: A New Concept in the Theory of Development.* Lanham, Maryland: University Press of America, 1985.

Green, Martin, *The Challenge of the Mahatmas.* New York: Basic Books, Inc., Publishers, 1978.

————, *Tolstoy and Gandhi: Men of Peace.* New York: Basic Books, 1983.

————, *The Origins of Nonviolence. Tolstoy and Gandhi in Their Historical Setting.* University Park, Pennsylvania: The Pennsylvania State University Press, 1986.

————, *The Mountain of Truth: The Counterculture Begins.* Hanover, N.H., University Press of New England, 1986.

Gregg, Richard B., *The Power of Non-violence.* Introduction by Rufus M. Jones, New York: Fellowship Publications, 1944.

————, *To Which Way Lies Hope? Examination of Capitalism, Communism, Socialism and Gandhi's Programme.* Ahmedabad: Navajivan, 1959.

Gremillion, Joseph, *The Church and Culture since Vatican II: The Experience of North and Latin America.* Notre Dame, Indiana: University of Notre Dame Press, 1985.

————, ed., *The Gospel of Peace and Justice: Catholic Social Teaching since Pope John.* Maryknoll, New York: Orbis Books, 1976.

Grover, Verinder, *Gandhi and Politics in India.* New Delhi: Deep & Deep Publications, 1987.

Gudorf, Christine, *Catholic Social Teaching on Liberation Themes.* Lanham, Maryland: University Press of America, 1980.

Guha, Ranajit and Gayatri Chakravorty Spivak, *Selected Subaltern Studies.* With a Foreword by Edward W. Said, New York: Oxford University Press, 1988.

Gustafson, James M., "Context vs Principles: A Misplaced Debate in Christian Ethics." *Harvard Theological Review* 58 (1965): 171-202.

————, *Christ and the Moral Life*. Chicago: The University of Chicago Press. 1968.

————, *Theology and Christian Ethics*. Philadelphia: Pilgrim Press, 1974.

————, *Can Ethics be Christian?* Chicago: The University of Chicago Press, 1975.

————, *Protestant and Roman Catholic Ethics*. Chicago: The University of Chicago Press, 1978.

————, *Ethics from a Theocentric Perspective*. 2 volumes. Chicago: The University of Chicago Press, 1981, 1984.

Gutiérrez, Gustavo., "Toward a Theology' of Liberation." (July 1968) in *Liberation Theology: A Documentary History*. Edited with Introductions, Commentary, and Translations by Alfred T. Hennelly, S. J., 62-76. Maryknoll, New York: Orbis Books, 1990.

————, "Liberation Development." *Cross Currents* (Summer 1971): 243-56.

————, *A Theology of Liberation: History, Politics, and Salvation*. Translated and edited by Caridad Inda and John Eagleson. Maryknoll, New York: Orbis Books, 1973. Fifteenth anniversary edition. Maryknoll, New York: Orbis Books, 1988.

————, "Liberation Movements and theology." *Concilium* 93, *Jesus Christ and Human Freedom*, eds. Schillebeeckx and van Iersel, 135-46 New York: Herder and Herder, 1974.

————, "Liberation, Theology and Proclamation." *Concilium* 96, *The Mystical and Political Dimension of the Christian Faith*, eds. Claude Geffre and Gustavo Gutiérrez, 57-77. New York: Herder and Header, 1974.

————, "Faith as Freedom: Solidarity with the Alienated and Confidence in the Future." *Horizons* 2 (Spring 1975): 25-60.

————, "Faith and Freedom." In *Living with Change, Experience, and Faith*, ed., Eigo, 15-54. Villanova: Villanova University Press, 1976.

————, "The Poor in the Church." *Concilium* 104, *The Poor and The Church*, eds., Greinacher and Muller, 11-16. New York: Seabury Press 1977.

————, "Freedom and Salvation: A Political Problem." In *Liberation and Change*, edited and introduced by Ronaid H. Stone, 1-94. Atlanta: John Knox Press. 1977.

————, "Two Theological Perspectives: Liberation Theology and Progressivist Theology." In *The Emergent Gospel*, eds., Sergio Torres and Virginia Fabella, 227-55. Maryknoll. New York: Orbis Books, 1978.

————, "Liberation Praxis and Christian Faith." In *Frontiers of Theology in Latin America*, ed. Rosino Gibellini, 1-33. New York: Orbis Books, 1979.

————, "The Irruption of the Poor in Latin America and the Christian Communities of the Common People." In *The Challenge of Basic Christian Communities*, 107-23. Edited by Sergio Torres and John Eagleson, Maryknoll. New York: Orbis Books. 1981.

————, *The Power of the Poor in History*. Translated by Robert R. Barr, Foreword by Robert McAfee Brown, New York: Orbis Books. 1983.

————, "Reflections from a Latin American Perspective: Finding our Way to Talk about God." In *Irruption of the Third World: Challenge to Theology*, 222-34. eds. Virginia Fabella, M.M., and Sergio Torres, New York: Orbis Books, 1983.

————, *We Drink from Our own Wells: The Spiritual Journey of a People*. Translated by Matthew J. O'Connell, Maryknoll, New York: Orbis Books, 1984.

————, "Speaking about God" *Concilium* 171 (1/1984): 24-32.

————, "I am a Christian First." An interview by Michael De Mott, Maryknoll (November 1986): 14-19.

————, *On Job: God-Talk and the Suffering of the Innocent.* Translated by Mathew J. O'Connell, Maryknoll, New York: Orbis Books, 1987.

————, *Diós o el oro en las Indias*. Lima: CEP and instituto Bartolome de Las Casas-Rimac, 1989.

————, *El Diós da la vida*. Lima: CEP, 1990.

——, *The Truth Shall Make You Free.* Maryknoll, New York: Orbis Books. 1990.

——, *The God of Life.* Translated from the Spanish by Mathew J. O'Connell, Maryknoll, N.Y.: Orbis Books, 1991.

——, *Las Casas: In Search of the Poor of Jesus Christ.* Translated by Robert R. Barr, Maryknoll, N.Y., Orbis, 1993.

——, *Sharing the Word Through the Liturgical Year.* Maryknoll, N.Y., Orbis Books, 1997.

Haight, Roger, *An Alternative Vision: An Interpretation of Liberation Theology.* Maryknoll, New York: Orbis Books, 1985.

Hardiman, David, *Gandhi in his time and ours.* Delhi: Permanent Black, 2003.

Häring, Bernard, *The Healing Power of Peace and Nonviolence.* New York: Paulist Press, 1986.

Harrison, Beverly Wildung, "Theological Reflection in the Struggle for Liberation." In *Making the Connections: Essays in Feminist Social Ethics,* 235-63. ed., Carol S. Robb, Boston: Beacon Press, 1985.

Hartman, Robert H., ed., *Poverty and Economic Justice: A Philosophical Approach.* New York: Paulist Press, 1984.

Haughey, John C., ed., *The Faith That Does Justice: Examining the Christian Sources for Social Change.* New York: Paulist Press, 1977.

Heilbroner, Robert L., *In the Name of Profit.* Garden City, New York: Doubleday & Company, Inc., 1972.

Hennily, Alfred T., *Theologies in Conflict: The Challenge of Juan Luis Segundo.* Maryknoll, New York: Orbis Books, 1979.

Heredero, R:, *Rural Development and Social Change — An Experiment in Non-Formal Education.* New Delhi: Manohar book House, 1977.

Hettne, Bjorn., "The Vitality of Gandhian Tradition." *Journal of Peace Research* XIII (3/1976): 227-45.

Hick, John, and Lament C. Hempel, ed., *Gandhi's Significance for Today.* New York: St. Martin's Press, 1989.

Hildebrandt, Rainer, *Von Gandhi Bis Walesa: Gewaltfreier kampf fur Menschenrechte.* Berlin: Verlag Haus am Checkpoint Charlie, 1987.

Hiriyanna, M., *Outlines of Indian Philosophy.* London: Allen & Unwin, 1932.

Hollenbach, David, *Claims in Conflicts: Retrieving and Renewing the Catholic Human Rights Tradition.* New York: Paulist Press, 1979.

————, *Nuclear Ethics: A Christian Moral Argument.* New York: Paulist Press, 1983.

Horowitz, Irving Louis, *Three Worlds of Development.* New York: Oxford University Press, 1972.

Horsburgh, H.J.N., *Nonviolence and Aggression: A Study of Gandhi's Moral Equivalent of War.* New York: Oxford University Press, 1968.

Houtart, Francis, *The Challenge to Change.* New York: Sheed and Ward, 1964.

Hug, James E.S.J., ed., *Tracing the Spirit: Communities, Social Action, and Theological Reflection.* New York: Paulist Press, 1983.

Inkeles, Alex., "The Modernization of Man." In *Modernisation: The Dynamics of Growth.* ed., Myros Weiner. New York: Basic Books, 1966.

Irwing, Horowitz L., *Three World of Development,* New York: Oxford University Press, 1966.

Iyer, Raghavan N., *The Moral and Political Thought of Mahatma Gandhi.* New York: Oxford University Press, 1973.

————, ed., *The Moral and Political Writings of Mahatma Gandhi.* 3 volumes. Oxford: Clarendon Press. 1986 & 1988.

Jain, Pratibha, *Gandhian Ideas, Social Movements, and Creativity.* Jaipur: Rawat Publications, 1985.

Jesudasan, Ignatius, S. J., *A Gandhian Theology of Liberation.* New York: Orbis Books, 1984.

Jha, Rama. "Gandhi's Encounter with Wetern Thought." *Gandhi Marg* (July 1983): 209-21.

Jha, S.N., *A Critical Study of Gandhian Economic Thought.* Agra: Lakshmi Narayan Aggarwal, 1961.

Jonas, Hans, *The Imperative of Responsibility: In Search of an Ethics for the Technological Age.* Chicago: The University of Chicago Press, 1984.

Jones, E. Stanley, *Mahatma Gandhi: An Interpretation.* London: Hodder & Stoughton, 1948; New York: Albingdon-Cokesbury Press, 1948.

Juergensmeyer, Mark, *Fighting with Gandhi: A Step-by-step Strategy for Resolving Everyday Conflicts*. San Francisco: Harper & Row, Publishers, 1984.

Kammer III, Charles L, *Ethics and Liberation: An Introduction*. Maryknoll, New York: Orbis Books, 1988.

Kappen, Sebastian, *Jesus and Freedom*. Maryknoll, New York: Orbis Books, 1977.

Kappen, Mercy, ed., *Gandhi and Social Action Today*. New Delhi: Sterling Publications, 1990.

Kee, Alistair, *Marx and the Failure of Liberation Theology*. London: SCM Press; Philadelphia: Trinity Press International, 1990.

Kerans, Patrick, *Sinful Social Structures*. New York: Paulist Press, 1974.

Khanna, J.K., *Gandhi: On Recent Indian Political Thought*. New Delhi: Ess Ess Publications, 1982.

Khanna, Suman, *Gandhi and the Good Life*. New Delhi: Gandhi Peace Foundation, 1985.

———, " 'Of Faith': A Study in Gandhi and Marcel." *Gandhi Marg 5* (May 1983): 88-108.

Kierkegaard, Soren, *Works of Love*. Translated by Howard and Edna Hong. New York: Harper and Brothers, 1962.

King, Martin Luther, Jr., *The Trumpet of Conscience*. Foreword by Coretta Scott King, San Francisco, Harper & Row Publishers, 1968.

———, *Strength to Love*. Third Printing. Philadelphia: Fortress Press. 1983.

Kirk, Kenneth E., *The Vision of God: The Christian Doctrine of the Summum Bonum*. Abridged Edition. Reprint. Greenwood: The Attic Press, Inc., 1977.

Krasner, Stephen D., ed., *International Regimes*. Second Printing, Ithaca: Cornell University Press, 1984.

Kruijer, Gerald J., *Development Through Liberation: Third World Problems and Solutions*. Translated by Arnorl Pomerans. Atlantic Highlands, New Jersey: Humanities Press International, Inc., 1987.

Lamb, Mathew L., *Solidarity with Victims: Toward a Theology of Social Transformation*. New York: The Crossroad Publishing Company, 1982.

Land, Philip, ed., *Theology Meets Progress*. Rome: Gregorian University Press, 1971.

Land, Philip S., "The Social Theology of Pope Paul VI." *America* 140 (May 1979): 390-95.

Lanza del Vasto, Joseph Jean, *Warriors of Peace: Writings on the Technique of Nonviolence*. Edited by Michel Random and Translated from the French by Jean Sidgwick. New York: Alfred A. Knopf, 1974.

Lerner, Daniel, *The Passing of Traditional Society: Modernizing the Middle East*. New York: Free Press, 1958.

Lernoux, Penny, *Cry of the People: The Struggle for Human Rights in Latin America — The Catholic Church in Conflict with U.S. Policy*. New York: Penguin Books, 1982.

Lonergan, Bernard, J.F., *Insight: A Study of Human Understanding*. New York: Philosophical Library, 1957.

Lonergan, Bernard, J.F., *Method in Theology*. Third Printing. New York: The Seabury Press, 1972.

Lutz, Mark A., "Human Nature in Gandhian Economics: The Case of Ahimsa or 'Social Action'." *Gandhi Marg* 4 (March 1983): 941-55.

Machiavelli, Niccolo, *The Prince*, translated by Leo Paul S. de Alvarez, Texas: University of Dallas Press, 1980.

Mahadevan, T.M.P., "The Philosophy of Mahatma Gandhi." *Indian Philosophical Annual* 5 (1969): 95-106.

Mahan, Brian and L. Dale Richesin, ed., *The Challenge of Liberation Theology: a First World Response*. Introduction by David Tracy, Maryknoll, New York: Orbis Books, 1981; second printing 1984.

Mahoney, John, *The Making of Moral Theology: A Study of the Roman Catholic Tradition*. Oxford: Clarendon Press, 1987.

Maritain, Jacques, *Integral Humanism: Temporal and Spiritual Problems of a New Christendom*. Translated by Joseph W. Evans, Reprint. Notre Dame, Indiana: University of Notre Dame Press, 1973.

Markovits, Claude, *The Un-Gandhian Gandhi: The life and Afterlife of the Mahatma*. Delhi: Permanent Black, 2003.

Martinez, Gaspar, *Confronting the Mystery of God: Political, Liberation, and Public Theologies.* New York: Continuum, 2001.

Matson, Floyd W., *The Broken Image.* New York: Doubleday, 1966.

McCann, Dennis, P., *Christian Realism and Liberation Theology: Practica Theologies in Creative Conflict.* Maryknoll, New York: Orbis Books. 1981; second printing 1982.

McCormick, Richard and Paul Rarnsey, ed., *Doing Evil to Achieve Good: Moral Choice in Conflict Situations.* Chicago: Loyola University Press, 1978.

McGovern, Arthur F., *Liberation Theology and Its Critics: Toward an Assessment.* Maryknoll, New York: Orbis Books, 1989.

Mehta, Saryu R., and Bhogilal, G. Sheth, *Shrimad Rajchandra: A Great Seer.* Anand, Gujarat: Raojibhai C. Desai, 1971.

Merton, Thomas, *Gandhi on Non-Violence.* Edited with an Introduction. Seventh Printing. New York: New Directions Publishing Corporation. 1965.

———, *The Asian Journal of Thomas Merton.* Edited by Naomi Burton, Brother Patrick Hari & James Laughlin. Tenth printing. New York: A New Directions Book, 1975.

———, *The Hidden Ground of Love: Letters.* Selected and Edited by William H. Shannon, Third Printing. New York: Farrar. Straus. Giroux. 1986.

Metz, Johann Baptist, *Faith, History and Society: Toward a Practical Fundamental Theology.* New York: The Seabury Press, 1980.

Miller, W.R., *Nonviolence, A Christian Interpretation.* New York: Schocken Books, 1966.

Minz, Nirmal, *Mahatma Gandhi and Hindu Christian Dialogue.* Madras: The Christian Literature Society, 1970.

Miranda, José Porfirio, *Marx and the Bible: A Critique of the Philosophy of Oppression.* Maryknoll, New York: Orbis Books, 1974.

———, *Marx Against the Marxists: The Christian Humanism of Karl Marx.* Translated by John Drury, Maryknoll, New York: Orbis Books, 1980.

Mische, Gerald and Patricia Mische, *Toward a Human World Order: Beyondthe National Security Straitjacket.* New York: Paulist Press, 1977.

Moser, Antonio, "The Representation of God in the Ethic of Liberation." *Concilium* 172 (2/1984): 42-47.

Mott, Stephen Charles, *Biblical Ethics and Social Change.* New York: Oxford University Press, 1982.

Mukerjee, Hiren, *Gandhi a Study.* Calcutta: National Book Agency Ltd., 1958.

Mukhopadhyay, Subrata and Ramaswamy, Sushila, ed., *Political Ideas of Mahatma Gandhi.* New Delhi: Deep & Deep Publications, 1998.

Murray, John Courtney, *We Hold These Truths: Catholic Reflections on the American Proposition.* New York: Sheed and Ward, 1960.

Naess, Arne, *Gandhi and Group Conflict.* Oslo-Bergen-Troms: Universitetsforlaget, 1984.

Nanda, B.R., *Mahatma Gandhi: A Biography.* London: George Allen and Unwin Ltd., 1959.

———, *Gandhi and His Critics.* New Delhi: OUP, 1985.

Nandy, Ashis, "From Outside the Imperium: Gandhi's Cultural Critique of the West." Chap. In *Traditions, Tyranny and Utopia: Essays in the Politics of Awareness.* Delhi: Oxford University Press, 1987.

Naravane, V.S., *Modern Indian Thought.* Bombay: Asia Publishing House, 1964.

Narayan, Jayaprakash, *Research on Gandhian Thought.* Bombay: Round Table on Research Programme on Gandhian Thought, 14th-15th June, 1969. Papers and Proceedings. December, 1970.

Narayan, Sriman., ed., *The Selected works of Mahatma Gandhi,* 5 volumes. Ahmedabad: Navajivan Publishing House, 1968.

Nash, Ronald H., ed., *Liberation Theology.* Grand Rapids, Michigan: Baker Book House, 1984

Nath, Bhupendra, "Significance of Suffering in Gandhian Ethics." *Gandhi Marg* 66 (September 1984): 475-82.

Nelson, Jack A., *Hunger for Justice: The Politics of Food and Faith.* Fourth Printing. Maryknoll, New York: Orbis Books, 1981.

Niebuhr, H. Richard, "War as the Judgement of God." *The Christian Century* 59 (1942): 630-33.

———, *Christ and Culture.* New York: Harper & Row, 1951.

————, *The Responsible Self.* New York: Harper & Row, 1963.

Niebuhr, Reinhold, *Moral Man and Immoral Society.* New York: Charles Scribner's Sons, 1932.

————, *The Nature and Destiny of Man.* 2 volumes. New York: Charles Scribner's Sons. 1941. 1943.

Ogden, Schubert, *Faith and Freedom: Toward a Theology of Liberation.* Nashville: Abingdon, 1979.

————, "The Concept of a Theology of Liberation: Must a Christian Theology Be So Conceived?" In *The Challenge of Liberation Theology*, 127-40. ed., Mahan and Richesin. Maryknoll, New York: Orbis Books. 1981.

Oglesby, Enoch H., *Ethics And Theology From The Other Side: Sounds of Moral Struggle.* Washington: University Press of America, 1979.

O'Gorman, Angie, ed., *The Universe Bends Toward Justice: A Reader on Christian Nonviolence in the U.S.* Philadelphia: New Society Publishers, 1990.

Outka, Gene., *Agape: An Ethical Analysis.* New Haven: Yale University Press, 1972.

Palkhivala, N.A., "Relevance of Gandhi Today." *Gandhi Marg* (April 1984): 3-14.

Parekh, Bhikhu, *Gandhi's Political Philosophy: A Critical Examination.* Notre Dame, Indiana: University of Notre Dame Press, 1989.

Parel, Anthony J., ed., *Hind Swaraj and Other Writings.* Cambridge: Cambridge University Press, 1997.

Parel, Anthony J., ed., *Gandhi, Freedom and Self-Rule.* London: Lexington Books, 2000.

Parsons, Talcott, "Evolutionary Universals in Society." *American Sociological Review* 29 (1964): 339-57.

————, *Societies: Evolutionary and Comparative Perspectives.* Englewood Cliffs, New Jersey: Prentice-Hall, 1966.

Parulekar, N.B., *The Science of the soul force or Mahatma Gandhi's Doctrine of Truth and Non-Violence.* Bombay: Hind Kitabs Ltd., 1962.

Pasricha, Ashu, *Gandhian Approach to Integrated Rural Development.* New Delhi: Shipra, 2000.

Patil, V.T., ed., *New Dimensions and Perspectives in Gandhism*. New Delhi: Inter-India Publications. 1988.

Pattery, George, S. J., *Gandhi the Believer· An Indian Christian Perspective*. Delhi: ISPCK, 1996.

Payne, Robert, *The Life and Death of Mahatma Gandhi*. New York: E.P. Dutton & Co., Inc., 1969.

Pegis, Anton C., ed., *Basic Writings of Saint Thomas Aquinas*, 2 volumes. New York: Random House, 1945.

Pieris, Aloysius, S. J., *An Asian Theology of Liberation*. Maryknoll, New York: Orbis Books, 1988.

Planas, Ricardo, *Liberation Theology: The Political Expression of Religion*. Kansas City: Sheed & Ward, 1986.

Polak, H.S.L., Brailsford, H.N. and Lawrence Lord Pathick, *Mahatma Gandhi*, London: Odhams Press Ltd., 1949.

Portes, Alejandro, "On the Sociology of Natural Development: Theories and Issues," *American Journal of Sociology* 82 (July 1976): 55-85.

Power, Paul F., ed., *The Meanings of Gandhi*. Hawaii: The University Press of Hawaii, 1971.

Prabhu, R.K., and U. R. Rao, comp. *The Mind of Mahatma Gandhi*. Bombay: Oxford University Press, 1960.

Prasad, Mahadeva, *Social Philosophy of Mahatma Gandhi*. Gorakhpur: Vishwavidyalaya Prakashan, 1958.

Prasad, K.M., *Sarvodaya of Gandhi*. Edited by Ramjee Singh, New Delhi: Raj Hans Publications, 1984.

Puri, Rashmi-Sudha, *Gandhi on War and Peace*. New York: Praeger Publishers, 1987.

Pyarelal, *Mahatma Gandhi: The Last Phase*. 2 volumes. Ahmedabad: Navajivan Publishing House, 1956, 1966.

Quade, Quentin L., ed., *The Pope and Revolution: John Paul II Confronts Liberation Theology*. Washington: Ethics and Public Policy Center, 1982.

Radhakrishnan, S., *Religion and Society*. London: George Allen & Unwin Ltd., 1947.

Radhakrishnan, S., ed., *Mahatma Gandhi: 100 Years*. New Delhi: Gandhi Peace Foundation, 1968.

Rahner, Karl, "Conversion." In *Encyclopedia of Theology: The Concise Sacramentum Mundi*. New York: The Seabury Press, 1975.

Rawls, John, *A Theory of Justice*. Cambridge, Massachusetts: Harvard University Press, 1971.

Ray, Baren, ed., *Gandhi's Campaign Against Untouchability, 1933-34: An Account from the Raj's Secret Official Reports*. New Delhi: Gandhi Peace Foundation, 1996.

Ray, Sibnarayan, ed., *Gandhi India and the World: An International Symposium*. Philadelphia: Temple University Press, 1970.

Rejón, Francisco Moreno, "Seeking the Kingdom and its Justice: The Development of the Ethic of Liberation." *Concilium* 172 (2/1984): 35-41.

Richards, Glyn, *The Philosophy of Gandhi: A Study of His Basic Ideas*. Totowa, New Jersey: Barnes & Noble Books, 1982.

Richards, Michael, "Towards a Theology of Development." *The Clergy Review*. 54 (1969): 510-18.

Ricoeur, Paul, *Freedom and Nature*, Chicago: Northwestern University Press, 1966.

Roach, Richard, "New Sense of Faith." *The Journal of Religious Ethics* 5 (Spring 1977): 135-54.

Rolland, Romain, *Mahatma Gandhi*. England: Allen & Unwin, 1924.

Ross, David F., and Mahendra S. Kanti, *Gandhian Economics: Sources, Substances and Legacy*. Bangalore: Prasad Publications, 1983.

Rostow, Walt W., *The Stages of Economic Growth: A Non-Communist: Manifesto*. Cambridge: Harvard University Press, 1960.

Rothermund, Indira, *The Philosophy of Restraint*. Bombay: Popular Prakashan, 1963.

Rudolph, Susanne Hoeber and Lloyd L. Rudolph, *Gandhi: The Traditional Roots of Charisma*. Chicago: The University of Chicago Press, 1983.

Ruskin, John, *"Unto This Last": Four Essays on the First Principles of Political Economy*. Edited with an introduction by Lloyd J. Hubenka, Lincoln: University of Nebraska Press, 1967.

Ryan, John A, *Distributive Justice: The Right and Wrong of Our Present Distribution of Wealth*. New York: The Macmillan Company, 1922.

————, *The Christian Doctrine on Property.* New York: Paulist Press, 1923.

Ryan, John A., and Francis J. Boland, *Catholic Principles of Politics.* New York: The Macmillan Company, 1940.

Sankhdher, M.M., *Understanding Gandhi Today.* New Delhi: Deep & Deep Publications, 1996.

Saxena, Sushil Kumar, *Ever Unto God: Essays on Gandhi and Religion.* New Delhi: Indian Council of Philosophical Research, 1988.

Schreiter, Robert J., *Constructing Local Theologies.* Foreword by Edward Schillebeeckx, Maryknoll, New York: Orbis Books, 1985.

Schumacher, E.F., *Small is Beautiful: Economics as if People Mattered.* New York: Harper & Row, Publishers, 1973.

Second General Conference of Latin American Bishops. *The Church in the Present-Day Transformation of Latin America in Light of the Council* (Medellin Documents). Washington, D.C., United States Catholic Conference, n.d.

Second Vatican Council, *Gaudium et Spes* (*Pastoral Constitution on the Church in the Modern world*). In The Gospel of Peace and Justice: Catholic Social Teaching since Pope John, 243-335. Edited by Joseph Germillion, Maryknoll, New York: Orbis Books, 1976.

Segundo, Juan Luis, *Grace and Human Condition.* Maryknoll, New York: Orbis Books, 1973.

————, *The Liberation of Theology.* Third printing. Maryknoll, New York: Orbis Books. 1982.

————, *Faith and Ideologies.* Maryknoll, New York: Orbis Books; Melbourne, Australia: Dove Communications; London, England: Sheed and Ward. 1934.

Sethi, J.D., *International Economic Disorder and a Gandhian Solution.* Shimla: Indian Institute of Advanced Study. 1990.

Shannon, William H., ed., *The Hidden Groud of Love: The Letters of Thomas Merton.* New York: Farrar, Straus & Giroux, 1985.

Sharma, Chandradhar, *A Critical Survey of Indian Philosophy.* Delhi: Motilal Banarsidass, 1976.

Sharma, Jai Narain, *Alternative Economics: Economics of Mahatma Gandhi and Globalisation.* New Delhi: Deep & Deep Publications Pvt. Ltd., 2003.

Sharma, Jai Narain, *Power, Politics and Corruption: A Gandhian Solution*. New Delhi: Deep & Deep Publications Pvt. Ltd., 2004.

Sharma, Rashmi, *Gandhian Economics: A Humane Approach*. New Delhi: Deep & Deep Publications, 1997.

——, *Autobiographical Writings of Mahatma Gandhi*. New Delhi: Deep & Deep Publications Pvt. Ltd., 2004.

Sharp, Gene, *Gandhi as a Political Strategist: With Essays on Ethics and Politics*. Introduction by Coretta Scott King. Boston: Porter Sargent Publishers, Inc., 1979.

——, *Gandhi Wields the Weapon of Moral Power*. Ahmedabad: Navajivan Publishing House, 1960.

——, *The Politics of Non-Violent Action*. Boston: Porter Sargent Publishers. 1973.

Shriridharani, Krishnalal Jethalal, *War Without Violence: A Study of Gandhi's Method and Its Accomplishments*. New York: Harcourt Brace and Company, 1939.

Siddharaj, Dhadda, *Gandhian Alternative*. Varanasi: Sarva Seva Sangh Prakashan, 1997.

Singh, Ramjee, *The Gandhian Vision*. New Delhi: Manak Publications, 1998.

Skinner, Quentin, *Foundations of Modern Political Thought*. 2 volumes. Cambridge; New York: Cambridge University Press, 1978.

Skurski, Roger, ed., *New Directions in Economic Justice*. Notre Dame, Indiana: University of Notre Dame Press, 1983.

Soares-Prabhu, George M., "Good News To the Poor, The Social Implications of the Message of Jesus." *Biblebhashyam*, IV (September 1978): 193-212.

——, "Class in the Bible: The Biblical Poor a Social Class?" in *Vidyajyoti* 49 (1985): 325-46.

——, *Collected Writings of George M. Soares-Prabhu, S. J.* 4 volumes, Pune: Jnana-Deepa Vidyapeeth Theology Series, 1999-2001.

Sobrino, Jon, *Christology at the Crossroads: A Latin American Approach*. Maryknoll, New York: Orbis Books, 1978.

Sobrino, Jon, *The True Church and the Poor*. Translated from the Spanish by Mathew J. O'Connell, Maryknoll, New York: Orbis Books, 1984.

Sobrino, Jon, and Pico, Juan Hernandez, *The Theology of Christian Solidarity*. Maryknoll, New York: Orbis Books, 1985.

Sonnieitner, Michael W., "Gandhian Satyagraha & Swaraj: A Hierarchical Perspective." A Paper presented at the 15th Annual Conference on South Asia, University of Wisconsin at Madison, 1986.

Spohn, William C., S. J., *What Are They Saying About Scripture and Ethics?* New York: Paulist Press, 1984.

Srisang, Koson, ed., *Perspectives on Political Ethics: An Ecumenical Enquiry*. Geneva: World Council of Churches Publications, 1983.

Suxena, S.K., "Gandhi and the Commitment to Truth." *Gandhi Marg* 68 (November 1984): 588-595.

Swomley, John M., *Liberation Ethics*. New York: The Macmillan Company, 1972.

Synod of Bishops. "Justice in the world." In *The Gospel of Peace and Justice: Catholic Social Teaching since Pope John*, 513-29. Edited by Joseph Germillion, Maryknoll, New York: Orbis Books, 1976.

Tagore, Rabindranath, *Gitanjali* (Song Offerings). Introduction by W.B. Yeats, Reprint. Delhi: The Macmillan Company of India Limited, 1980.

Tanner, Norman P., S. J., *Decrees of the Ecumenical Councils*. 2 volumes. London: Sheed and Ward, and Washington: Georgetown University Press, 1990.

Tellis-Nayak, V., "Gandhi on the dignity of the Human Person." *Gandhi Marg* 7 (January 1963): 40-52.

Tendulkar, D.G., *Mahatma: Life of Mohandas Karamchand Gandhi*, 8 vols. Bombay: Jhaveri and Teldulkar, 1952.

Thomas, Norman E., "Liberation for Life: A Hindu Liberation Philosophy." *Missiology* XVI (April 1988): 149-62.

Tolstoy, Leo, *The Kingdom of God is Within You: Christianity not as a Mystic Religion but as a New Theory of Life*. Translated from the Russian by Constance Garnett. Lincoln: University of Nebraska Press, 1984.

———, *Writings on Civil Disobedience and Nonviolence*. Introduction by David H. Albert, Philadelphia: New Society Publishers, 1987.

Topa, Ishwara, *Ethos of Non-Violence*. Ahmedabad: Navajivan Publishing House, 1964.

Tracy, David, *Blessed Rage for Order: The New Pluralism Theology.* New York: The Seabury Press, 1978.

———, *The Analogical Imagination: Christian Theology and the Culture of Pluralism.* New York: The Crossroads Publishing Company, 1981.

———, *Plurality and Ambiguity: Hermeneutics, Religion, Hope.* San Francisco: Harper & Row, Publishers, 1987.

Troeltsch, Ernst, *The Social Teaching of the Christian Churches,* 2 vols. Translated by Olive Wyon; with an Introduction by H. Richard Niebuhr London: George Allen & Unwin Ltd., and New York: The Macmillan company, 1931. Reprint. Chicago: The University of Chicago Press, 1981.

Tutu, Desmond Mpilo, *Hope and Suffering: Sermons and Speeches.* Edited by John Webster with a Foreword by the Right Reverend Trevor Huddleston, CR., Reprint. Grand Rapids, Michigan: William B. Eerdmans Publishing Company, 1986.

Ul Haq, Muhbub, *The Poverty Curtain: Choices for the Third World.* New Delhi: Oxford University Press, 1978.

Varma, V.P., *The Political Philosophy of Mahatma Gandhi and Sarvodaya.* Agra: Lakshmi Narain Agarwal, Educational Publishers, 1959.

Vasudev, Kasthuri., "The Metaphysical Basis of Gandhian Political Philosophy." *Indian Philosophical Annual* 5 (1969): 188-95.

Verma, V.P., *The Political Philosophy of Mahatma Gandhi and Sarvodaya.* Agra: Lakshmi Narain Aggarwal, 1981.

Vettickal, Thomas, *Gandhian Sarvodaya: Realizing a Realistic Utopia.* New Delhi: Gyan Publications, 2002.

Von Rad, Gerhard, *Old Testament Theology*, vol. II, trans. D.M.G. Stalker, New York: Harper & Row Publishers, 1965.

Wallerstein, Immanuel, *The Modern World System: Capitalist Agriculture and the Origins of the European World Economy in the Sixteenth Century.* New York: Academic Press, 1974.

———, "The Present State of the Debate on World Inequality." In *World Inequality: Origins and Perspectives on the World System*, ed., Immanuel Wallerstein, 12-28 Montreal; Blank Rose Books. 1975.

Weber, Max, *The Protestant Ethic and the Spirit of Capitalism.* Translated by Talcott Parsons with an Introduction by Anthony Giddens. New York: Charles Scribner's Sons, 1976.

Weiner, Myros, *Modernization: The Dynamics of Growth.* New York: Basic Books, 1966.

Williams, Preston N., "An Analysis of the Conception of Love and Its Influence on Justice in the Thought of Martin Luther King, Jr." *The Journal of Religious Ethics* 18 (Fall 1990): 15-31.

Wogaman, Philip J., *The Great Economic Debate: An Ethical Analysis.* Philadelphia: The Westminster Press, 1977.

Wolpert, Stanley, *Gandhi's Passion: The Life and Legacy of Mahatma Gandhi.* New York: Oxford University Press, 2001.

Younger, Paul, *Introduction to Indian Religious Thought.* Philadelphia: Westminster Press. 1972.

Index

Active and acting God, 108-12

Ahiṁsā
concept of, 24, 68, 70, 81-82, 102, 133-40, 150-52, 155, 163-65, 168, 171-72, 229-31, 235, 237, 239-40

healing power of, 163-64

Ahiṁsātmaka satyāgraha, 7, 10-11, 13, 81, 97, 102, 141-60, 205, 221-22, 225, 230-35, 239
as technique, 156-57
conflict resolution method, 160-64
healing power of *ahiṁsā*, 163-64
ideal *satyāgrahī*, 157-60
implication of non-violence, 150-53
individual and social transformation method, 160-64
method of individual and social transformation, 160-64

origin and meaning, 141-4
passive resistance/pacifism and, 143-46
positive meaning of, 146-48
theory and praxis of, 154-55
virtue of strong, 148-49

Alvarez, Leo Paul S. de, 175n

Alves, Ruben, 232n

Amin, Samir, 34n, 81n

Amin, Shahid, 5n, 18n

Anselm principle, 78

Appār, Tamil Śaivite poet, 65

Aquinas, Thomas, 59n, 63n, 84, 97n, 170, 132n

Aristotle, 62, 92, 97n, 99n

Arya, Victor, 49n, 105, 106n, 108n-09n, 129, 215n, 217n-18n

Ashe, Geoffrey, 97n

Aspiration, liberation as, 33

Ātman, concept of, 64, 88, 153, 171

Augustine, St., 70n, 85, 94-95, 132n

Ballou, Robert O., 131n, 133n

Barr, Robert R., 35n

Barth, Hans, 67n, 103

Barth, Though, 85n

Bartholomew, 103n

Baum, Gregory, 34n

Becker, Ernest, 2n

Bernstein, H., 34n

Besant, Annie, 16

Bhagavad-Gītā, 3

Bhuskute, 64n

Blondel, Maurice, 187n

Bodenheimer, Susanne J., 34n

Boff, Leonardo, 216n, 218n

Bondurant, Joan V., 167n, 172n

Bonhoeffer, Dietrich, 103-04, 110

Bonino, José Miguez, 31n, 195n, 215n

Bose, Nirmal Kumar, 75n, 82n, 212

Bourke-White, Margaret, 146n

Bradlaugh, Charles, 62, 76

Brahman, 56, 62, 153

Brown, Robert McAfee, 195n-96n, 197

Bultmann, 103

Cahill, Lisa Sowle, 63n

Camus, Albert, 60n

Cardenal, Ernesto, 180n

Chander, Jag Parvesh, 167n

Chatterjee, Margaret, 76n, 136n, 151n, 170n, 209

Chiang Kai Shek, 5

Chopp, Rebecca S., 37n

Christ, Jesus, 38-39, 42, 104, 110-11, 117-20, 188-94, 196-200, 205, 213-15, 219, 223-24

Christo-centric spirituality, 188-91, 223-24

Churchill, 162

Clark, T.T., 85n

Cockroft, James D., 34n

Coleman, John A., 151n

Communion and commitment, God of, 112-13

Communion mechanism, 235-37

Community enterprise, 193

Comte, Auguste, 133n

Cone, J., 31n

Confessions, 94

Conflict resolution, 160-67

Conversion, spirituality of, 202-04

Cormie, Lee, 34n

Cosmic pervading power, God as, 56-61

Creator, God as, 52-54
Culliton, Joseph T., 144n
Curren, Charles, 231n

Danto, Arthur C., 46n
Daridranārāyaṇa, God as, 64-65, 101
Dasgupta, Surendranath, 48n
Dayal, John, 3n
De Jouvenel, 22
De Maistre, 132n
Dear, John, 173n, 177n
Desai, Mahadev, 50n, 52n-53n, 69n, 75n, 78n, 91n
Desai, V.G., 142n
Dey, Nirmal Chandra, 50n
Dhawan, G.N., 86n, 156

Doke, Joseph J., 45n, 142, 143n
Donahue, John R., 195n
Douglass, Jim, 177n
Dumas, Andre, 110
Duquoc, Christian, 181n
Durkheim, 97n
Dynamic spirituality, 187-88, 223

Eagleson, John, 3n, 35n, 195n
Easwaran, 173n
Edwards, Paul, 21n
Einstein, 133n

Empowerment, 229
    spirituality of, 198-99
Erasmus, 132n
Erikson, 139n
Evans, Joseph W., 100n
Existential Force, God as, 56-61

Fabella, 200n-201n
Fabri, Charles, 55
Fisher, Louis, 94
Floristan, Casiano, 181n
Forest, Jim, 178n
Frank, Andre Gunder, 34n
Freedom, as *swarāj*, 19-25
Freud, Sigmund, 2n, 133n
Fuchs, Josef, 231n

Gaete, Arturo, 180n
Gandhi, Mangalal, 142
Gandhi, Manilal, 158
Gandhi, Mohandas Karamchand, 212, 223-24, 227-29
    ahiṁsātmaka satyāgraha, 7, 10-11, 13, 141-60, 141-78, 205, 221-22, 225, 230-35
    belief in God, 28
    conditions of *ahiṁsā*, 150
    conflict resolution method, 160-67
    contemporary political leaders, 5-6

convictions to resort to *satyā-graha*, 147-48
ethics of action, 6
form of social action, 6-7
foundational basis of liberation, 45-46
God (Truth), 11, 46-70
Gustavo and, 3-13, 220-41
human, 85-95
individual and social transformation method, 160-64
law of suffering, 164-65
liberative transformation goal of, 207-13
liberative transformation paradigam, 12
liberative transformation process, 44-102
means-end nexus and, 173-76
new agenda for liberative trans-formation, 237-41
non-violent creed, 176-77
notion of *swarāj*, 7-8
novelty and contribution to liberative transformation, 132-81
option for truth, 220-27
quest for liberation, 6
Rāmarājya, 208-13, 229-30
reasons against use of violence, 167-73
reconciliation and communion mechanism, 235-37

satya and *ahiṁsā* concept, 134-40, 150-52
self-suffering concept, 7, 13
swarāj concept of, 207-08
theological origin of socio-political action of, 95-102
truth, 70-79
views of liberation, 14-31
views on political economy, 6
way of the cross, 164-65
Gandhi, Narandas, 69n, 74n, 139
Gandhi, Purushottam, 77n
Gandhian homo, 85-95
human inter-relatedness, 93-95
human the brute, 86-87
socio-political action 95-102
soul within, 87-93
Gandhian liberation, foundational basis of, 45-46
Gandhian socio-political action, theological origin of, 95-102
Gandhian *swarāj*, 207-08, 212, 223-24, 227-28
Ganguli, B.N., 100n-101n
Garnett, Constance, 135n
Gaur, V.P., 136n
Gibellini, Rosino, 36n
Giddens, Anthony, 33n
Gilkey, Langdon, 110, 111n

Gilleman, S.J. Gerald, 141n

Gilson, E., 183n

Gispert-Sauch, George, 3n

Gītāñjali, 65

God,

  as *ātmā*, 49 as existential force, non-embodied conscious-ness, unalterable law, ulti-mate value and cosmic per-vading power, 56-61

  as one creator, master and father of us all, 52-54

  as prime source and summit of all moral norms, 61-62

  as protector/saviour, 61

  as truth, 67-70

  beyond morality, 62

  beyond reason, 63-64

  hidden, present, active and acting, 108-12

  human encounter, 124-29

  image and likeness of, 120-21

  in and of history, 107-08

  of communion and commit-ment, 112-13

  of Gandhi, 49-70

  of Gutiérrez, 105-29

  of life, 106-07

  of love, 113-15

  of preferential love, 115-17

  preferential lover, 64-67

  present, active and interested in human history and affairs, 54-56

  saving action of, 123-24

  ultimate end and final telos, 50-52

God of the Poor, 105

Godwin, William, 133n

Goethe, 50

Grass-root intimacy spirituality, 192-93

Gray, J. Glenn, 3n

Green, Martin, 3n, 136n

Gregg, Richard B., 158n

Grotius, 132n

Guha, Ranajit, 5n

Gustafson, James M., 9n, 72, 73n, 97n, 225, 231n

Gutiérrez, Gustavo,

  biblical theology, 11

  christo-centric spirituality, 188-91

  communion and recon-ciliation mechanism, 235-37

  contemplative in action, 201-02

  conversion spirituality, 202-04

  dynamic spirituality, 187-88

  empowerment spirituality, 198

foundational basis of liberation, 102-29

Gandhi and, 3-13, 220-41

God of, 105-29

grass-root intimacy spirituality, 192-93

historical consciousness, 8

historically-involved commu-nity enterprise, 193

homo, 118-20

human-God encounter, 124-29

human responsibility, 124

kingdom of God according to, 213-19, 229-30

liberation agenda, 8-10

liberation concept of, 228-29

liberation spirituality, 183-85

liberative transformation goal of, 207, 213-19

liberative transformation para-digam, 12

liberative transformation process, 44, 102-29, 232-34

life-affirming spirituality, 185-86

Magnificat, 204

methodology spirituality, 199-200

new agenda for liberative trans-formation, 237-41

option for poor, 220

preferentially-opted spirituality, 194-98

religious vision, 8

spirituality of, 180-206, 230-35

view of liberation, 31-43

way of walking according to the spirit, 191-92

Haight, Roger, 183n, 201n, 214n

Haight, S.J. Roger, 32n, 41

Hamilton, Hamish, 60n

Harijan, 55, 150

Häring, Bernard, 2n, 81, 83n, 86, 87n, 97n

Haughey, John C., 195n

Hegel, 47n

Hennlly, Alfred T., 181n

Hettne, Bjorn, 159, 160n

Hidden God, 108-12

Hildebrandt, Rainer, 4n

Hind Swarāj, 19, 137

Hindustan Times, 212

Hiriyanna, M., 48n

History, God of and in, 107-08

Hitler, Adolph, 5, 162

Hobbes, 97n-98n

Hollenbach, David, 3n

Hong, Howard, 141n

Horowitz, Irwing Louis, 34n

Houtart, Francois, 14

Human actions, 58, 62

Human-God encounter, nature of, 124-29

Human history and affairs, God interest in, 54-56

Human inter-relatedness, 93-95

Human nature, brutal element in, 86-87

Human quest, 35-36

Human responsibility, 124

Human soul (*ātman*), 87-93

Humanization process, liberation as, 34

Hume, 98n

Huxley, Aldous, 175n

Ideal *satyāgrahī*, 157-60

Inda, Caridad, 3n

Individual *swarāj*, 24

Individual transformation, method of, 160-64

Inkeles, Alex, 34n

Iyer, Raghavan, 17n, 19n-20n, 24n, 26, 49n-50n, 52n, 55n, 57n, 59n-60n, 68n-69n, 86n, 98n, 130n, 133n-35n, 142n, 160n, 163n

Jain, Pratibha, 176n

Jesudasan, S.J. Ignatius, 14n, 16n-17n, 19n, 51n, 66n, 85, 96, 161, 210n

Joad, C.E.M., 145n

Johnson, Dale L., 34n

Johnson, Raynor, 84n

Jones, Stanley E., 157n, 174n

Juergensmeyer, Mark, 151n

Kairos, liberation as, 36

Kamaraj, 4n

Kant, Immanuel, 92, 97n, 132n

Kasamali, 50n

Kaur, Amrit, 71n

Kerans, Patrick, 2n

Kevalajñāna, Jain goal of, 27

Khanna, Suman, 60n

Kierkegaard, Soren, 18n, 141n

King Jr., Martin Luther, 4n, 81n, 164n-65n

Kingdom of God, Gutiérrez vision of, 213-19, 224, 229-30

Kingdom of God is Within You, 141

Lamb, Mathew L., 2n

Lenin, 5

Lerner, Daniel, 33n

Liberated society, Gandhian vision of, 211

Liberation,
    as aspiration, 33
    as graced Kairos, 36
    as human quest, 35-36
    as process of humanization, 34

as salvation, 38-43

as *swarāj*, 15-30

as transformation, 29-30, 36-38

Gandhian view of, 14-31

Gutiérrez view of, 31-43

levels of, 32

making of, 31-43

meaning of, 43

theology of, 14, 31

Liberation spirituality, nature of, 183-85

Liberative transformation, foundational basis of, 44-45

Gandhian novelty and contri-bution to, 132-81

ahiṁsātmaka satyāgraha, 141-78

conflict resolution method, 160-67

individual and social transformation method, 160-64

law of suffering, 164-65

means-end nexus, 173-76

non-violent creed, 176-77

reasons against use of violence, 167-73

satya and *ahiṁsā*, 134-40

way of the cross, 164-65

new agenda for, 237-41

spirituality of, 130-206

Liberative transformation goal of,

Gandhi, 207-13, 219

Gutiérrez, 207, 213-19

Life,

affirming spirituality, 185-86

God of, 106-07

Lincoln, Abraham, 81

Locke, 97n-98n

Lonergan, Bernard, 2

Love, God of, 113-15

Machiavelli, Niccolo, 175n

Madhva, 47n, 97n

Magnificat, 204

Mahoney, John, 231n

Mao Tse Tung, 5

Marcel, Gabriel, 60n

Marcos, Ferdinand, 4n

Maritain, Jacques, 99, 100n

Marx, Karl, 2n, 98n, 133n

Master and father of all, God as, 52-54

Matson, Floyd W., 2n

May, Rollo, 2n, 82

Mayor, Dios, 111

Mazumdar, Haridas T., 15n

McCleland, David C., 33n

McGovern, Arthur F., 187n, 188, 195n, 236n

Menon, Esther, 84n

Merton, Thomas, 177, 178n

Methodology, as spirituality, 199-200

Migne, P.L., 183n

Mill, 97n-98n

Miller, W.R., 144n

Miller, Webb, 157-58

Minz, Nirmal Kumar, 69n, 142n

Modern Review, 154

Mokṣa, 50, 83
    swarāj as, 26-29

Moltmann, 109

Monier-Williams, 68n, 134n

Montague, E.S., 55

Moral norms, God as summit of, 61-62

Morality, God beyond, 62

Muhbub Ul Haq, 34n

Mukerjee, Hiren, 143n

Murray, John Courtney, 95

Nadkarni, 62

Naidu, Sarojani, 157

Naoroji, Dadabhai, 17

Naravane V.S., 48n

Narayan, Jayaprakash, 98n

Narayan, R.K., 5n

Narayan, Sriman, 29n, 73n

National *swarāj*, 24

Nehru, Jawaharlal, 4n, 81n

Niebuhr, Reinhold, 95

New Christendom movement, 37

Nicholas, Tsar, 5

Nicomachean Ethics, 62

Niebuhr, H. Richard, 29, 97n, 105

Nietzsche, 60, 136

Non-embodied consciousness, God as, 56-61

Non-violence, implications to *satyāgraha*, 150-53

Non-violent creed, 176-77

Nouwen, Henri J.M., 189n, 192n-93n

O'Connell, Matthew J., 36n

Outka, Gene, 140

Pacifism, and *satyāgraha*, 143-46

Palkhivala, N.A., 83n

Paoli, Arturo, 180n

Parekh, Bhikhu, 48n, 59n, 89n, 141n, 146-47, 166

Parsons, Talcott, 33n-34n

Partridge, P.H., 21n

Passive resistance, 142-46
    and *satyāgraha*, 143-46

Patāñjali, 236

Pauline, 97

Pearce, Brian, 34n

Pegis, Anton C., 59n

Plato, 97n, 230

Poor, Gutiérrez's option for, 220-27

Portes, Alejandro, 34n

Prabhu, R.K., 94n-95n, 156

Prasad, Janakadhari, 83n

Prasad, K.M., 145n-46n, 163, 172n, 174n

Prasad, Mahadev, 93

Preferential lover, God as, 64-67, 115-17

Preferentially-opted spirituality, 194-98

Prime source, God as, 61

Protector, God as, 61

Pūrṇa swarāj, concept of, 24-25

Pyarelal, 92n, 94n, 179n

Radhakrishnan, S., 97n, 130n, 135n, 145n, 162n

Rahner, 97n

Rajkotwala, Ibrahimji, 63

Ramakrishna, 83

Rāmānuja, 47n, 97n

Rāmarājya, 139, 155, 177, 180
    Gandhi's vision of, 207-13, 223, 229-30

Rao, U.R., 94n-95n, 156

Rawls, John, 97n, 223n

Reason, God beyond, 63-64

Reconciliation mechanism, 235-37

Ricoeur, Paul, 2

Rolland, Romain, 5n, 45, 79, 97n

Roosewelt, Franklin, 6

Rostow, W.W., 33n-34n

Rudolph, Lloyd I., 5n, 142n, 154n

Rudolph, Susane Hoeber, 142n

Ruskin, 135n, 141

Russell, Bertrand, 20

Ryan, William, 141n

Ryle, Gilbert, 98n

Saint-Simon, 133n

Salvation,
    humanization process, 41
    language of, 39
    liberation as, 38-43
    meaning of, 39
    process character of, 41

Śaṅkara, 47n, 97n

Santayana, George, 83n, 84

Santos, Theotonio Dos, 34n

Sarvodaya samāj, 208-09

Satya, concept of, 24, 26, 133-40, 229

Satyāgraha, see also, *Ahiṁsātmaka satyāgraha*
    as virtue of strong, 148-49
    conflict resolution, 160-67

individual and social trans-
    formation method, 160-64
non-violence implications,
    150-53
origin and meaning of, 141-
    48
passive resistance/pecifism
    and, 143-46
satya and *ahiṁsā* as
    dimensions of, 134-40
satyāgrahī, 157-60
technique, 156-57
theory and praxis of, 154-55

Saving action, of God, 123-24

Saviour, God as, 61

Saxena, 180n

Schumacher, F., 23n

Segundo, Juan Luis, 181n

Self-determination, spirit of, 23-
    24

Self-government, concept of, 17

Self-reliance, 23

Self-rule,
    concept of, 17
    Platonic and Stoic ideals of,
        20
    swarāj as, 25-26

Self-suffering (*tapasyā*), 7, 13

Shankaran, 50n, 57

Shannon, William H., 178n

Sharma, Chandradhar, 48n

Shukla, 68n

Sin, fact of, 121-23

Singh, Ramjee, 145n

Skinner, 96n-97n

Smuts, Jan Christian, 173n

Soares-Prabhu, George M., 194n-
    95n

Sobrino, Jon, 181n, 188n, 218n

Social transformation, method
    of, 160-64

Socio-political, action theo-
    logical origin of, 95-102

Socrates, 153, 177

Sonnleitner, Michael W., 78n

Sorel, 133n

Soul, 87-93

Spinoza, 47n

Spirit, way of walking according
    to, 191-92

Spirituality,
    Christo-centric, 188-91, 223-
        24
    contemplative action, 201-02,
        223
    dynamic, 187-88, 223
    empowerment, 198-99
    grass-root intimacy, 192-93
    liberation spirituality, 183-85
    life-affirming, 185-86
    methodology, 199-200
    of conversion, 202-04
    preferentially-opted, 194-98

search of by Gutiérrez, 180-206

traits of, 182

way of walking according to, 191-92

Spivak, Gayatri Chakravorty, 5n

Srivastava, Rama Shanker, 48n

Stalin, 5

Stanton, 81

Suarez, 96n

Suffering, law of, 164-65

Sun Yat Sen, 5

Swadeśī, 24

Swarāj,
  and *swadeśī*, 24
  as freedom, 19-25
  as *mokṣa*, 26-29, 38
  as self-rule, 25-26
  as transformation, 29-30
  Gandhi's conception of, 207-08, 212, 223-24, 227-28
  liberation as, 15-30
  pillars of, 30

Tagore, Rabindranath, 53-55, 65, 84, 206, 211

Tapasyā (self-suffering), 210, 213, 239

Telegram, 158

Tellis-Nayak, V., 98n

Tendulkar, 99n, 157n, 167n

Theology of Liberation, 188

Theosophical Society, 16

Thompson, Edward, 130n

Tilak, Bal Gangadhar, 17

Tillich, 97n, 103

Tolstoy, Leo, 133n, 135n, 141

Torres, Sergio, 35n, 107n, 195n, 200n-01n

Transformation,
  liberation as, 36-38
  swarāj as, 29-30

Trujillo, Alfonso Lopez, 236n

Trusteeship, Gandhian theories of, 79

Truth,
  Gandhi's option for, 220-27
  God as, 67-70
  impact of, 79-85
  nature of, 70-79

Ultimate truth (*parama satya*), 79

Ultimate value, God as, 56-61

Unalterable law, God as, 56-61

Unto This Last, 141

Vachon, S.J. Andre, 141n

Vallabha, 47n

Vanderheaar, Gerard A., 3n

Venkataramani, K.S., 5n

Verma, V.P., 143n

Violence, reasons against use of, 167-73

Virginia Fabella, M.M., 107n

Vivekananda, 7n, 97n

Voltaire, 2n

Von Rad, Gerhard, 110, 125

Von Weizacker, Carl Friedrich, 2n

Wallas, Graham, 20

Wallerstein, Immanuel, 34n

We Drink from Our Own Wells, 131, 183, 185, 189

Weber, Max, 33n, 68

Weiner, Myros, 34n

Weizacker, 83n

Wilhelm, Kaiser, 5

Wilson, Woodrow, 6

Yeats, W.B., 54n-55n

Young India, 62

Younger, Paul, 48n

Zeno, 131n